# Piatto Unico

D1247372

# Piatto Unico

## WHEN ONE COURSE MAKES A REAL ITALIAN MEAL

BY **Toni Lydecker**

*PHOTOGRAPHY BY TINA RUPP*

LAKE ISLE PRESS | NEW YORK

Recipes copyright © 2011 by Toni Lydecker
Photography copyright © 2011 Tina Rupp

All rights reserved. No part of this book may be reproduced, stored in a retrieval system, or transmitted, in any form, or by any means, electronic or mechanical, including photocopying and recording, without prior written consent from the publisher.

Published by:
Lake Isle Press, Inc.
2095 Broadway, Suite 301
New York, NY 10023
(212) 273-0796
E-mail: lakeisle@earthlink.net

Distributed to the trade by:
National Book Network, Inc.
4501 Forbes Boulevard, Suite 200
Lanham, MD 20706
1(800) 462-6420
www.nbnbooks.com

Library of Congress Control Number:  2011933324

ISBN-13: 978-1-891105-48-7
ISBN-10: 1-891105-48-5

Book and cover design:  Anna Raff
Editors: Stephanie White, Jennifer Sit

This book is available at special sales discounts for bulk purchases as premiums or special editions, including customized covers. For more information, contact the publisher at (212) 273-0796 or by e-mail, lakeisle@earthlink.net

First edition
Printed in the United States of America

10 9 8 7 6 5 4 3 2 1

## DEDICATION

This book is dedicated, in the true Italian spirit, to my family.

## ACKNOWLEDGMENTS

*Tante grazie* to all the Italian cooks, chefs, and gardeners who have shared their knowledge with me through the years; quite a few are credited by name in head notes for particular recipes. Special thanks to Sara Matthews-Grieco and Allen Grieco, owners of Il Poggiolo, a hilltop farm in Tuscany's Valdarno. Many recipes in this cookbook were developed and tested during a two-month period when my husband Kent and I house sat for them. That sojourn turned out to be a phenomenal opportunity for me to market every day, form rewarding relationships with our Italian neighbors, and cook in a well-appointed kitchen.

Many thanks to Hiroko Kiiffner and her editorial team, Stephanie White and Jennifer Sit, who gave their all to making *Piatto Unico* the best it can be. Kudos to Tina Rupp for her evocative photography and to Anna Raff for her design. I am also thankful for the help of Clare Pelino, my agent.

Finally, *un forte abbraccio* to my food-loving family and friends, always happy to taste and never afraid to say what they think.

# CONTENTS

# INTRODUCTION

As you have no doubt heard and observed, a real Italian meal consists of several courses. Except when it doesn't.

Launching the meal with a *primo*, most often pasta, and continuing with a *secondo* of meat or fish with a vegetable or salad: This leisurely sequence is indeed the norm in Italy, and may it ever be so. For a special occasion, the meal might expand to include an antipasto and always concludes with dessert, if only fresh fruit. At the same time, the concept of a one-course meal, or *piatto unico*, is well established and growing in popularity. Italians are eating this way more often at home, and restaurants are finding ways to accommodate customers who choose to eat just one course.

Elena Cecchi, a Tuscan friend, describes one-course meals as *cucina di moda*—that is, an approach to cooking and eating that's very much in style. "They are so convenient, given the chaotic lives we lead," she adds. Italians are beset by many of the same challenges Americans are, ranging from busier and more complicated lives to concern about pounds creeping on, and the simplicity of a single course for lunch or dinner holds considerable appeal. There are circumstances when lunch turns out to be a greasy slice of pizza or mediocre bowl of pasta eaten on the run, but Italians care too much about food to make a habit of eating slap-dash meals.

Instead, Italian one-course meals, whether traditional or contemporary, tend to be delicious and nourishing. In that spirit, *Piatto Unico* abounds in recipes for substantial soups, stews, pastas, entrée salads, and pizzas of the knife-and-fork variety. Americans have always enjoyed eating Italian food this way and, increasingly, Italians agree that this kind of meal merits a role in contemporary life.

A health-related Italian website I came across calls attention to the *piatto unico* phenomenon not only because it's sensible from a nutritional point of view but also because it is "as old as the world." Indeed, one-course meals such as a frugal bowl of soup or a plate of beans and polenta have existed for centuries. They are at the center of the classic peasant cooking known as *cucina povera*, which emphasizes grains, legumes, and vegetables, while incorporating smaller quantities of costly meat, seafood, and cheese. Ironically, a way of eating once associated with poverty is now celebrated as the essence of true Italian cooking and a healthful Mediterranean-style diet. Traditionally, *piatti unici* are also linked to religious festivals or funerals, times when regular meal-making is interrupted and people rely instead on dishes that can be made in advance and reheated. In Sicily, for example, a meat or fish pie might be taken to a bereaved family or to a potluck dinner during Holy Week.

Not surprisingly, given this history, *piatti unici* are associated with the idea of eating well in both the gastronomical and nutritional senses, without overindulging. Nutrition is taken into account in a natural, non-calorie-counting sort of way. As Katia Amore, owner of a cooking school in Modica, points out, "In the same way in which many vegetable-based dishes are part of our diet without being singled out as vegetarian, people seek a good carbohydrate-protein balance when preparing a *piatto unico*—without acknowledging the process." Italians are accustomed to using the freshest and best ingredients, and they behave no differently when preparing one-course meals.

Gastronomic versatility is a hallmark of *piatti unici*, as Alberto Capatti and Massimo Montanari observe in their definitive book, *Italian Cuisine*: "Minestrone, pizza, and pasta will tolerate the most diverse ingredients." These are what we'd call one-pot meals in America, but I found that in Italy the idea of a *piatto unico* also encompasses meat or fish with a side dish such as a vegetable or salad—served at the same time, though not necessarily on the

same plate—and recipes for these kinds of combinations are also included in *Piatto Unico*.

In contemporary Italy, one-dish meals are most often eaten by choice, not because of hard times or convention, so the range of possibilities is broad. Many dishes considered appropriate are traditional in derivation—*pasta e fagioli*, for example, or grilled chicken with a vegetable—but a more luxurious dish such as egg pasta with a creamy seafood sauce or eggs garnished with truffles can be part of the picture, too. Though many dishes in this cookbook come together rapidly, and therefore qualify as *cucina veloce*, others (notably soups and stews) call for long, slow cooking or a more intricate preparation. Because the *piatto unico* concept is more elastic than that of a traditional multicourse meal, there is more room for improvisation on the part of the cook and for introducing foreign ingredients and unusual combinations. What all of these have in common is the appealing simplicity of one dish, abundantly portioned to provide a satisfying meal.

The subject matter of this book has given me cause to think about the social changes that are giving *piatti unici* a more prominent role in meal preparation, as well as the countervailing force of tradition in preserving what Italians value about their incomparable table. Woven through this book are my observations on this tug of war, together with practical advice on shopping and

cooking in contemporary Italy as well as in America.

For the past three decades, I've been making the comforting vegetable and bread soup called *ribollita* from a recipe given to me by a Florentine gardener. It's in this collection, along with a few others gathered one year when we lived near Florence's Porta Romana. While my husband researched his art history dissertation in the state archives, I wheeled our baby to markets and tried to learn the rudiments of cooking like an Italian. Making the rounds of the produce vendor, butcher, dairy store, and the like took a good part of the morning, and I sometimes felt a bit sorry for myself until, on occasional afternoon outings, spotting the familiar faces of other matrons, I realized with a shock that some marketed not once but twice a day, before lunch *and* dinner.

During the intervening years I've traveled all over Italy and continued what has turned into a lifelong education in that country's fascinating food ways. But the bookend for that initiation was a recent two-month sojourn in a Tuscan farmhouse, when I resumed the daily discipline of marketing and cooking *all' italiana*. I found myself comparing my experiences, past and present. Some things were unaltered; in both times and places, I kneaded dough or prepped ingredients on the same marble-topped kitchen table where we ate our meals. Whether I was buying eggs from free-range chickens, sheep's milk ricotta, or a bottle of locally pressed olive oil, I could count on an impressive level of quality. If I wanted cooking advice or recipes, virtually any Italian was an enthusiastic source—even a carpenter or computer programmer who never touches a sauté pan could describe his grandmother's *lasagne* in loving detail.

But I noticed changes as well. Even in cities, many consumers find price- and time-saving advantages in buying their food at a supermarket or an even larger *iper coop* (similar to a Costco) at least some of the time. These often well-stocked stores offer the option of personalized service from butchers and staff at the deli, bakery, and pasta counters. All the same, they are clearly nudging some mom-and-pop stores out of business.

In Montevarchi, the nearest town to our hilltop living quarters, I learned to distinguish between the offerings of the "covered market," open daily, which sold only cheeses, produce, wines, dried beans, and olive oils produced locally; the weekly outdoor market, some of whose vendors came from other parts of Italy or even other European countries; and the occasional "Slow Food" markets, where one could conduct a conversation with artisans on their techniques for making pecorino or curing prosciutto. Beyond a remarkable range of choices, such as these, Italy is home to a proliferation of food and wine festivals celebrating not only the harvest seasons for white truffles or wine grapes, but paying

homage to such modest comestibles as zucchini or crostini. These happy occasions are tinged with nostalgia, an awareness that some traditions linked to an agricultural economy are fading from common use.

The same mixed response to change— regret and acceptance—surfaces when the subject of cooking comes up. Families can't necessarily count on their *nonna* (grandmother) spending her days in the kitchen. Lina, a middle-aged woman who continues to cook two meals a day for her family, told me sadly that none of her friends routinely do this anymore—and then she cheerfully gave me a recipe for *panzanella*, the tomato and bread salad she herself prepares when she "doesn't feel like cooking." Paolo and Leda are retirees who enjoy gardening and cooking, but quite often a *piatto unico* is what they want at the end of the day. That's also what Alexandra and Tommaso, young professionals who live in an urban neighborhood and relish good food, put together on a weeknight.

Trattoria del Carmine is among the restaurants we frequented as a young family in Florence and, to my pleasure, the grilled porcini mushrooms and veal chops I remember are still on the menu. But, in the same way as Italian markets, many restaurants have adapted to global influences. The steady flow of chefs-in-training between major Italian and American cities benefits both, perhaps at a cost of some homogenization. A contemporary dish such as zucchini carpaccio, though created by an Italian chef, could well be rooted in foreign soil.

Some restaurants, especially those in urban areas, have responded to changes in dining patterns by offering *piatti unici* or an assortment of *piattini* (small plates) for those who want to eat in a lighter or more flexible way; at Gran Caffe Orientale in Parma, for instance, I ordered a *piatto unico* consisting of not one but two rectangular dishes, one with a small portion of mushroom risotto and the other containing cold roast beef and tomato wedges. I wouldn't have encountered this option years ago, but the appetizing, nutritionally balanced dinner was exactly what I wanted that night.

Some recipes in *Piatto Unico* are relatively faithful interpretations of classic dishes, while others are what Italians call "personal recipes"—but all are tethered to Italy in some way. I found I was equally interested in home cooks and chefs who cling to tradition, those who strike out in new directions, and those of us who do a little of each. I learned not to inquire in a general way about one-course meals, but to ask my acquaintances and friends what they had eaten the day before for lunch and for dinner. Quite often, one of those meals could be classified as a *piatto unico*. I take pleasure in sharing their recipes, stories, and techniques, along with my own one-course favorites.

# ABOUT the RECIPES

Because the dishes in *Piatto Unico* are each meant to constitute a satisfying meal, the serving sizes are more ample than if intended as appetizers or another meal component. In this book you'll find plenty of hearty all-in-ones and generously portioned helpings of meat or fish with a vegetable or grain on the side. But I've also included lighter dishes—notably in the vegetable and grains chapter—that may be just the right fit for your appetite and mood. For those occasions when it's not, suggestions for easy add-ons (such as bread or a green salad) make the meal more substantial.

Most recipes can be made with ordinary ingredients from local markets, plus core ingredients in the section on Italian kitchen staples (page 15). But I also wanted to capitalize on a wonderful development of recent years: the availability of Italian products that were once obscure or impossible to get in the U.S. I've incorporated a number of these in recipes, both to share some of their uses and in the hope that readers will be intrigued enough to seek them out. At the same time, I've tried always to give alternatives if, for example, you can't find *friselle*, *Crucolo* cheese, or *vin santo*. There's dinner to be made and, in the Italian spirit of using what's on hand or easily obtained, I encourage you to go ahead with one of the suggested substitutes (or one you think of yourself).

Along the same lines, many of the recipes offer ideas for following a basic technique or recipe, such as for a frittata or risotto, while improvising with seasonal ingredients. Using locally made cheeses and cured meats in Italian applications is another promising option.

Medium-grind sea salt was used in recipe testing, except for salting pasta water, when less costly kosher salt was used. Kosher salt, listed as an alternative, is acceptable for all uses. Most recipes call for seasoning to taste rather than specifying an amount, in part because preferences vary so widely and because some readers are on special diets, but also because developing the judgment to season properly is an essential cooking skill. In most cases, black pepper and hot chiles are also added at the cook's discretion.

In many recipes, olive oil is listed among the ingredients but a quantity is not given. Instead, the procedure might call for adding enough to lightly (or generously) coat the bottom of a sauté pan—as in the case of key seasonings such as salt, my motive is to encourage cooks to judge how much is necessary, based on the dimensions of their pan and other variables. When precision is important, as in the case of making pizza dough, an exact quantity is given.

# KITCHEN STAPLES

Italian cooking depends on a core group of ingredients that are easy to keep on hand. These are the ones I can't live without. I've made suggestions for brands in some cases, but these are far from comprehensive. I encourage you to sample products that are available where you live and, through a process of tasting thoughtfully, develop a list of your own favorites.

### AGED CHEESE

Because it contains less moisture, an aged grating cheese keeps considerably longer than younger cheeses, and I always keep a chunk in my cheese drawer for a multitude of uses. Most often it's rich-tasting, nuanced Parmigiano Reggiano, but sometimes I choose versatile Grana Padano or a sharper-tasting aged pecorino. Though harder to find, Piave, Montasio, and Bra Duro are other good choices. To allow the cheese some breathing room, wrap it first in cheesecloth or waxed paper and then in plastic wrap. For maximum flavor and moistness, grate the cheese only when you need it.

### BROTH

Instructions for easily made meat and mushroom broths appear in this cookbook (pages 99 and 247), and some recipes generate their own broth. When you buy broth, choose an organic one free of additives such as sugar. Use a reduced-sodium or unsalted broth if possible; otherwise, dilute the broth with water when cooking, and season cautiously.

### CAPERS

Capers preserved in salt (available in jars or by the ounce in some Italian delis) are superior in taste to those pickled in brine; the best are from Pantelleria and the Aegean Islands. The smaller ones are nice because they can be used whole; larger capers might need to be chopped, but they taste the same. Regardless of how they are cured, capers should be soaked in water for a few minutes to eliminate some of the salt.

### CURED ANCHOVIES

Meaty preserved anchovies from the Mediterranean are great for strewing on a pizza or salad, but their utility as an ingredient for sauces or a *soffritto* is even more impressive. Just a fillet or two gives savory depth without a hint of fishiness. Good-quality tinned anchovy fillets preserved in olive oil are a convenient pantry staple; Recca and Sclafani are two labels to look for. Salt-cured whole anchovies, available by the ounce in some specialty stores, are even better; they keep well in the refrigerator. (For filleting instructions, see page 211.)

### DRIED BEANS AND LENTILS

I keep a can or two of chickpeas around—in my opinion, they are the only legume that retains its firmness once canned—but otherwise, my collection of beans and legumes are in dried form. A serviceable assortment might consist of cannellini (small white beans; Great Northern are a close match), *borlotti* (cranberry beans, for which pintos can be substituted), and lentils.

Even industrially produced dried beans are a step above canned, and artisanal beans and legumes can be incredible. They're not easy to find, but that's changing as demand grows. I find an especially big difference between supermarket-quality lentils, which can turn mealy or mushy when cooked, and small, firm greenish-brown Tuscan or French lentils. Your beans and legumes horizon can also be broadened by experimenting with heirloom varieties such as *pavoni*, large beans tasting of chestnuts, and small cream-colored *zolfini* beans.

For the delicious virtues of bean liquid, a by-product of cooking beans and legumes from scratch, see page 85.

## DRIED PASTA AND GRAINS

My pantry is always stocked with several varieties of made-in-Italy dried pasta, one of which is likely to be appropriate for whatever I decide to make. The mix includes noodles (spaghetti, linguine, etc.), short shapes such as penne, *gemelli* ("twins") and *farfalle* ("butterflies"), and *pastine*, orzo, and other small shapes for soup. I'm a pushover for unusual cuts such as calamari (yes, squid shaped) and

C-shaped *spaccatelle*. Artisanal pasta is extruded through bronze dies and dried more slowly than industrially made pasta; it costs considerably more, but rewards the buyer with good looks, a toothsome texture, and sauce-trapping talents. (For brand recommendations, including whole-grain and gluten-free pastas, see page 47.)

A supply of Italian short-grain rice (such as Arborio, Carnaroli, and *vialone nano*), couscous (including larger-grained pearl couscous and Sardinian *fregola*), and whole grains (farro, barley, stone-ground cornmeal) provides the foundation for many one-course meals. (For buying and cooking tips, see page 100.)

## HERBS

Dried thyme, rosemary, sage, oregano, and bay leaves are used often in Italian cooking. Buy whole leaves rather than powders, and in the smallest quantities available; the flavors diminish over time, so frequent replenishing is advisable. Mediterranean oregano branches can be found in some specialty shops; just rub the leaves between your fingers to crumble the herb. Italian seasoning blends contain most or all of these herbs, but I have mixed feelings about them; though handy, they can give a boring sameness to the seasoning of dishes. Most of the time, I prefer to tailor the use of herbs to what a particular dish seems to call for.

In addition to dried herbs, I usually have a fresh herb or two on hand. Flat-leaf parsley is so ubiquitous in Italian cooking that you don't have to worry about using it up. Place the bunch in a liquid measuring cup or vase, like a bouquet of flowers, with the stem ends immersed in an inch of water, and loosely enclose it with a plastic bag (tied at the bottom). Held this way, parsley stays fresh for about a week; basil can be handled the same way, though its shelf life is shorter. Fresh herbs such as mint, thyme, or rosemary can be wrapped in a damp paper towel, slipped into a plastic bag, and refrigerated. Even better, devote a window box or a patch of your garden to fresh herbs for as much of the year as is feasible.

## NUTS

Small bags of pine nuts, almonds, and unsalted pistachios are always tucked away in my freezer. They can be tossed, still frozen, into whatever I'm making or, if the recipe decrees, lightly toasted in a toaster oven or skillet. Walnuts and hazelnuts are also used in Italian cooking, though somewhat less frequently.

## OLIVES

Olives are not only used frequently in Italian cooking, but they're nice to have on hand for pre-dinner nibbling. So why not keep a supply in the refrigerator? The selection of Italian-grown olives available in American markets ranges from small Gaetas to medium-sized Nocellaras to fat green Sicilian olives. Olives from other Mediterranean countries, such as widely available Greek Kalamatas, French Picholines, and wrinkled, sun-cured black Spanish or Moroccan olives, are other good

choices. Unpitted olives are more versatile and seem to maintain their quality longer. Marinated olives are best avoided, because the flavorings may limit their uses—and olives are very easy to marinate at home.

## OLIVE OIL

For all-purpose use, choose extra-virgin oil with a mild but definite flavor, pleasantly fruity and well balanced. Olive oil does not improve with age, so check the label for a harvest date, which should be no earlier than the previous year. If you use olive oil regularly, as I do, consider getting high-quality oil at a good price by buying a four-liter tin at an Italian market. Using a funnel, decant it as needed into a smaller tinted glass bottle.

In addition to a general-purpose, moderately priced olive oil, it's lovely to have on hand an extra-virgin or two with more distinctive qualities—an unfiltered Tuscan oil with pepper and pine notes, for instance, or a luscious single-estate Sicilian oil. These are the ones to bring out when the flavor of the oil counts in a big way, such as in a salad dressing or for drizzling on a fine steak or bowl of bread soup.

## PANCETTA

Pancetta is pork belly cured with salt and seasoned with pepper and sometimes spices; it is usually (though not always) unsmoked. Pancetta is sometimes sold as a flat slab (especially in Italy) but more often in rolled form. Buy a chunk or, if purchasing by the ounce, have it cut into thickish,

1/4-inch slices that can be cut into small dice to add to a *soffritto* (flavor base); in Italy, pancetta is sold in diced form. *Guanciale*, sometimes called "face bacon" because it comes from the pig's jowl and cheeks, is a wonderful alternative; like pancetta, it is available here only from U.S. producers.

## SALT

Italians believe mineral-rich sea salt holds nutritive properties, but a flavor bonus is the more important reason to choose this kind of salt. I find that medium-grind white sea salt is best for all-purpose use; keep it in a jar by the stove and get accustomed to using your fingers or hand for gauging an appropriate amount when seasoning foods. It's worth noting that Italian chefs are experimenting with exotic salts, such as pink Himalayan salt, from elsewhere in the world.

Medium-grind kosher salt can be used as a substitute for sea salt, and it is a sensible choice for such tasks as seasoning pasta water.

## SPICES AND OTHER SEASONINGS

Black pepper is not an automatic companion of salt in Italy; instead, it is used judiciously, sometimes sparingly, sometimes emphatically, and sometimes not at all. Hot red peppers, whether in the form of dried *peperoncini*, whole or crumbled, or dried flakes, are employed in an equally thoughtful way: perhaps just a hint or, at the other end of the spectrum, an all-out assault in the company of garlic, anchovies, and the like.

Saffron is indispensable to some risottos and sauces; though its cultivation has been resurrected in Tuscany, the most reliable source for saffron threads is Spain. Fennel seed comes into occasional play—most memorably in sausage, but also in breads and other baked goods.

In any survey of key seasonings for Italian cooking, however brief, dried porcini mushrooms must be included. These days, many packages make a guessing game of their origin, claiming that they were harvested in Italy *or* China.

## TOMATOES

When the fresh tomato season is over, it's reassuring to know that their flavor can be captured for use in cooking. I learned that it's usually best to buy whole plum tomatoes canned in purée or juice, even if you plan to chop the tomatoes; crushed and puréed tomatoes may be from lower-grade, damaged produce. San Marzano is a variety of tomato as well as a famous Italian tomato-growing region; *D.O.P.* on the label certifies that both conditions are met, and that's pretty much top of the line. I make an exception to the whole-tomato rule for a small producer's bottle of *passata*, a simple essence of fresh sieved tomatoes, or Pomì's strained and chopped tomatoes in aseptic boxes, which seem consistently good.

I also keep a tube of tomato paste on a refrigerator shelf—if you can get your hands on a jar of Sicilian *stratto*, a laboriously sun-dried concentrate, that's the best—as well as a jar of sun-dried tomatoes preserved in olive oil.

## VINEGAR

White and red wine vinegars are used in salad dressings, sweet-sour sauces, and stews, among other things. They can be used interchangeably, though white may be preferable for seafood and other light-colored dishes. Quality can be hard to judge, but a label promising that the vinegar is made from aged wine or a particular varietal (such as Chardonnay or Cabernet) may be a good bet.

For everyday use, choose a mid-range balsamic vinegar (*aceto balsamico di Modena*) that is a blend of aged wine vinegar with traditionally made balsamic. *Condimento balsamico*, when made traditionally without long aging, and products that blend *vincotto* (cooked grape must) with wine vinegar can also be quite good. Producers to seek out: Acetaia San Giacomo, Acetaia Leonardo, Cavalli, La Vecchia Dispensa, and Mazzetti.

## Chapter 1
# PRIME-TIME PASTAS
∞

Although there are exceptions, pasta is normally eaten in Italy as a *primo*, not a main course. But, day to day, lots of people eat a single-course *piatto unico* for lunch or dinner, and pasta is perhaps the top choice. This trend is evident in many restaurants in Italy, where it's now accepted to order just a plate of pasta, especially at lunchtime. And, of course, eating pasta as a main course has long been the norm in the U.S. When the topping supplies some protein and plenty of vegetables, it's as balanced a meal as any.

I think everyone loves sauces that are quickly readied in a bowl or skillet, waiting for hot pasta to join them. *Tagliolini* with fresh tomato sauce and arugula pesto fits into that category and, in another recipe, the same pasta is tossed with a shrimp, prosciutto, and leek sauce.

I'm also fond of stockpiling a batch of meat *sugo*—slow in the simmering, but lightning fast when it need only be heated and mixed with the pasta of your choice. Baked pastas such as eggplant and sausage rigatoni call for a multistep campaign. Once in the pan, the casserole can be heated a few hours hence, and when it's time to eat you're likely to conclude it was well worth the trouble.

Italians have their version of crêpes, called *crespelle*. As in the case of fresh pastas such as cannelloni, they succeed in capturing a variety of fillings, with a sauce slathered on top. I've also included a recipe for gnocchi, Italian dumplings that fit into a broad definition of pasta.

Pasta is an enormous topic, about which entire books are written. Here I hope not to cover it comprehensively but to offer a few of my favorite recipes, along with some ideas on how to improvise pastas that take choice ingredients in pleasing directions.

# PRIME-TIME PASTAS

*Fettuccine with Tuscan Kale and Walnut Pesto*

*Trofie with Pesto Genovese, Green Beans,
and Potatoes*

*Orecchiette with Chickpeas and Dandelion Greens*

*Tagliolini with Cherry Tomatoes and Arugula Pesto*

*Penne or Pici with Lina's Meat Sugo*

*Fettuccine with Lamb Ragu*

*Orecchiette with Creamy Tomato, Leek,
and Bacon Sauce*

*Baked Rigatoni with Eggplant and Sausage*

*Shells with Broccoli Rabe, Sausage, and Peppers*

*Spaghetti with Tuna, Fresh Tomatoes, and Olives*

*Tagliolini with Shrimp, Leeks, and Prosciutto*

*Tagliatelle with Scallops and Amalfi-Style
Lemon Sauce*

*Asparagus-Spinach Crêpes with Taleggio*

*Green Gnocchi ("Gnudi") with Mushroom-Sage Sauce*

# FETTUCCINE with TUSCAN KALE and WALNUT PESTO

*Fettuccine con pesto di cavolo nero e noci*

MAKES 4 TO 6 SERVINGS | PREP: 10 MINUTES | COOK: 10 TO 12 MINUTES

*Dusky green Tuscan kale, well-browned onions, and walnuts share their earthy flavors in a pasta dish that makes a warming fall or winter meal. It's just as easy to make a big batch of this pesto and I always do, freezing whatever I don't need at the moment.*

**Sea salt or kosher salt**
**1 pound dried fettuccine or** *pici* **noodles**
  **(see Note, page 34)**
**1¼ cups Tuscan kale and walnut pesto (recipe follows)**

1. Fill a large saucepan about two-thirds full with cold water. Bring to a boil and add a handful of salt. Cook the fettuccine for 8 to 12 minutes until al dente.

2. Meanwhile, place the pesto in a large serving bowl. Drain the pasta, reserving about ½ cup of the cooking water, and turn it into the bowl. Mix well, adding as much cooking water as needed for a saucy consistency.

# Tuscan Kale and Walnut Pesto

MAKES 2½ CUPS *(enough for 2 pounds pasta)* | PREP: 30 MINUTES
COOK: 15 MINUTES

1 large onion
4 cloves garlic
1 cup extra-virgin olive oil
1 large bunch *cavolo nero* (Tuscan kale) (see Note)
¼ cup walnuts or pecans
2 teaspoons sea salt or kosher salt
¼ teaspoon freshly ground pepper
½ cup grated Parmigiano Reggiano or Grana Padano cheese

1. Halve the onion, end to end, and cut in thin slices. Roughly chop the garlic. Heat ¼ cup of the olive oil in a large sauté pan. Sauté the onion over medium-high heat until it softens and turns golden brown, about 15 minutes; reduce the heat if there's danger of burning. Stir in half of the garlic during the last few minutes of cooking.

2. Meanwhile, fill a large saucepan about two-thirds full with water and bring to a boil. Strip off the kale leaves, discarding the stems. Shred by cutting crosswise with a large knife (you should have about 8 packed cups). Add the kale to the boiling water and cook until wilted and tender, 3 to 5 minutes (depending on the size and freshness of the kale). Drain and cool.

3. Combine the kale, onions and garlic, the remaining raw garlic, walnuts, salt, pepper, and remaining ¾ cup olive oil in a food processor bowl. Purée until the mixture is well combined but the texture is slightly chunky.

4. Scrape the pesto into a bowl. With a spatula, fold in the cheese. Chill or freeze any of the pesto you don't plan to use immediately.

## NOTE

*Cavolo nero* means "black cabbage," but the greenish-black fronds are actually a delicious variety of kale, also known as Tuscan kale or lacinato. Your best chance for finding it is at a farmers' market.

# TROFIE with PESTO GENOVESE, GREEN BEANS, and POTATOES

*Trofie con pesto genovese, fagiolini e patate*

MAKES 4 TO 6 SERVINGS | PREP: 10 MINUTES | COOK: 10 TO 15 MINUTES

*In this Ligurian specialty, green beans echo the verdant look of the pesto, and the potatoes compliantly absorb some of the garlicky snap. Richard Goldthwaite, a friend who lives in Florence, often eats it as a piatto unico. He likes to go heavy on the potatoes and green beans, making the dish more substantial, and so do I. In some recipes, the three ingredients go into the boiling water at the same time, but this one calls for a slightly lengthier method ensuring that the pasta, potatoes, and green beans are each cooked to the proper point.*

Sea salt or kosher salt
2 small boiling potatoes (about 8 ounces), peeled and diced into
  medium pieces
8 ounces green beans, preferably small, thin *fagiolini*, trimmed
  and cut or snapped into short lengths
1 pound dried or fresh *trofie* or other short, twisted pasta such
  as *gemelli* ("twins") or *strozzapreti* ("strangled priests")
  (see Note)
1 cup homemade *pesto genovese* (recipe follows)
  or purchased pesto

**1.** Fill a large saucepan about two-thirds full with cold water. Bring to a boil and add a handful of salt. Cook the potatoes at a brisk simmer until tender but not falling apart. Scoop them out with a long-handled strainer or pasta spoon and place in a bowl. Add the green beans to the boiling water and cook for a few minutes until crisp-tender, then scoop into the bowl with the potatoes.

**2.** Add the pasta to the boiling water, giving a big stir to separate the strands. Cook until tender; for fresh pasta, this will take 1 to 3 minutes and, for dried, about 5 to 12 minutes.

3. Scoop the pesto into a bowl large enough to hold the cooked pasta. Reserving a cupful of the cooking water, drain the pasta and add it to the bowl with the pesto. Gently mix until well coated with the sauce; mix in the potatoes and green beans, adding cooking water as needed.

## Pesto Genovese

MAKES 1 CUP | PREP: 10 MINUTES

2 cups firmly packed basil leaves
2 cloves garlic, roughly chopped
2 tablespoons pine nuts, lightly toasted
1 teaspoon sea salt or kosher salt
2/3 cup extra-virgin olive oil
1/2 to 2/3 cup grated Parmigiano Reggiano or Grana Padano cheese

1. Combine the basil, garlic, pine nuts, and salt in a food processor bowl. Process until chopped. Through the funnel, slowly add the olive oil, processing until puréed.

2. Scrape the pesto into a small bowl. With a spatula, mix in the cheese.

### NOTES

*Trofie*, the classic pasta for this dish, are available fresh or dried. When made by hand, short strips of pasta are rolled until tapered at both ends and then twisted.

Once you are familiar with this dish, try this shortcut method: After the potatoes have cooked for 5 minutes, add the green beans. If you're using dried pasta, it goes in at this point, too; if fresh, add it a minute or two later. When all the ingredients are cooked through, drain and mix with the pesto.

### VARIATIONS

My feeling is that this dish can accommodate one additional ingredient, judiciously chosen. I'd recommend halved grape tomatoes, baby shrimp, or—to keep the focus on Liguria—tiny cubes of Genoa salami.

# ORECCHIETTE with CHICKPEAS and DANDELION GREENS

*Orecchiette con ceci e tarassaco*

MAKES 6 SERVINGS | PREP: 20 MINUTES | COOK: 20 MINUTES

*This nutritionally balanced pasta dish captures the Southern Italian delight in balancing assertive flavors: the bitterness of dandelion greens, heat of red pepper, sharpness of ricotta salata, and sweetness of currants.*

*Some chickpeas remain whole, while the rest are puréed to help thicken the sauce. Boiling water also does double duty, blanching the greens and then cooking the pasta. By the time the orecchiette are cooked, the skillet sauce is ready.*

3 tablespoons currants
1 (19-ounce) can chickpeas, drained and rinsed
1 cup canned plum tomatoes with some of their purée
¼ cup extra-virgin olive oil
1 medium onion, halved and sliced
1 thick-cut (¼-inch) slice pancetta, cut into small cubes
  (about ⅓ cup) (optional)
Sea salt or kosher salt
Hot red pepper flakes
1 bunch dandelion greens, thick stems removed, shredded
  crosswise (3 to 4 cups packed) (see Note)
1 pound *orecchiette* ("little ears"), cavatelli, or other short
  pasta shape
2 cups crumbled *ricotta salata* cheese
¼ cup pine nuts or almonds, lightly toasted

**1.** Place the currants in a small bowl with warm water to cover. Combine half of the chickpeas and all of the tomatoes with 1 cup water in a food processor or blender bowl; process until smooth.

**2.** Heat the olive oil in a large skillet over medium heat. Sauté the onion and (if using) the pancetta, stirring often, until lightly browned, about 10 minutes. Stir in the chickpea-tomato purée and whole chickpeas. Season to taste with salt and hot red pepper flakes. Lower the heat so that the mixture cooks at a bare simmer.

**3.** Meanwhile, fill a large saucepan about two-thirds full with cold water. Bring to a boil and add a handful of salt. Cook the dandelion greens until tender, about 5 minutes; scoop up with a long-handled strainer and stir into the chickpea mixture. Keep warm.

**4.** Add the pasta to the boiling water, stirring well. When the *orecchiette* reach the al dente stage, in 8 to 12 minutes, drain them, reserving about 1 cup of the water. Return the pasta to the empty saucepan and mix in the sauce, adding the reserved cooking water as needed for a saucy consistency. Stir in half of the *ricotta salata* and the currants along with their soaking water.

**5.** To serve: Spoon the sauced pasta into shallow soup bowls. Sprinkle the remaining *ricotta salata* and the pine nuts on top.

**NOTE**
If you can't find dandelion greens, substitute kale or broccoli rabe.

# TAGLIOLINI with CHERRY TOMATOES and ARUGULA PESTO

*Tagliolini con pomodorini e pesto di rucola*

**MAKES 3 OR 4 SERVINGS | PREP: 10 MINUTES | COOK: 10 MINUTES**

*Even foreign students with a tenuous grasp of Italian understand perfectly when Luisa Moscucci Neri demonstrates how to make arugula pesto at Siena's Dante Alighieri School. "Mi apre," she says, handing a jar of pine nuts to one student, and "Grazie" when it's returned, opened. Luisa urges her students to press the food processor's pulse button just long enough to blend the ingredients without overheating and "cooking" them. And, for the pesto to remain "bello vedere" ("beautiful to see"), it must be mixed with the pasta off heat, not on the burner.*

*These small but important attentions pay off in Luisa's recipe for thin egg noodles dressed with a rustic tomato sauce and bright-tasting pesto.*

Extra-virgin olive oil
1 clove garlic, finely chopped
1¼ pounds cherry tomatoes, quartered (see Note)
Sea salt or kosher salt
1 pound fresh *tagliolini*, linguine, or other thin egg noodles
Arugula pesto (recipe follows)

**1.** Heat a large skillet over medium heat. Drizzle enough oil to coat the bottom (about 3 tablespoons); add the garlic and let it sizzle for a few seconds, until fragrant, before adding the tomatoes. Cook, stirring, until they collapse and give off some juices, about 5 minutes. Season to taste with salt. Turn the heat to low, keeping the sauce warm.

**2.** Fill a large saucepan about two-thirds full with cold water. Bring to a boil and add a handful of salt. Cook the pasta until tender, 1 to 3 minutes; the fresher the pasta, the shorter the cooking time.

**3.** Drain the pasta, reserving ½ cup of the cooking water. Turn the pasta into the skillet with the cherry tomatoes, combining thoroughly with a pasta spoon or 2 forks; add reserved pasta water as necessary for a saucy consistency.

*continued*

4. Divide the pasta among 3 or 4 shallow soup bowls or plates. Add 1 to 2 tablespoons of the arugula pesto to each serving and, with a fork, swirl it into the pasta. Pass any remaining pesto at the table.

**NOTE**

Look for plump, ripe, thin-skinned cherry tomatoes for this dish. Large round tomatoes can be substituted if they are thin-skinned; trim the ends and dice them.

## Arugula Pesto

MAKES 3/4 CUP PESTO | PREP: 10 MINUTES

2 cups firmly packed torn arugula leaves
1/2 cup extra-virgin olive oil
1 large clove garlic, roughly chopped
1/2 teaspoon sea salt or kosher salt
1/4 cup grated Parmigiano Reggiano, Grana Padano, or aged
   pecorino cheese

1. In a food processor bowl, combine the arugula, olive oil, garlic, and salt. Pulse to chop and blend the ingredients until smooth.

2. Transfer the pesto to a small bowl. Using a spoon, blend in the grated cheese.

# PENNE or PICI with LINA'S MEAT SUGO

*Penne con sugo di carne alla Lina*

MAKES 5 OR 6 SERVINGS | PREP: 10 MINUTES | COOK: 20 MINUTES

I'd heard about Lina Romei's killer *sugo*, so I was thrilled when her son Luciano brought us a jar. Indeed, it's a formidable example of the long-simmered meat sauces made all over Italy, and we enjoyed every bite of pasta glossed with this meaty essence.

Enthusiastically, I requested the recipe. It didn't materialize, but we did receive an invitation to dinner in the Romei family's home in Mercatale, a small town in Tuscany's Arno Valley. Lina presented a steaming pan of lasagne, layered with her signature *sugo*. The evening was filled with lively conversation about Italian and American politics, the antics of the family's rambunctious black Lab, and the arrival of aromatic platters from Lina's kitchen—leaving no time to delve into the mysteries of the *sugo*.

Shortly before our return to the U.S., Lina invited me for a morning visit. We toured her garden, inspecting basil and tomato plants and commiserating over the latest hole dug by Luna, the dog. We made small talk over coffee. And then, just before I left, Lina told me all about her *sugo*.

**3 to 4 cups Lina's meat *sugo* (recipe follows)**
**Sea salt or kosher salt**
**1 pound penne or dried *pici* noodles (see Note)**
**1 cup grated Parmigiano Reggiano cheese**

**1.** Place the meat *sugo* in a small saucepan and heat over medium-low heat.

**2.** Fill a large saucepan about two-thirds full with cold water. Bring to a boil and add a handful of salt. Cook penne for 8 to 12 minutes, or until al dente; dried *pici* noodles need to cook longer, up to 20 minutes.

**3.** Drain the pasta, reserving about ½ cup of the cooking water. Return the pasta to the saucepan, and mix in the hot meat sauce. Dilute with some of the cooking water as needed.

*continued*

**4.** To serve: Spoon the pasta into shallow bowls and sprinkle a little of the cheese on top. Pass the remaining cheese at the table.

## NOTE

*Pici* are medium-length to long noodles that, in Tuscany, are sold both fresh and dried. The fresh kind is often made by hand, typically from semolina and soft-wheat flour mixed with water and no eggs. Alternatively, the noodles are made from semolina flour, cut with copper dies, and dried very slowly. The fresh kind, which you're unlikely to find outside Tuscany, cooks quickly, while dried *pici* require an unusually long time to cook; the latter can be purchased in specialty stores or from online sources.

## Lina's Meat Sugo

MAKES 1 QUART | PREP: 10 MINUTES | COOK: 2 1/2 HOURS

1 small onion, cut into chunks
1 small carrot, cut into chunks
1 medium stalk celery, cut into chunks
1 pound meatloaf mix (equal parts ground beef, veal, and pork)
2 tablespoons extra-virgin olive oil
1/2 cup white wine
1 cup strained tomatoes (such as Pomì ) or chopped canned plum
   tomatoes with some of their purée
2 tablespoons tomato paste
1/2 teaspoon sea salt or kosher salt, plus more to taste
1 or 2 pinches hot red pepper flakes
1/2 cup dried porcini mushrooms (optional)

**1.** Combine the onion, carrot, and celery in a food processor bowl. Pulse several times until the vegetables are finely and uniformly chopped but not mushy.

**2.** Turn the vegetables into a medium saucepan with the meatloaf mix and olive oil. Over medium heat, cook until the meat loses its raw look and browns to a warm hazelnut color, about 15 minutes.

3. Add the white wine and continue to cook at a brisk simmer, stirring often, for about 5 minutes. Stir in the tomatoes, tomato paste, salt, pepper flakes, and 1 cup water. Bring to a simmer; reduce the heat to low and cook, covered, until the sauce is dense and the flavor well developed, about 2 hours. Stir occasionally and add more water and salt if needed.

4. Meanwhile, if using the porcini, place the pieces in a small bowl and cover with warm water; soak until fairly soft, about 15 minutes. Drain the mushrooms (reserving the liquid) and rinse away any grit. Chop medium fine, and add to the sauce. Through a small strainer lined with a double thickness of paper towel, strain about 1/2 cup of the soaking liquid into the *sugo*. Cook a few minutes longer. If you are not using the sauce immediately, it can be covered and refrigerated for several days or frozen.

# FETTUCCINE with LAMB RAGU

*Fettuccine con ragù d'agnello*

MAKES 4 TO 6 SERVINGS | PREP: 30 MINUTES | COOK: 2 HOURS

*It takes a patient cook to wait while aromatic stewing liquid works its alchemy on tough chunks of lamb shoulder stew. When fork tender, the meat is shredded and returned to the soupy sauce...to wait, in turn, for the pasta to reach readiness.*

1½ pounds bone-in lamb shoulder
Sea salt or kosher salt
1 thick-cut (¼-inch) slice pancetta
1 medium carrot
1 medium stalk celery
1 medium onion
1 or 2 cloves garlic
2 tablespoons extra-virgin olive oil or vegetable oil, plus more if needed
½ cup red wine
1 cup canned plum tomatoes, chopped or squished with your
   fingers, with some of the purée
Freshly ground black pepper
1 pound dried fettuccine (or 20 ounces fresh) or other egg pasta
1 cup grated Parmigiano Reggiano or Grana Padano cheese

1. Blot the lamb dry with paper towels. Sprinkle generously with salt (about 1 teaspoon) and let the lamb come to room temperature. Cut the pancetta into small dice (about 3 tablespoons). Cut the carrot and celery into small dice and finely chop the onion and garlic.

2. Heat the olive oil in a large skillet over medium-high heat. Add the lamb and cook on both sides until well browned, about 10 minutes. Transfer to a medium saucepan, breaking apart the meat to fit.

3. Lower the heat under the skillet to medium and add up to 1 tablespoon oil, if needed. Add the onion and pancetta and sauté, stirring often, until the onion is golden and the pancetta has yielded most of its fat. Stir in the carrot and celery and cook a few minutes longer, until soft and lightly browned. Add the garlic, cooking just until fragrant.

**4.** Add the red wine, letting it sizzle while scraping the bottom of the pan with a heatproof spatula to loosen any browned-on bits. Pour the contents of the skillet over the lamb. Add the tomatoes, 1/4 teaspoon black pepper, and enough water to cover the lamb.

**5.** Bring the mixture to a boil. Adjust the heat so that it remains at a bare simmer with a few bubbles lazily cracking the surface. Simmer, partially covered, until the meat is fork tender, 1 1/2 to 2 hours, checking several times to make sure the cooking pace remains slow and skimming off any fat that rises to the surface.

**6.** Using tongs, transfer the lamb pieces to a plate; cool until just warm, and shred the meat with your fingers, discarding bones, fat, and gristle. Return the shredded meat to the sauce. Taste and add more salt and pepper, if needed. (At this point, you can proceed with the rest of the recipe, keep the sauce warm for an hour, or refrigerate for up to 24 hours.)

**7.** Fill a large saucepan about two-thirds full with cold water. Bring to a boil and add a handful of salt. Add the fettuccine, stirring well to separate the strands. Boil until tender, 3 to 5 minutes for dried egg pasta and 1 to 3 minutes for fresh. Drain the pasta, reserving 1/2 cup of the cooking water, and return to the pasta pot. Ladle in about half of the sauce, mixing well and adding pasta water as needed for a saucy consistency. Cook for 1 to 2 minutes to heat through. The sauce should be brothy with bits of meat.

**8.** Divide the pasta among shallow bowls or plates. Ladle some of the remaining sauce on top of each serving. Sprinkle with half of the cheese and pass the rest at the table.

# ORECCHIETTE with CREAMY TOMATO, LEEK, and BACON SAUCE

*Orecchiette al fumo*

MAKES 4 SERVINGS | PREP: 20 MINUTES | COOK: 30 MINUTES

*I've seen many references to this classic dish from Cortona but have never tasted it in that lovely hill town. I improvised this version anyway and must say that, once the bowl is before me, I can't put my fork down.*

1 medium carrot

3 slices good-quality bacon

1 medium leek (white part plus 1 inch green), halved lengthwise
  and washed (see Note)

Extra-virgin olive oil

1 tablespoon finely chopped fresh rosemary leaves or 1 teaspoon
  dried rosemary (optional)

1 or 2 cloves garlic, finely chopped

1 tablespoon tomato paste

1 carton (about 26 ounces) strained plum tomatoes (such as
  Pomì) or 1 similar-size can of plum tomatoes with purée, puréed
  in a blender

¼ to ½ cup heavy cream

Sea salt or kosher salt

Freshly ground black pepper

1 pound *orecchiette* or other short pasta shape

2/3 to 1 cup grated Parmigiano Reggiano cheese

1. Peel and chop the carrot. Cut the bacon lengthwise in thin strips; cut crosswise in small squares. Cut the leek crosswise in thin slices.

2. Combine the leek and carrot with enough olive oil to coat the bottom of a saucepan or skillet large enough to accommodate the pasta later (about 3 tablespoons). Cook over medium heat, stirring often, until the vegetables soften, about 5 minutes. Add the bacon, cooking until the fat is rendered but the bacon is not yet crisped.

*continued*

**2.** Stir in the rosemary (if using) and garlic, cooking just until fragrant. Add the tomato paste and stir until it darkens. Stir in the strained tomatoes. When the sauce begins to bubble, reduce the heat to low; stir in the cream and season to taste with salt and pepper. Simmer very slowly, adding a little water if the sauce thickens too much, while cooking the pasta.

**3.** Fill a large saucepan about two-thirds full with cold water. Bring to a boil and add a handful of salt. Add the *orecchiette*, stirring to separate, and boil until al dente, 8 to 12 minutes. Drain, reserving 2 cups of the pasta water.

**4.** Immediately add the hot pasta to the skillet, stirring well to combine. Add as much of the pasta water as needed for a saucy consistency (the sauce should coat the pasta fairly thickly).

**5.** Stir half of the cheese into the pasta and spoon into shallow bowls; sprinkle with the remaining cheese or pass at the table.

**NOTE**

Pushing up through the earth, a leek can trap a fair amount of soil. After halving the leek lengthwise, wash each layer under running water. If the recipe permits, as this one does, slice the leek crosswise and place the pieces in a bowl of cold water; the leek will remain at the top, while any dirt sinks; after a few minutes, scoop out the leek.

# BAKED RIGATONI with EGGPLANT and SAUSAGE

*Rigatoni con melanzana e salciccia al forno*

**MAKES 6 TO 8 SERVINGS | PREP: 30 MINUTES | COOK: 1 HOUR**

*This dish takes some doing, but the payoff is a made-ahead casserole. When you're ready to reheat it for family or company, the secret to crisping the top without drying out the filling is a high temperature.*

**Extra-virgin olive oil**
**½ cup fresh bread crumbs**
**1 cup grated aged pecorino cheese**
**1 medium eggplant, peeled, halved lengthwise, and cut into
  2-inch chunks**
**1 pound Italian sausage links**
**2 cloves garlic, finely chopped**
**1 (28- or 35-ounce) can whole plum tomatoes packed in purée**
**1 teaspoon dried oregano**
**Sea salt or kosher salt**
**½ cup Mediterranean black or green olives, pitted and slivered**
**Freshly ground black pepper**
**1 pound rigatoni**
**1½ to 2 cups coarsely grated mozzarella cheese**

1. Preheat the oven to 425°F. Line a roasting pan with aluminum foil. Lightly coat the bottom of a large baking dish (about 8x12") with olive oil. In a small bowl, combine the bread crumbs and pecorino.

2. Pile the eggplant on a rimmed baking sheet; drizzle with ¼ cup olive oil and mix with your hands to coat the pieces; spread out in a single layer. Place the sausages in the foil-lined roasting pan; roll them in a little olive oil.

3. Roast the eggplant and sausages on middle racks in the oven. Remove the sausages after 15 minutes or so, when they are browned and cooked through; cool on a plate lined with paper towels. Roast the eggplant about 15 minutes longer, until browned and tender.

*continued*

4. Meanwhile, fill a large saucepan about two-thirds full with cold water and bring to a boil.

5. To make the tomato sauce: Combine the garlic with 2 tablespoons olive oil in a large saucepan. Over medium-low heat, cook the garlic until fragrant. Add the tomatoes, crushing them with your fingers, and the purée. Stir in the oregano and ½ teaspoon salt. Simmer briskly until fairly dense, about 10 minutes. Add the olives and black pepper to taste.

6. Transfer the eggplant to a bowl and sprinkle with salt while still warm. Cut the sausage into ½-inch slices.

7. Add a handful of salt to the boiling water and dump in the rigatoni; stir well and cook until very al dente, about 7 minutes. Drain the pasta, reserving a cup of the cooking water, and return it to the pan; stir in the tomato sauce, followed by the eggplant and sausage. Add as much of the cooking water as needed for a fairly loose sauce (it will become more concentrated in the oven). Taste and add more salt and pepper if needed.

8. Turn the sauced pasta into the prepared baking dish. Sprinkle with the mozzarella. Top with the pecorino and bread crumbs. Cover with aluminum foil. (At this point, the dish can be held 1 to 2 hours at room temperature or, if refrigerated, up to 12 hours.)

9. Bake the pasta until heated through, 15 to 20 minutes. Remove the foil and cook until the topping is lightly browned, about 5 minutes.

## VARIATIONS

This recipe takes well to tweaking. You can choose hot sausage or the "sweet," fennel-flavored variety, mellow black olives or tart green ones, fresh mozzarella or the ordinary supermarket kind.

In place of mozzarella, mix the same quantity of *ricotta salata* into the pasta. For the topping, omit the pecorino, increase the quantity of bread crumbs to 1 cup, and toss with 2 tablespoons olive oil.

To make a vegetarian version: Omit the sausage and use a large rather than medium eggplant, or roast 1 pound of sliced white or crimini mushrooms with the eggplant.

# SHELLS with BROCCOLI RABE, SAUSAGE, and PEPPERS

*Conchiglie con cime di rapa, salsiccia e peperoni*

MAKES 4 TO 6 SERVINGS | PREP: 20 MINUTES | COOK: 20 MINUTES

*To me, broccoli rabe tastes outrageously good. I can't get enough of its seductive bitterness, especially when set in counterpoint to the savory sweetness of the sausage and peppers.*

2 small yellow and/or red bell peppers, cores and
   seeds discarded
1 large bunch broccoli rabe (see Note)
1 pound sweet Italian sausage or other mild sausage
Extra-virgin olive oil
2 cloves garlic, lightly crushed
1½ cups chopped canned plum tomatoes with some of
   the purée
Sea salt or kosher salt
1 pound shells, *spaccatelle*, or other short pasta
Hot red pepper flakes or freshly ground black pepper
2 tablespoons pine nuts, toasted (optional)
½ to 1 cup grated Parmigiano Reggiano or other aged cheese

1. Cut the bell peppers in 1-inch square pieces. Cut the broccoli rabe crosswise in lengths about 1½ inches long. Cut the sausage in small pieces.

2. In a medium skillet, cook the sausage with 1 tablespoon olive oil over medium heat, stirring often, until browned.

3. Fill a large saucepan about two-thirds full with cold water and set over high heat to boil for the pasta.

4. Meanwhile, drizzle 2 to 3 tablespoons olive oil into a skillet large enough to hold the pasta and sauce. Over medium heat, sauté the peppers and garlic until the peppers are fairly tender and the garlic turns golden; remove the garlic, chop, and return to the pan. Add the tomatoes, browned sausages, and ½ cup water. When the mixture comes to a simmer, reduce the heat to low and cook slowly.

*continued*

**5.** When the pasta water comes to a boil, add a handful of salt and the broccoli rabe. Cook until just tender, about 3 minutes. Scoop it out of the water with a long-handled strainer or large slotted spoon and add to the skillet with the peppers and sausage.

**6.** Boil the shells in the same water until al dente, 7 to 9 minutes. Drain, reserving 1 cup of the water, and turn immediately into the skillet with the sauce. Stir gently but thoroughly, adding pasta water as needed for a saucy consistency. Season to taste with salt (you won't need much, if any, because of the sausage) and red pepper flakes and cook a little longer to blend the flavors.

**7.** Spoon the pasta into shallow soup bowls. Sprinkle the pine nuts (if using) and grated cheese on top.

## NOTE
Young broccoli rabe with slender stems can be sautéed with the peppers rather than blanched in the pasta water.

## VARIATIONS
To make a vegetarian version of this pasta, leave out the sausage and substitute 6 to 8 ounces of feta or other soft sheep's milk cheese. Season more assertively with salt and pepper to compensate for the loss of the seasoning in the sausage.

Serve the sauce over soft polenta or gnocchi rather than pasta.

# SPAGHETTI with TUNA, FRESH TOMATOES, and OLIVES

*Spaghetti con tonno, pomodori e olivi*

MAKES 4 OR 5 SERVINGS | PREP: 10 MINUTES | COOK: 8 TO 12 MINUTES

*When everyone's starving at some weird hour like midnight, it's time for a spaghettata—a pasta feast improvised from ready-to-go ingredients. This tuna-tomato sauce and the anchovy variation are not only satisfying, but require no cooking.*

Sea salt or kosher salt
1 pound spaghetti or other pasta shape
2 cups diced fresh tomatoes or quartered cherry tomatoes
1/3 to 1/2 cup extra-virgin olive oil
2 tablespoons fresh lemon juice
1/2 cup black Mediterranean olives, pitted and cut into slivers
1 can (about 7 ounces) good-quality tuna packed in olive oil
1/2 cup chopped flat-leaf parsley
Hot red pepper flakes
1/2 cup toasted bread crumbs (optional) (recipe follows)

**1.** Fill a large saucepan about two-thirds full with cold water and set over high heat to boil for the pasta. Add a handful of salt and the spaghetti, pressing with a wooden spoon until fully immersed; stir well. Cook until al dente, 8 to 12 minutes.

**2.** Meanwhile, in a bowl large enough to hold the cooked pasta, combine the tomatoes, olive oil, lemon juice, and olives. Flake the tuna into the bowl, adding any olive oil remaining in the can. Stir in the parsley and season to taste with salt (sparingly) and hot red pepper flakes.

**3.** Drain the spaghetti, reserving about 1 cup of the cooking water and turn into the bowl with the tuna-tomato sauce, and mix well, adding the cooking water as needed for a saucy consistency. Sprinkle with the toasted bread crumbs (if using) and stir briefly.

*continued*

# Toasted Bread Crumbs

MAKES 1 CUP | PREP: 5 MINUTES | COOK: 5 MINUTES

**2 slices firm white bread, crusts trimmed**
**Extra-virgin olive oil**

1. Tear the bread into pieces, placing them in a food processor bowl. Process until medium-fine.

2. Smear the bottom of a heavy medium saucepan with a little olive oil (about 2 teaspoons) and place over medium-high heat. Add the bread crumbs and stir them as they steam, change color, and turn golden brown, over the course of about 5 minutes. Reduce the heat or lift the skillet if they seem in danger of burning.

3. Use the warm crumbs immediately or cool and store in a resealable plastic bag for several days.

## VARIATION

### *Penne with Tomatoes, Anchovies, and Baby Arugula*
For the tuna, substitute 8 anchovy fillets (or more), pinched into small pieces. Use only ¼ cup olives; in place of the parsley, fold 3 cups baby arugula into the hot pasta.

## Stand-Out Pastas, Step by Step

*Choose pasta brands that can be relied on* to deliver toothsome results. I'm partial to Italian-made pastas; De Cecco and Barilla are two moderately priced, good-quality brands that are widely available. Occasionally, treat yourself and your fellow diners to artfully shaped artisanal pasta, extruded through copper dies and dried at low temperatures to produce a surface that catches sauces in a wonderful way. Recommended brands: Cavalieri, Rustichella d'Abruzzo, Di Benedetto, Latini, Martelli, and Fara S. Martino.

*Pay attention to taste and texture* as well as nutritional attributes when experimenting with whole-grain pastas, a growing category. Some of the companies just mentioned make whole-grain pastas that pass those tests; Rustichella d'Abruzzo, for example, produces excellent farro pasta. Tinkyada's rice-based pasta is free of the strong flavors in some gluten-free pastas made with corn or legumes.

*Play with pasta shapes and colors.* To make sure an alternate shape is compatible with your sauce, pick one in the same category as the original—for example, substitute spinach *tagliatelle* for the thinner egg noodles called *tagliolini*. Or, if you find tubular *garganelli* on your grocer's pasta shelf, use it as an alternative to familiar penne.

*Get your pasta pot going.* For one pound of pasta, you'll need about six quarts of cold water. Bring it to a boil and add a handful of kosher or sea salt—about two tablespoons. A relatively small amount is absorbed, but salt is essential to the flavor of the cooked pasta; otherwise, it will taste flat, and no amount of tinkering with the sauce can fix that.

*Cook the pasta correctly.* Dried semolina pasta such as spaghetti and macaroni should be boiled until al dente—still slightly chewy and definitely not mushy.

*continued*

It might be ready in seven minutes or even earlier (many cook times given on pasta packages are too long); whole-grain pastas usually take longer than regular semolina pasta. Whether dried or fresh, egg pastas such as *tagliatelle* should be cooked until tender, from one to five minutes.

*Don't squander the pasta water!* Sometimes a vegetable such as spinach or green beans can be blanched in the boiling water before the pasta is cooked. And, it's often a good idea to save some of the starchy water after cooking the pasta, usually by scooping some out before draining. Added at the cook's discretion, it dilutes the sauce while, paradoxically, slightly thickening it.

> *"Often the best way to 'marry' the two is to add the cooked pasta to the bowl or skillet with the sauce."*

*Calculate the right proportion of sauce to coat*, but not drown, the cooked pasta. If you suspect there may be too much sauce, add it gradually to the pasta rather than all at once. If there's not enough sauce to coat and fully season the pasta, you may want to add more of a key ingredient—whether canned tomatoes, olive oil, or broth. Adding more of a flavor-enhancing ingredient such as fresh herbs or capers can also help.

*Allow the pasta and sauce to spend time together.* Often the best way to "marry" the two is to add the cooked pasta to the bowl or skillet with the sauce. The components are mixed thoroughly and, in some cases, cooked together for several minutes.

*Garnish pasta with ingredients that add flavor*, make it look pretty, and need no additional cooking. Sometimes it's a good idea to mix some grated cheese into the finished pasta and save the rest to sprinkle on top. Other topping ideas: a dollop of ricotta, fresh herbs, toasted nuts, or bread crumbs. ෴

# TAGLIOLINI with SHRIMP, LEEKS, and PROSCIUTTO

*Tagliolini con gamberi e prosciutto*

MAKES 4 TO 6 SERVINGS | PREP: 20 MINUTES | COOK: 12 MINUTES

*This wonderful dish comes from Alberto Rossetti of Al Tramezzo, a jovial chef known for his seafood expertise. The restaurant is in Parma, and he makes brilliant use of the locale's famous prosciutto, crisping it for this* mare e montagna *specialty.*

2 to 4 thin slices (about 1 ounce) prosciutto di Parma or other
   high-quality prosciutto (see Note)
1 medium leek, washed well (see Note, page 40)
3 sun-dried tomatoes (preferably the semisoft kind preserved
   in oil) (see Note)
¾ pound small shrimp, peeled (see Note)
1 tablespoon unsalted butter
Extra-virgin olive oil
½ cup white wine
⅓ cup chopped flat-leaf parsley
Sea salt or kosher salt
Hot red pepper flakes
1 pound thin fresh noodles such as *tagliolini* or angel hair pasta

**1.** Cut the prosciutto into small pieces with kitchen shears or a knife. Thinly slice the leek crosswise, including the white and an inch of the tender green part. Cut the sun-dried tomatoes in thin strips (kitchen shears work best). Unless the shrimp are really small (about 40 per pound), cut each one in half.

**2.** Melt the butter over medium heat in a small skillet. Cook the prosciutto, stirring and separating the pieces with a wooden spoon or heatproof spatula, until crisp, about 3 minutes. Remove from the heat but leave in the pan.

**3.** Fill a large saucepan about two-thirds full with cold water and set over high heat to boil for the pasta.

**4.** Meanwhile, heat about 3 tablespoons olive oil over medium heat in a skillet large enough to hold all the ingredients. Sauté the leek until tender but not browned. Stir in the shrimp, cooking just until it loses its raw look. Add the white wine, letting it sizzle for 1 to 2 minutes. Stir in the crisped prosciutto, sun-dried tomatoes, and parsley. Season sparingly with salt (because prosciutto and sun-dried tomatoes contain sodium) and red pepper flakes.

**5.** Add a handful of salt to the boiling water and the pasta, shaking each handful a few strands at a time (to avoid tangling); stir well. Boil just until tender, 1 to 3 minutes (depending on freshness). Drain, reserving 2 cups of cooking water, and transfer the noodles to the skillet with the shrimp-leek mix. Stir gently but thoroughly to coat the pasta with the sauce; add as much of the cooking water as needed for a saucy consistency.

## NOTES

Some delis sell prosciutto ends, usually at a lower cost than center-cut slices. Cut in small cubes, an end will work well in this recipe; thick-cut pancetta is another option.

Sun-dried tomatoes that are so hard they cannot be folded over must be soaked in water until soft.

In Italy, I use the smallest, sweetest shrimp, no bigger than a baby's pinkie, for this dish. Those are hard to find in the U.S.—the closest you might come are tiny, sweet Maine rock shrimp or the smallest Florida Key West pinks. Other varieties of wild Gulf shrimp have a lot of flavor, too.

# TAGLIATELLE with SCALLOPS and AMALFI-STYLE LEMON SAUCE

*Fettuccine con capesante al limone*

MAKES 3 TO 4 SERVINGS | PREP: 15 MINUTES | COOK: 10 MINUTES

*Anyone traveling along the Amalfi coast has seen lemon trees tucked among the cliffs, covered by protective netting. I found their unforgettable perfume and flavor particularly compelling in creamy sauces clinging to tagliatelle and other fresh pasta—so much so that some kind of pasta al limone became my default restaurant order there.*

*Back home, I tried to replicate those citrusy epiphanies. The sauces I made were good but just a bit less aromatic, a bit less memorable—that's why Amalfi lemons are famous, after all. I did discover, however, the affinity of sweet, briny sea scallops for a creamy lemon sauce. This seafood sauce is set off especially well by the warm-toned, slightly earthy flavor of artisanal whole-wheat pasta made with farro.*

1 large lemon
1 pound "dry" bay scallops or sea scallops (see Note)
2 tablespoons unsalted butter
2 tablespoons finely chopped shallot or onion
1/2 cup heavy cream
Sea salt or kosher salt
Freshly ground black pepper
1 tablespoon extra-virgin olive oil
9 ounces fresh or dried regular or whole-wheat *tagliatelle*
2 to 4 tablespoons snipped chives, parsley, basil, or mint

**1.** Grate the lemon zest (yellow part only); halve and juice the lemon. Blot the scallops on both sides with paper towels; if using sea scallops, cut them in half to form half-moons.

**2.** In a medium saucepan, melt 1 tablespoon of the butter over medium-low heat. Sauté the shallot until soft, about 5 minutes. Stir in the cream and season to taste with salt and pepper. Simmer for several minutes until it begins to thicken. Stir in the lemon juice and zest and keep warm over low heat.

**3.** Fill a large saucepan two-thirds full with cold water and set over high heat to boil for the pasta.

**4.** Meanwhile, heat a large skillet over medium-high heat. Melt the remaining tablespoon of butter with the olive oil. Sear the scallops until well browned and heated through, turning once. Transfer them to the saucepan with the lemon sauce. Add a little water to the skillet, stirring to loosen any browned bits, and add to the pan with the lemon cream sauce; stir to combine. Keep warm over low heat.

**5.** Add a handful of salt and the pasta to the boiling water and cook until tender, 1 to 5 minutes. Scoop out the pasta with a long-handled strainer and add to the skillet along with the chives. Mix thoroughly, adding a bit of the pasta water if needed to dilute the sauce.

**6.** Heap the pasta on broad, shallow bowls or plates.

### NOTE
Question your fishmonger closely to make sure you are buying "dry" scallops free of tripolyphosphate, a preservative that also whitens and adds water weight to seafood. Scallops that do not brown properly have most likely been treated with this chemical, or frozen, or both.

# ASPARAGUS-SPINACH CRÊPES with TALEGGIO

*Crespelle agli asparagi e spinaci con salsa al Taleggio*

MAKES 4 OR 5 SERVINGS | PREP: 30 MINUTES | COOK: 25 MINUTES

*Crespelle,* the Italian version of crêpes, can be filled and sauced in many ways. This combination offsets the richness of the sauce with fresh green vegetables.

4 tablespoons unsalted butter, plus more for pan
8 ounces asparagus (at least 15 spears), trimmed
1 pound spinach, tough stems trimmed
1/2 cup chopped shallot or onion
Sea salt or kosher salt
Freshly ground black pepper
1 1/2 cups half-and-half
2 tablespoons unbleached all-purpose flour
4 ounces Taleggio cheese, cubed (about 2/3 cup)
12 to 15 crêpes (recipe follows)
2 to 3 ounces thinly sliced Italian prosciutto (optional)

1. Lightly butter a rectangular Pyrex or ceramic baking dish (about 11x14"). Fill a large saucepan two-thirds full with water; bring to a boil. Cook the asparagus until barely tender, about 2 minutes; with tongs, transfer to a colander and cool under running water. Add the spinach to the boiling water, cooking just until it wilts. Drain in a colander; cool under running water, squeeze out some of the moisture, and chop.

2. Melt 2 tablespoons butter over medium-low heat in a medium skillet. Add the shallot and cook, stirring, until tender, about 5 minutes. Stir in the chopped spinach, cooking briefly until fairly dry; season to taste with salt (if needed) and pepper, and transfer to a bowl.

3. To make the Taleggio sauce: Microwave the half-and-half in a liquid measuring cup until steaming, about 30 seconds, or heat in a small saucepan. Meanwhile, melt 2 tablespoons butter over medium-low heat in a small saucepan. Add the flour and cook, stirring, for 1 to 2 minutes. Gradually add the hot half-and-half, whisking constantly to avoid lumps. Bring the mixture to a simmer and cook, stirring often, for about 10 minutes. The consistency of the sauce should be fairly loose, similar to that of heavy cream. Stir in the Taleggio cheese, cooking just until it melts. Season to taste with salt and pepper. Keep warm over low heat.

**4.** Preheat the oven to 400°F. Line up the crêpes, Taleggio sauce, spinach, prosciutto (if using), and asparagus, assembly-line fashion. Laying out one crêpe at a time, spread a little Taleggio sauce over it, followed by a light coating of the seasoned spinach. Tear off part of a prosciutto slice and lay it on top. Place an asparagus spear (or several, if they are thin) so that the tips are peeking out, and roll up the crêpe. Place it in the prepared baking dish. Repeat with the remaining crêpes and ingredients, gauging quantities so that you come out more or less even.

**5.** Drizzle the crêpes with the remaining Taleggio sauce, using a spatula to distribute it evenly. Cover the dish with aluminum foil. (At this point, the crêpes can be held for 1 to 2 hours at room temperature or refrigerated for up to 12 hours.)

**6.** Bake the crêpes until heated through and the sauce is bubbly, about 15 minutes. Move to the top rack of the oven and broil briefly to brown the top.

## Crêpes

MAKES 12 TO 15 CRÊPES | PREP: 10 MINUTES | COOK: 20 MINUTES

2 tablespoons unsalted butter, plus more if needed
1 cup milk
2 eggs, beaten
1 cup unbleached all-purpose flour
Large pinch sea salt or kosher salt

**1.** Melt 1 tablespoon butter in a microwaveable container or small saucepan over low heat; add to the milk. In a small bowl, whisk the eggs. Add the milk mixture.

**2.** Combine the flour and salt in a food processor. Pulse to blend. With the processor running, add the liquid through the funnel. Process until smooth, scraping down the sides of the bowl once or twice. Scrape the crêpe batter into a bowl. Refrigerate for at least half an hour or up to 4 hours.

*continued*

**3.** Heat a 7-inch carbon-steel crêpe pan or another small skillet over medium heat. Melt the remaining tablespoon of butter and brush a little over the skillet. Ladle ¼ cup of the batter into the pan; lift the pan and tilt to distribute in a thin layer over the bottom of the pan. Cook until lightly browned on the bottom, about 20 seconds (you may need to reduce the heat a little). Using a small spatula, flip the crêpe and cook a few minutes longer until lightly browned on the other side. Transfer to a plate. Repeat with the remainder of the batter, brushing the pan with butter before cooking each crêpe. Stack the crêpes on top of one another. They can be used right away or made a day or two in advance and refrigerated. Or, layer them between pieces of waxed paper, wrap well, and freeze.

# GREEN GNOCCHI ("GNUDI") with MUSHROOM-SAGE SAUCE

*Gnocchi verdi con salsa ai funghi e salvia*

**MAKES 4 SERVINGS | PREP: 40 MINUTES | COOK: 15 MINUTES**

*These ricotta-and-greens gnocchi also go by the name ravioli gnudi ("nude ravioli") because of their resemblance to ravioli filling. The delicate mixture morphs into dumplings with the addition of flour. It is important to resist the temptation to add the amount of flour needed to make the gnudi mixture truly easy to handle, in the interest of producing dumplings that are light, not leaden.*

*When served as a first course, these gnocchi are usually glossed with a butter-and-sage or tomato sauce. But larger servings and a heartier mushroom sauce enable this dish to stand on its own.*

1 pound fresh spinach
2 cups whole-milk or part-skim ricotta cheese (see Note)
2/3 cup unbleached all-purpose flour, or more as needed
2 large eggs, beaten
Sea salt or kosher salt
1/8 teaspoon nutmeg
1 cup grated Parmigiano Reggiano or Grana Padano cheese
Mushroom-sage sauce (recipe follows)

1. Remove and discard spinach stems if they are thick; wash the leaves, changing the water until no grit remains behind. Place the wet spinach in a saucepan. Cover and cook over medium heat, stirring once or twice, until wilted, about 8 minutes. Drain the spinach and cool it under running water; squeeze with your hands until very dry. Chop roughly.

2. In a medium bowl, with a spatula or wooden spoon, mix together the ricotta, flour, eggs, 1 teaspoon salt, nutmeg, and half of the Parmigiano Reggiano. Add the spinach and blend thoroughly. The mixture will be very soft and somewhat damp. If it seems too wet, add a bit more flour, but be sparing—too much flour results in leaden gnocchi.

*continued*

**3.** Preheat oven to 250°F. Fill a large saucepan two-thirds full with cold water; bring to a boil and add a handful of salt. Dust your hands with flour. Scoop up a bit of the mixture with a teaspoon and gently roll to form an oval pellet about 1 inch long. Test it by cooking in the boiling water. If it disintegrates, add a little more flour—again, as little as possible. Taste for seasoning and adjust if necessary in the rest of the dough. Form the rest of the gnocchi, dusting your hands with flour as needed, and place gnocchi on a cutting board or other surface lined with waxed paper. (Alternatively, scoop up a larger amount of gnocchi dough; place on a well-floured surface and roll between your hands to form a rope; cut into 1-inch lengths.)

**4.** Drop the gnocchi into the boiling water, about 10 at a time; they will sink. After the water returns to a boil, cook 3 to 4 minutes, until the gnocchi rise to the surface. With a slotted spoon, transfer each batch to a casserole dish. Spoon some of the mushroom-sage sauce over them. Keep warm in the oven while cooking and saucing the remaining gnocchi.

**5.** To serve: Spoon the hot gnocchi and sauce into shallow soup bowls and sprinkle with the remaining cheese.

**NOTE**

Choose a high-quality brand such as Montena Taranto or Calabro, which come in metal containers with a perforated bottom. Or, if you are fortunate enough to find it, buy freshly made ricotta in your farmers' market.

## Mushroom-Sage Sauce

MAKES 4 SERVINGS | PREP: 20 MINUTES | COOK: 20 MINUTES

1 pound white mushrooms or a mixture such as white, crimini, and shiitake
2 tablespoons unsalted butter
½ tablespoon extra-virgin olive oil
½ cup finely chopped shallots or onion
½ cup dry white wine
½ cup heavy cream
Sea salt or kosher salt
Freshly ground black pepper
Leaves from 3 sage sprigs, snipped into small pieces
  (about 2 heaping tablespoons)

1. Trim mushroom ends if they are dry and clean the mushrooms by dunking in cold water and wiping clean with paper towels (if shiitake are part of the mix, use only the caps, saving the stems to flavor a broth or for some other use). Halve the mushrooms lengthwise (quarter larger ones) and cut crosswise into thin slices.

2. Melt the butter with the olive oil in a large skillet over medium-high heat. Sauté the shallots until soft. Add the mushrooms and cook until they soften and give up some of their moisture. Stir in the wine and cook until absorbed. Add the cream and up to ½ cup water for a saucy consistency; season to taste with salt and pepper. Stir in the sage leaves and cook just until wilted.

## VARIATIONS

For the cream in the mushroom sauce, substitute 1 cup puréed plum tomatoes (such as Pomì); add water as needed for a saucy consistency.

To take the sauce in a sweetly aromatic direction, substitute Marsala or *vin santo* for the white wine.

A sprinkle of crisp, crumbled bacon would be delicious on this dish. Or, sauté finely diced pancetta with the shallot when preparing the sauce.

# Chapter 2

# MINESTRONI and OTHER BIG, BOUNTIFUL SOUPS

In his famous treatise on the Italian kitchen, Pellegrino Artusi leads with soups — specifically, diminutive pasta shapes floating in broth, the kind of elegant soup meant to tantalize taste buds without making much of a dent in the appetite. The assumption, of course, is that soup is merely a prelude to the meal—and, indeed, the word *minestra* originally referred to any first course.

Eventually *La Scienza in Cucina e L'Arte di Mangiar Bene* moves on to *minestroni* ("big soups"), dense with seasonal vegetables, beans, and grains, and to *zuppe*, even heartier soups thickened or topped with stale bread. Long before the musings of a nineteenth-century bourgeois gentleman, such soups sustained populations through hard times. People gathered available makings, stretching them by adding water to make a nourishing one-dish meal.

Ask a Piemontese born before World War II about chestnut soup or a Sicilian of similar age about *maccu* (whose main components are beans or other pulses). They remember soups like these in the most vivid way. What's interesting is that these humble dishes haven't been left behind in more prosperous times, but rather are considered the essence of *cucina povera*. They are eaten with relish, albeit with more luxurious touches. The reason: They're not only satisfying but, assuming a good cook is stirring the pot, absolutely delicious.

Take *pasta e fagioli*, a big soup with impeccable nutritional credentials. More often than not, the cook lays down a flavor base with *soffritto*, consisting at its most simple of onions sautéed in olive oil to the desired hue. Selections of produce and other ingredients are attuned to the season, with sensitivity to compatible flavors and an eye to an appetizing combination of colors and shapes. With judiciously chosen seasonings, those components yield a flavorful soup, usually without the addition of broth. Pasta goes into the pot in time to cook through, without overcooking.

In Italy, soups are typically served as a *primo*, or first course. But there's no question that, with the portion sizes ramped up a little, substantial soups make wonderful meals in a bowl. And that's the focus of this chapter, which ranges from *acquacotta*, a minestrone topped with a poached egg, to a thick, flavorful chickpea and porcini soup.

# MINESTRONI and OTHER BIG, BOUNTIFUL SOUPS

# LIGURIAN-STYLE MINESTRONE with GREEN GARNISHES

*Minestron*

MAKES 8 TO 10 SERVINGS | PREP: 30 MINUTES | COOK: 30 MINUTES

*This summer soup from the Italian Riviera is cousin to the Provençal soupe au pistou, made with seasonal vegetables and, invariably, finished with a dollop of garlicky pesto. To preserve their bright color and fresh taste, I like to blanch green vegetables at the start of cooking and return them to the soup pot at the end.*

2 medium leeks (white and tender green parts), halved lengthwise
    and washed well (see Note, page 40)
1 baby eggplant
2 medium yellow summer squash or zucchini, or 1 of each
1 boiling potato, peeled
1 stalk celery
8 ounces green beans, trimmed
2 cups firmly packed spinach leaves
1 large tomato, peeled (see Note)
1 or 2 cloves garlic
Sea salt or kosher salt
Piece of Parmigiano Reggiano rind (optional)
½ cup *pastine* (soup pasta) or other small pasta
Up to 1 cup *pesto genovese* (see Note)

**1.** Cut the leeks crosswise into thin slices. Peel the eggplant and squash only if the skins are tough. Cut the eggplant, squash, and potato into medium (½-inch) dice. Thinly slice the celery and cut the green beans in short lengths. With a knife, shred or chop the spinach. Cut the tomato into medium dice and finely chop the garlic.

**2.** Bring 3 quarts cold water to a boil in a large saucepan. Add the green beans and half of the leeks; cook for a couple of minutes, until beans are crisp-tender; add the spinach and cook for a few seconds until wilted; scoop out the vegetables with a long-handled strainer, cool under running water, and set aside.

**3.** To the simmering water, add the remaining leeks, the eggplant, squash, potato, celery, 2 teaspoons salt, the garlic and, if using, the cheese rind. Bring to a boil, reduce the heat, and simmer until the vegetables are tender, about 20 minutes.

**4.** Stir in the *pastine* and tomato. Simmer briskly until the pasta is just tender, about 7 minutes. Stir in the blanched green beans, leeks, and spinach. Season with salt as needed.

**5.** To serve: Ladle the soup into broad, shallow soup bowls. Garnish each with a heaping teaspoon of pesto; pass the remainder at the table.

## NOTES

You can blanch the tomato in boiling water for a few seconds to loosen the skin but, for a single tomato, it's easier to strip off the skin with a sharp knife.

Follow the recipe for *pesto genovese* on page 27, omitting the pine nuts and using only ½ cup olive oil and ½ teaspoon salt.

# BROTHY BREAD SOUP with POACHED EGGS

*Acquacotta*

**MAKES 4 SERVINGS | PREP: 20 MINUTES | COOK: 30 MINUTES**

*On a visit to the Maremma, I was hoping to see the wild boars used to make a much-prized prosciutto. Not a glimpse. I did have plenty of opportunities, however, to sample a brothy vegetable and bread soup for which this area of coastal Tuscany and Lazio is also known.*

*Despite an unpromising name meaning "cooked water," acquacotta is full of flavor. When broken with a spoon, the poached egg releases its richness into the broth, while the croutons add body.*

1 cup medium bread cubes cut from a country-style white or
  whole-wheat loaf (about 2 slices)
Extra-virgin olive oil
1 small onion, chopped
1 small carrot, thinly sliced
1 small stalk celery, thinly sliced (about ½ cup)
1 large clove garlic, finely chopped
1 teaspoon chopped fresh rosemary or ½ teaspoon dried
  rosemary
⅛ teaspoon hot red pepper flakes, or to taste
Sea salt or kosher salt
1 cup chopped or shredded chard (any variety) or spinach leaves
1 cup chopped canned plum tomatoes with some of the purée
4 eggs
1/2 cup grated Parmigiano Reggiano cheese, or more to taste

**1.** Preheat an oven or toaster oven to 400ºF. Toss the bread cubes on a baking sheet with 1 tablespoon olive oil. Cook until dry to the touch and lightly browned, about 5 minutes. Turn off the heat, leaving the cubes in the oven.

**2.** Add a little olive oil (about 1 tablespoon) to a large saucepan over medium heat. Sauté the onion until soft but not colored, stirring often. Reduce the heat and add the carrot and celery, sautéing for a couple of minutes longer. Add the garlic, rosemary, and red pepper flakes, cooking just until the garlic is fragrant.

*continued*

**3.** Add 2 quarts cold water and 2 teaspoons salt; bring to a boil. Stir in the chard and tomatoes; reduce the heat to low and simmer for 10 to 15 minutes to blend the flavors. Taste the broth and season as needed with more salt and hot red pepper.

**4.** Bring 1 quart water to a very gentle simmer in a deep skillet or saucepan just wide enough to accommodate 4 poached eggs. Break an egg into a small dish and, holding it close to the surface of the water, slide it in. When the water returns to a simmer, add the next egg. Poach the eggs until the whites are opaque and the yolks firm up slightly but are still soft, about 2½ minutes. Remove the eggs (in the same order you poached them) with a skimmer or slotted spoon.

**5.** Meanwhile, ladle the soup into 4 broad, shallow bowls. Top each serving with a poached egg, a sprinkle of Parmigiano Reggiano, and croutons.

### NOTE

For ease of preparation and a more rustic look, poach the eggs right in the soup pot. They will sink from sight but rise to the surface when almost fully cooked. Transfer eggs to the soup bowls as described above, and ladle the soup around them.

### VARIATION

In addition to the other garnishes, add small strips of prosciutto, torn by hand, to the bowls just before serving.

# MINESTRONE with CHICKEN, for a CROWD

*Minestrone con pollo, per la folla*

**MAKES ABOUT 7 QUARTS** *(14 servings)* | **PREP: 1 HOUR** | **COOK: ABOUT 1½ HOURS**

*I had agreed to make homemade minestrone for a church gathering of about fifty people, which would normally translate into a lot of chopping. Short of time, I resorted to the shredded vegetables now on hand in just about any produce department. The soup came out great and, at the end of lunch, not a ladleful remained in the pot. Simmering the chicken for just 30 to 40 minutes creates a light but flavorful broth; the meat hasn't been cooked to oblivion, so it can also be used in the soup.*

*Because feeding fifty isn't an everyday enterprise, this downsized version produces soup for a smaller group.*

2½ pounds bone-in chicken thighs
1 pound beef bones (optional)
2 bay leaves
1 large onion
2 or 3 cloves garlic
3 stalks celery
Extra-virgin olive oil
1 small package (8 ounces) shredded carrots (see Note)
1 small package (8 ounces) shredded or julienned zucchini
1 small package (8 ounces) shredded cabbage or slaw mix
1 (28-ounce) can or carton diced tomatoes with juice (such as Pomì)
Sea salt or kosher salt
1 tablespoon dried Italian seasoning blend or a combination of
   dried oregano and thyme
Freshly ground black pepper
2 cups mini *rotelli*, *pastine* (soup pasta), or other small pasta
3 cups white beans with sage and garlic with some of their broth (page
   72) or the same quantity of canned beans, drained and rinsed
2 cups grated Parmigiano Reggiano, Grana Padano, or aged
   pecorino cheese, or more to taste
Country bread (optional)

*continued*

1. Place the chicken and beef bones (if using) in a 6- to 8-quart saucepan. Add the bay leaves and fill about two-thirds full with cold water. Bring to a boil. Reduce the heat and simmer for 30 to 40 minutes, skimming off the scum that rises to the top.

2. Meanwhile, chop the onion, finely chop the garlic, and cut the celery into small dice. In a skillet, sauté the onion in a generous quantity of olive oil (about ¼ cup) over medium heat until tender and golden brown, about 10 minutes. Add the garlic and cook briefly until fragrant.

3. With tongs, transfer the chicken thighs to a bowl; cool until they can be handled. Cut the chicken meat into bite-size pieces, discarding the skin and bones. Discard the beef bones if you used them.

4. Add the onion-garlic mixture to the broth in the saucepan. Add the celery, carrots, zucchini, cabbage, tomatoes, 2 heaping tablespoons salt, the Italian seasoning, and 1 teaspoon pepper. Over medium-high heat, bring the mixture to a boil. Reduce the heat and simmer until the vegetables are tender, about 15 minutes. (At this point, the soup and chicken thighs can be held separately, refrigerated, for up to a day; skim any fat off chilled soup before reheating).

5. If the saucepan is nearly full at this point, transfer half of the contents to another saucepan. Add water if the soup seems too dense. When it comes to a simmer, add the pasta and cook until al dente, about 10 minutes. Stir in the chicken and beans; taste and add more salt and pepper if needed. Simmer a few minutes longer to blend the flavors and finish cooking the pasta.

6. Serve with the grated cheese and hunks of country bread.


NOTE

As an alternative to buying shredded carrots, zucchini, and cabbage, prepare them in your food processor, using the shredding attachment.

# ESCAROLE, WHITE BEAN, and PLUM TOMATO SOUP

*Minestra di scarola, cannellini e pomodoro*

MAKES 6 SERVINGS | PREP: 15 MINUTES | COOK: 25 MINUTES *(plus soaking and cooking time for the beans)*

*Escarole is lovely in summer—pale green, crisp, and with just enough bitterness to make it interesting. So I decided to do this warm-weather take, finished with fresh tomatoes, on a classic minestra. Once the beans are done, it's a quick soup to make.*

1 medium onion, chopped
Extra-virgin olive oil
2 cloves garlic, finely chopped
3 cups white beans with sage and garlic (recipe follows),
  including the bean cooking liquid (see Note)
3 cups chicken or vegetable broth or water
Piece of Parmigiano Reggiano rind (optional)
4 cups shredded escarole
4 fresh plum tomatoes, diced small, or 4 chopped canned
  plum tomatoes
Sea salt or kosher salt
Hot red pepper flakes
Grated Parmigiano Reggiano or Grana Padano cheese

1. In a large saucepan over medium heat, sauté the onion in olive oil (about 3 tablespoons) until golden, about 10 minutes. Stir in the garlic, cooking just until fragrant.

2. Add the bean cooking liquid, chicken broth, and Parmigiano Reggiano rind (if using). Bring to a boil. Stir in the beans, lower the heat, and bring to a simmer.

3. Add the escarole and tomatoes and cook just until the greens wilt and the tomatoes soften. Season to taste with salt and hot red pepper flakes.

4. Divide among bowls and sprinkle with grated cheese. Serve warm, not scaldingly hot.

*continued*

**NOTE**

If it's almost dinnertime and you're out of time to cook the beans from scratch, substitute 3 cups canned chickpeas, drained and rinsed. Use additional chicken or vegetable broth to make up for the lack of bean cooking liquid.

# White Beans with Sage and Garlic

MAKES ABOUT 3 CUPS | PREP: 10 MINUTES *(plus up to 6 hours soaking time for the beans)* | COOK: 1 TO 2 HOURS

**1 cup small dried white beans**
**1 large sprig fresh sage**
**2 cloves garlic, lightly crushed**
**Sea salt or kosher salt**

1. Place the beans in a medium saucepan and cover with cold water; soak for 6 hours or as directed on the package.

2. Drain the beans and wash under running water, picking them over to remove any pieces of grit. Return the beans to the saucepan and cover with fresh cold water to a depth of several inches above the beans. Add the sage and garlic.

3. Bring the bean mixture to a boil; reduce the heat to a bare simmer, partially cover, and cook until the beans are tender but still hold their shape, 1 to 2 hours. Remove and discard the sage and garlic; season lightly with salt.

**NOTE**

The same method can be used for other dried beans, including *borlotti* (cranberry beans), chickpeas, and various kinds of heirloom beans; *zolfini* (sulphur beans) require longer soaking, about twelve hours, as well as longer cooking, three to four hours.

# CANNELLINI, LENTIL, and PENNETTE SOUP

*Minestra di cannellini, lenticchie e pennette*

MAKES 6 SERVINGS | PREP: 30 MINUTES *(plus up to 6 hours soaking time for the legumes)* | COOK: ABOUT 1½ HOURS

*Soups like this one, belonging to the* pasta e fagioli *canon, bring to mind a long-ago summer when we were wandering central and northern Italy with our young daughters, recently minted vegetarians. They must have eaten several cauldrons of* pasta e fagioli, *cumulatively, in various restaurants. Our order was always preceded by ingredient queries, and we learned that the soup was sometimes entirely vegetarian and sometimes not. Calling a problem to the waiter's attention, I could almost see the thought bubble floating above his head: "What could a little* brodo *hurt?"*

*Personally, I'm pro-brodo in the case of this soup. I appreciate the little flavor push it gives—unless my daughters are coming to dinner!*

1 cup dried cannellini or other small white beans
1 cup lentils (preferably the small, greenish-brown Italian or
    French variety)
1 medium onion, halved
2 bay leaves
Extra-virgin olive oil
1 cup peeled, small-diced butternut squash (see Note)
1 stalk celery, diced small
1 clove garlic, finely chopped
1 cup chopped canned plum tomatoes with some of the purée
2 cups chicken broth or water
1 teaspoon dried thyme, or to taste
Sea salt or kosher salt
Freshly ground black pepper
1 cup *pennette* or other small pasta (see Note)
2 to 4 cups shredded spinach or chard
Aged Piave, or another hard grating cheese

*continued*

1. In separate bowls, soak the cannellini and lentils for 6 hours or as directed on the packages (see Note). Drain the legumes (keeping them separate) and rinse under running water, rubbing between your hands and picking out any pieces of grit, until the water runs clear.

2. Place the cannellini, one onion half, and the bay leaves in a large saucepan; cover with water to a depth of several inches above the beans. Bring to a boil; reduce the heat to low and simmer very slowly for 30 minutes. Stir in the lentils. Continue to simmer until both are perfectly tender, but still firm enough to hold their shape, about 30 minutes longer.

3. Meanwhile, chop the remaining onion half. In a skillet, combine the onion with a generous quantity of olive oil (2 to 3 tablespoons). Over medium heat, cook until tender but not browned. Stir in the squash and celery and continue to cook for a few minutes; add the garlic, cooking just until fragrant. Add the tomatoes, broth, and thyme. Season to taste with salt and pepper. Continue to simmer the mixture while the beans finish cooking.

4. In a small saucepan over high heat, bring 3 cups of water to a boil. When the simmering beans have absorbed most of their liquid, add 2 to 3 cups of the boiling water and 2 teaspoons salt to the beans. Add the pasta and bring to a boil. Reduce the heat and simmer until pasta is al dente, about 8 to 12 minutes. Add the tomato mixture and spinach, simmering until the pasta is tender and the spinach wilts. Taste and add more salt and pepper if needed.

5. Pass a chunk of the Piave with a small grater, or grate some of the cheese to serve in a bowl.

## NOTES

Peel the squash with a vegetable peeler, or use the peeled chunks sold in some produce departments. Acorn squash or carrots—or even sweet potatoes—could be substituted for the butternut squash.

In recent years miniature shapes such as *pennette* and mini fusilli have become more widely available. In soups, they offer a midsize alternative to regular pasta and tiny soup pasta.

Normally, lentils are not presoaked, but sitting in water does soften them, shortening the cooking time—and, since you're soaking the cannellini anyway, why not?

# LENTIL, SQUID, and GREENS SOUP

*Zuppa di lenticchie, calamari e tarassaco*

MAKES 6 SERVINGS | PREP: 20 MINUTES | COOK: 45 MINUTES

*To many people, calamari and fried are synonymous terms. Squid, an abundant, economical, and delicious source of protein, deserve more credit for their versatility—for instance, they take swimmingly to this comforting lentil and greens soup.*

*I enjoy these simple, straightforward flavors but, for an edgy extra, you might add a splash of red wine vinegar or hot sauce in the final moments of cooking.*

1 small onion
1 cup lentils (preferably the small greenish-brown Italian or
  French variety), washed well
1 small carrot, peeled and diced small
1 bay leaf
Sea salt or kosher salt
Freshly ground black pepper
½ pound cleaned baby squid or regular squid
Extra-virgin olive oil
1 clove garlic, finely chopped
2 cups firmly packed shredded greens such as baby dandelion,
  spinach, or chard leaves

**1.** Cut off one-third of the onion at the root end, reserving the end; peel and chop the remainder of the onion. Put the lentils in a medium saucepan and add water to about double their depth. Add the onion end, carrot, and bay leaf. Bring to a boil. Reduce the heat and simmer slowly, partially covered, until tender but not mushy, about 30 minutes. Season to taste with salt and pepper.

**2.** While the lentils are simmering, cut the squid bodies in thin rings; cut the tentacles into smaller clumps. In a small skillet, sauté the chopped onion over medium heat in 2 tablespoons of the olive oil until golden; add the garlic and cook just until fragrant. Add 1 tablespoon of olive oil and stir in the squid. Cook until it firms up and takes on an opaque look, about 3 minutes.

**3.** In a small saucepan over high heat, bring 2 to 3 cups water to a boil. Pour as much hot water over the lentils as needed for a thick but fluid consistency. Stir in the greens and cook just until tender. Add the squid and onions and heat through; taste and adjust the seasoning. Remove the onion end and bay leaf before serving.

# CRANBERRY BEAN, SAUSAGE, and FARRO SOUP

*Zuppa di borlotti, salsicce e farro*

**MAKES 8 SERVINGS | PREP: 20 MINUTES** *(plus soaking time for the beans)*
**COOK: 2 HOURS**

*This recipe brings together good ingredients and lets them do the work. The beans, sausage, and aromatic vegetables produce a rich-tasting broth, which is in turn thickened by the farro. Accompanied only by a crusty loaf of bread, this soup makes a perfect meal for a crisp fall day or winter night.*

1 pound dried cranberry or pinto beans
2 bay leaves
1 medium onion, chopped
Extra-virgin olive oil
½ pound mild or hot Italian sausage links, cut into small pieces
1 or 2 cloves garlic, finely chopped
2 medium carrots, diced
1 small fennel bulb or 1 stalk celery, diced
2 tablespoons tomato paste
1½ cups chopped canned tomatoes with purée
½ cup farro or barley (see Note)
Sea salt or kosher salt
Freshly ground black pepper (optional)

1. Place the beans in a large saucepan and cover with cold water; soak for 6 hours or as directed on the package. Drain and wash well under cold running water. Return the beans to the saucepan and cover with cold water to a depth a couple of inches above the beans. Add the bay leaves and bring to a boil. Reduce the heat and simmer, partially covered, until tender, about 1 hour.

2. Meanwhile, combine the onion with enough olive oil to coat the bottom of a skillet (about 3 tablespoons). Sauté over medium heat until soft. Add the sausages. Cook until the onion and sausage are golden brown, about 15 minutes. Stir in the garlic and cook briefly until fragrant. Add the carrots and fennel. Stir in the tomato paste and 1 cup water, simmering and stirring until the tomato paste is dissolved.

**3.** Add the sausage mixture and tomatoes to the beans (even if beans are not fully cooked). Stir in the farro, 1 tablespoon salt, and pepper to taste (if using). Bring to a boil. Reduce the heat and simmer until the farro is tender and the soup is fairly thick, about 30 minutes; dilute with water if it seems too dense. Taste and add more salt and pepper if necessary. Discard the bay leaves before serving.

### NOTE

Even if it doesn't say so on the label, farro and barley are normally sold "pearled" or "semi-pearled"—that is, processed to remove the outer hull so that the grain will become more tender when cooked. Even so, they retain more fiber and nutrients than more highly processed grains such as rice.

### VARIATION

To make a vegetarian version of this soup: For the sausage, substitute 10 ounces sliced white or crimini mushrooms; sauté with the onion and garlic as directed in the recipe.

# THICK CHICKPEA and PORCINI SOUP

*Zuppa di ceci e porcini*

**MAKES 4 SERVINGS | PREP: 10 MINUTES** *(plus up to 6 hours soaking time for the chickpeas)* **| COOK: 2½ HOURS**

*This soup won my heart at Ristorante La Mencia, in the town of Asciano. I found it creamy (though it possesses not a drop of cream) and deeply satisfying, but light enough to eat on a day when spring was edging into summer. Afterwards, owner Paolo Nocentini showed me a sackful of the chickpeas, grown by a nearby organic farmer. "It's a very simple soup to make!" he said enthusiastically. And so it is.*

1 cup high-quality dried chickpeas, preferably Tuscan (see Note)
2 cloves garlic
1 sprig sage
Sea salt or kosher salt
Freshly ground black pepper
1 ounce (about ½ cup) dried porcini mushrooms
1 small onion or 2 spring onions, coarsely chopped
Extra-virgin olive oil
1 cup canned peeled plum tomatoes with some of their purée
1 cup whole-wheat mini-rotini or other small pasta
Best-quality extra-virgin olive oil, for drizzling

**1.** Soak the chickpeas in cold water for 6 hours, or according to package directions. Drain and wash well, picking out any pieces of grit. Coarsely chop 1 garlic clove, leaving the other whole.

**2.** In a medium saucepan, combine the chickpeas with the whole garlic clove and the sage sprig. Cover with cold water to a depth 2 inches above the beans. Bring to a boil; reduce the heat and cook at a bare simmer, partially covered, until tender, 1 to 2 hours. Remove sage sprig. Stir in 1 teaspoon salt and ¼ teaspoon pepper.

**3.** Place the porcini in a small bowl and cover with warm water. In a medium skillet, combine the onion with 3 tablespoons olive oil. Cover and cook over medium-low heat, stirring often, until tender but not browned, about 5 minutes. Stir in the chopped garlic, cooking just until fragrant. Add the tomatoes and 2 cups of the chickpeas with some of their cooking liquid. Bring to a brisk simmer and cook, partially covered, for about 10 minutes.

**4.** Transfer the chickpea-tomato mixture to a blender container; add 1 cup bean cooking liquid or water; purée until very smooth. Add the purée to the cooked chickpeas.

**5.** Reserving the soaking liquid, briefly rinse the softened porcini and chop coarsely. Heat 1 tablespoon oil in a small skillet over medium heat; sauté the porcini for 1 to 2 minutes.

**6.** Add the porcini to the saucepan with the chickpeas. Bring to a simmer, taste, and add more salt and pepper if needed. Add the pasta and cook until tender, about 10 minutes. Strain about 1 cup of the porcini soaking liquid into the soup through a small strainer lined with a double thickness of paper toweling. Add more water if needed; the soup should have a fairly thick consistency.

**7.** Ladle the soup into crocks or shallow soup bowls. On each serving, from a teaspoon or through a bottle fitted with a small spout, form a "C" with your best olive oil.

## NOTES

For the dried chickpeas, you could substitute 3 cups canned chickpeas, drained and rinsed. Use chicken broth, vegetable broth, or water to make up for the lack of bean cooking liquid, and add the sage sprig to the soup (remove at the end). Taste the soup and adjust seasoning as needed.

This *zuppa* is a blend of puréed and whole chickpeas. You might choose to purée a lower or higher proportion of chickpeas, or even purée all of them, leaving only the porcini slices whole. If more puréed chickpeas are used, the soup may need to be diluted with additional water.

## VARIATION

Making this soup in Italy, I followed the lead of Ristorante La Mencia and used fresh porcini slices. You should do the same if you come across fresh porcini, which show up occasionally in farmers' markets; a small one weighing about 4 ounces is enough. Wipe it clean with a damp paper towel and cut into bite-size slices. Sauté the mushroom in a little olive oil over medium heat until it softens, about 5 minutes, and proceed as directed in the recipe.

# TUSCAN BREAD SOUP

*Ribollita*

MAKES 6 SERVINGS | PREP: 40 MINUTES *(plus soaking time for the cannellini)*
COOK: 2 TO 3 HOURS

*I learned to make* ribollita *more than three decades ago from Livio Cesari, then the gardener of one of Florence's grand villas. In truth, the recipe was his sister's, but Livio proved to be a discriminating judge of technique. After sampling a batch I'd made, he gave his verdict: nice enough but not the genuine article. How had I cooked the onions? As it turned out, they had not been browned sufficiently, the essential first step for this full-flavored soup. I tried again, and this time Livio gave his blessing to my* ribollita.

*The soup can be served right away, but the flavors will develop further if it is refrigerated overnight. True to its name, the soup is then "reboiled" or, more accurately, reheated gently and mixed with dry bread.*

1 large yellow or Spanish onion
2 large stalks celery
3 medium carrots
2 small zucchini, peeled
4 medium boiling potatoes, peeled
1 small bunch *cavolo nero* (Tuscan kale) or curly-leaf kale
  (see Note, page 25)
Extra-virgin olive oil
2 tablespoons tomato paste
1/4 cup chopped flat-leaf parsley leaves and stems
Sea salt or kosher salt
Freshly ground black pepper
2 cups white beans with sage and garlic (page 72)
4 slices white country-style bread, cut into cubes (about 4 cups)
  (see Note)
Best-quality extra-virgin olive oil, for drizzling

1. Cut the onion, celery, carrots, and zucchini in small (1/4-inch) cubes. Cut two of the potatoes into 1/4-inch dice; halve the other two. Tear or cut off the kale leaves, discarding the stems; thinly slice the leaves crosswise.

**2.** Heat a generous quantity of olive oil (about ¼ cup) over medium heat in a large saucepan. Add the onion, cooking and stirring until it softens, about 5 minutes. Reduce the heat to medium-low and cook, stirring often, until the *soffritto* reaches a deep golden brown color, about 20 minutes.

**3.** Stir in the tomato paste and 1 cup cold water. Simmer for 10 to 15 minutes, stirring from time to time, until the mixture is dense.

**4.** Add the celery, carrots, zucchini, diced and halved potatoes, kale leaves, parsley, 1 teaspoon salt, and ½ teaspoon pepper. Add enough cold water to barely cover the vegetables. Bring the mixture to a boil. Reduce the heat to medium-low and simmer, partially covered, until the vegetables are very tender, about 2 hours.

**5.** Cool the soup slightly. Use a food processor or food mill to purée the halved potatoes and 1 cup of the beans; return the purée mixture to the soup pot with the remaining whole beans. Taste and season with more salt and pepper if needed. Simmer at least 30 minutes longer.

**6.** Meanwhile, preheat the oven to 325°F. Unless the bread is stale, spread the cubes on a rimmed baking sheet and toast until dry to the touch but not browned, about 10 minutes.

**7.** Divide the bread cubes among 6 shallow soup bowls. Ladle the soup on top and mix gently. Pass a cruet of your best olive oil at the table to drizzle over the soup.

**NOTES**

Sturdy, salt-free Tuscan bread is the classic choice for *ribollita*, and with good reason. The stale bread absorbs moisture and feathers into crumbs without turning gluey. Unless you are making this soup in Tuscany, you'll likely have to settle for a substitute—look for a loaf that is not spongy but pushes back a little when pressed.

Another way to serve *ribollita*: Layer the bread cubes and soup in a tureen or casserole dish. Cover and reheat in a low oven. When this method is followed, the bread softens as it absorbs liquid—more so than when the *ribollita* is simply spooned onto bread cubes.

# SPRING GREENS and RICE SOUP

*Minestra di erbe e riso*

MAKES 6 TO 8 SERVINGS | PREP: 30 MINUTES | COOK: 1 HOUR

*Every spring Margherita Aloi puts together a "cleansing soup" made with Italian rice and spring greens. She tells me that the women in her Piedmont family have made this vitamin-rich soup for generations, believing that it helps their immune systems cope with changeable spring weather.*

*"This soup comes from a time when people went to work on the land," says Margherita. "During the planting season, they didn't have time to prepare dinner every day, and the soup could be heated up." Though few of us are farmers, it's nonetheless nice to find this soup waiting, like a good friend, at the end of a busy day.*

12 ounces to 1 pound spring greens such as baby spinach,
    dandelion greens, watercress, and pansies (choose at least two
    varieties), washed well, tough stems removed (see Note)
2 cups cleaned, thinly sliced leeks or spring onions (white and
    tender green parts) (see Note, page 40)
2 cloves garlic, chopped
¼ cup extra-virgin olive oil
2 cups peeled, medium-diced russet potatoes
3 quarts chicken broth or water, or a mixture
1 cup Carnaroli or Arborio rice
½ bunch asparagus, trimmed, cut into short lengths
1 small hot red pepper, seeded and slivered, or hot red pepper
    flakes to taste, or freshly ground black pepper
Sea salt or kosher salt
Best-quality extra-virgin olive oil, for drizzling
1 to 1½ cups freshly grated Parmigiano Reggiano or Grana
    Padano cheese

1. Leaving small leaves whole, thinly slice the spring greens (makes about 10 cups).

2. Heat a large saucepan over medium-low heat. Combine the leeks and garlic with the olive oil, stirring until coated. Cover the pan and cook, stirring often, until they soften but do not brown, about 10 minutes.

3. Add the potatoes and cover with broth (if using water, add 1 tablespoon salt). Bring to a boil; reduce the heat and simmer, partially covered, until barely tender. Stir in the rice and cook until al dente, about 10 minutes.

4. Add the asparagus, hot red pepper, and shredded greens. Season with salt and simmer just until the greens are tender, about 20 minutes.

5. Serve the soup warm, topping each serving with a thread of olive oil and a sprinkle of cheese. Pass the rest of the cheese at the table.

### NOTES

If you want to add pansies to your spring greens mix, buy them from a specialty food store; flowers meant for the garden may have been sprayed with chemicals.

My farmers' market sells bags of "braising greens"—a mix of whatever happens to be ready for market—that are ideal for this soup.

### VARIATION

To make a cold-weather version of this soup: For the spring greens, substitute a mixture of mild greens (such as chard and escarole), and bitter greens (such as kale, baby mustard, and turnip greens). In place of the asparagus, cut broccoli crowns or broccoli rabe into bite-size pieces.

## Italian Soup Ways

*S tart with soffritto.* Onions, sautéed slowly in olive oil or butter until their color and flavor deepens: This is the most elemental *soffritto* ("just short of frying"), the flavor base on which so many soups, stews, and other dishes depend. In addition, carrots, celery, and flat-leaf parsley often add their flavors to a *soffritto*; ask an Italian produce vendor for *odori* ("aromatics"), and she will gather up what you need for a pot of soup. Sometimes pancetta incorporated into a *soffritto* imbues the finished soup with meaty flavor. A particular *soffritto* might be cooked to a deep golden-brown, giving the soup a rich, slightly caramelized flavor, or to pale golden, for a more subtle broth—the cook decides.

*Think seasonal.* Drawing from the bounty of produce in season is a given. Some soups showcase a particular vegetable (example: spring peas in the Venetian rice-and-peas soup called *risi e bisi*), while others mingle the flavors of several (example: autumn root vegetables and greens). A fall or winter soup might be thickened with farro or barley, while rice is a more likely choice for warm-weather soups. In Abruzzo, a soup of seven grains and seven beans signifies the transition from winter to spring and, from a practical standpoint, amounts to a spring cleaning for kitchen cupboards.

*Temperature control.* The idea that every soup should be piping hot? Italians don't buy it. Soups are sometimes served warm, allowing subtle flavors to emerge more fully. And a light summer minestrone might be served tepid.

*Timing is all.* In many soups, ingredients are added in several stages, and for good reason. Dried herbs such as thyme could be incorporated into the *soffritto* at the beginning, while fresh basil goes in at the end. Pasta and rice should cook just long enough to turn tender, but not so long that they become bloated and sodden.

**Beans and broth.** Chickpeas retain most of their firmness, but the canning process turns most other beans and legumes soft or even mushy. That's one reason for taking time to cook them in dried form; another is the bean liquid, an asset that contributes greatly to the flavor of the soup. Similarly, even a simple meat or vegetable broth made at home is often superior to what you can buy; if you do purchase broth, choose an all-natural one without a mile-long ingredients list. The exception to my do-it-yourself advice, for both beans and broth, is when these ingredients constitute a fairly minor part of the soup.

> *"In Abruzzo, a soup of seven grains and seven beans signifies the transition from winter to spring..."*

**Purée pointers.** There's a type of soup, called a *passato*, that is entirely puréed, and sometimes strained, in pursuit of a silky texture. Delicious as these soups are, they are a relatively recent addition to the Italian canon—requiring a degree of fussing that, before the age of blenders and food processors, held little appeal for cooks. In the making of other soups, such as *ribollita*, a portion of the soup is puréed and then stirred back into the soup as a thickening agent.

**Garnishes.** A sprinkle of grated aged cheese, such as Parmigiano Reggiano, Piave, or pecorino, is a classic garnish for many but not all brothy soups (fish soups are an exception). Alternatively, a bowl of grated cheese can be passed at the table. Top a *passato* with tiny cubes of edible cheese rind (such as Parmigiano Reggiano) fried in olive oil until crisp or with chopped toasted hazelnuts. A drizzle of your best olive oil is another great garnish, especially for a thick bean or bread soup. ෨

# RICE and PEA SOUP with SHRIMP

*Minestra di riso, gamberi e piselli*

MAKES 4 SERVINGS | PREP: 20 MINUTES | COOK: 40 MINUTES

*I've always loved risi e bisi, the thick Venetian soup of rice and peas. Venice is famous for its seafood, of course, and that got me wondering whether a simple seafood broth could stand in for the usual chicken broth. By the time I finished, I was pretty far from a traditional risi e bisi, but happy with this pleasingly brothy soup. I like the hint of meaty richness contributed by the pancetta, but it can certainly be omitted if you wish.*

3/4 pound small or medium shrimp
6 scallions
3 tablespoons extra-virgin olive oil
Sea salt or kosher salt
Freshly ground black pepper
1 bay leaf
1 tablespoon unsalted butter
1/2 thick-cut (1/4-inch) slice pancetta, diced small
   (about 2 tablespoons) (optional)
1 cup Carnaroli or Arborio rice
1 cup frozen peas
1 or 2 parsley sprigs or snipped chives

1. Peel the shrimp, reserving the shells. Unless the shrimp are very small (in which case, leave them whole), cut them into bite-size pieces. Cut the scallions crosswise in half. Roughly chop the green part. Thinly slice the remaining white part (which may include some pale green).

2. Heat 2 tablespoons olive oil in a medium saucepan over medium heat. Add the shrimp shells and chopped scallion greens. Sauté for a couple of minutes, stirring more or less constantly, until the shells turn pinkish and the greens soften.

3. Add 8 cups water, 1 teaspoon salt, several grindings of pepper, and the bay leaf. Bring to a boil; reduce the heat, stir well, and simmer for 10 to 15 minutes. Keep warm over the lowest setting.

4. In a large saucepan, melt the butter with the remaining tablespoon of olive oil over medium heat. Cook the pancetta (if using) and the sliced scallions for a few minutes, stirring, until the pancetta yields its fat and the scallions soften; don't allow them to brown and crisp (the butter may cause a bit of brown crust to form on the bottom of the pan, however, and that's all right). Stir in the rice, cooking for a minute or so until it smells toasty.

5. Position a strainer over the saucepan; strain the warm broth through it into the saucepan with the rice; discard the solids that remain in the strainer. Adjust the heat to a simmer, cooking until the rice swells and approaches doneness, about 10 minutes. Stir in the peas and, as soon as the broth returns to a simmer, add the shrimp. Cook just until they turn pink, about 2 minutes.

6. Off heat, taste the soup and add more salt and pepper if needed. Pluck the leaves off the parsley sprigs, if using, and tear into small pieces, dropping them into the soup. Let the soup stand for a few minutes before ladling it into shallow soup bowls.

## VARIATION

### Venetian Rice and Pea Soup

For a soup closer to traditional *risi e bisi*, sauté sliced scallions (including the tender green parts) and pancetta in olive oil and butter. Stir in the rice, as in the recipe above, and then add hot seasoned chicken broth. When the rice is almost tender, stir in the peas and heat through. Serve with grated Grana Padano or Parmigiano Reggiano cheese.

# THREE-ONION SOUP with FONTINA CROSTINI

*Zuppa di tre cipolle con crostini con Fontina*

**MAKES 4 TO 6 SERVINGS** *(about 2 quarts)* | **PREP: 20 MINUTES** | **COOK: 40 MINUTES**

*Italians take as much pride in their onion soup as the French do in theirs. This thick, subtly flavored version is based loosely on an old Piedmont recipe.*

4 medium leeks, cleaned (see Note, page 40)
1 large yellow onion, halved lengthwise
4 shallots
2 cloves garlic
2 tablespoons unsalted butter
1 tablespoon extra-virgin olive oil
8 cups chicken or vegetable broth, or a mixture of broth
   and water
2 bay leaves
Several thyme or marjoram sprigs, or 1/2 teaspoon dried thyme
   or marjoram
Sea salt or kosher salt
Freshly ground black or white pepper
4 to 6 slices sturdy rye bread, crusts trimmed
About 6 ounces thinly sliced fontina cheese (preferably Fontina
   Valle d'Aosta)

1. Thinly slice the leeks, halved onion, and shallots crosswise (about 8 cups total). Chop the garlic.

2. Heat the butter and olive oil over medium-low heat in a large, broad-bottom saucepan. Add the leeks, onion, and shallots, cover, and cook, stirring from time to time, until they soften but do not color, about 15 minutes. Uncover, raise the heat to medium, and cook the onions until they take on a warm golden tone, about 10 minutes longer (lower the heat if they begin to brown); stir in the garlic towards the end of cooking.

3. Add the broth, bay leaves, and thyme. Bring to a boil, reduce the heat, and simmer slowly, partially covered, until the onions are very soft. Remove from heat. Season to taste with salt and pepper. Cool slightly.

4. Purée the soup briefly with an immersion blender (start on low speed to avoid splashing); the goal is a thick but chunky texture, with distinct pieces of onion. Alternatively, purée 2 cups of the soup with a countertop blender (holding down the lid with one hand) or food processor; return to the saucepan and keep warm.

5. Cut each slice of bread diagonally. Toast for 2 minutes in a toaster oven or under the oven broiler. Top with the fontina slices. Continue to toast until the bread is lightly browned and the cheese melts.

6. To serve: Spoon the soup into crocks or shallow soup bowls, topping each with 2 fontina crostini.

### NOTES

You can substitute just about any member of the onion family for the varieties specified here. Scallions, including the tender green parts, are best added during the simmering phase so that they retain their color. Snipped chives, sprinkled over the soup at the end, are a pretty finishing touch.

Look for rye bread with enough character to soften but not disintegrate or turn gummy when floated on the hot soup. If this doesn't work out, serve the cheese crostini on the side.

### VARIATIONS

To underline and enhance the soup's flavors, add up to ¼ cup grappa or brandy during the last few minutes of cooking.

A couple of pinches of fennel pollen, available from spice or Italian specialty vendors, does something magical to this soup. Omit the thyme if you go this route.

For caramelized flavor similar to that of a French onion soup, add a sprinkle of sugar and a dash of wine vinegar to the softened onions. Cook slowly until they caramelize, turning a deep golden brown. Proceed with the remainder of the recipe.

# GOLDEN SUMMER VEGETABLES, in a SMOOTH SOUP

*Passato di verdure dorate*

**MAKES 6 TO 8 SERVINGS** *(about 3 quarts)* | **PREP: 20 MINUTES** | **COOK: 50 MINUTES**

*A yellow bell pepper soup has appeared regularly on the menu of Cibreo since the '80s, when Florentine chef Fabio Picchi first spread the word that soups are more true to Tuscan traditions than pasta. (At the time, he made waves by refusing to serve pasta in that restaurant, and he has never wavered.)*

*Though I've made a version of Fabio's soup for decades, I only recently discovered the virtues of adding other summer vegetables that just happen to be yellow. In a face-off with a sackful of summer squash and fresh corn from a relative's garden, I won by tossing them into the soup pot. No high expectations, because it was all too easy. The next day, I tasted the puréed soup, or passato, then ladled out a generous serving. It looked and tasted like a bowlful of sunshine. Italians might eat a hot-weather soup warm or tepid, but not cold. In this case, I recommend breaking the rules—heat it up or really chill it down.*

1 medium yellow onion
1 large stalk celery
1 medium carrot
2 medium yellow summer squash (about 1 pound), ends trimmed
1 medium yellow bell pepper, trimmed and seeded
1 medium potato, peeled
2 cloves garlic
1 large ear fresh corn, husked
Extra-virgin olive oil
1 medium yellow tomato (optional)
2 quarts water or chicken broth, or a combination
Sea salt or kosher salt
Hot red pepper flakes
Good-quality ricotta cheese (preferably sheep's milk), for garnish
Chopped chives, for garnish

1. Coarsely chop the onion, celery, and carrot. Cut the squash, pepper, and potato into small chunks. Halve the garlic cloves. With a small knife, scrape the kernels off the corn ear; reserve the cob and the corn, breaking the cob in two.

2. Combine the onion, celery, and carrot with a generous amount of olive oil (about ¼ cup) in a wide, heavy-bottom saucepan. Over medium heat, cook these *odori* ("aromatics"), partially covered, until tender, but not browned, about 10 minutes.

3. Stir in the squash, bell pepper, and garlic. Sauté, stirring often, until the vegetables soften, about 10 minutes. Add the corn kernels and cobs, potato, tomato (if using), and water. Add salt (if using broth, hold off on the salt for the moment) and season lightly with hot red pepper flakes. Bring to a boil. Reduce the heat to medium-low and simmer, partially covered, until the vegetables are very soft, about 30 minutes. Taste the broth and add more salt and red pepper if needed. Cool the soup for 10 minutes.

4. Remove the cobs. Working in batches, fill a countertop blender two-thirds full of soup; holding down the lid with one hand, purée until smooth (alternatively, purée the soup in the pan with an immersion blender starting on low speed to avoid splashing). Return the puréed soup to the saucepan; reheat, diluting with water as needed for a thick, soupy consistency.

5. Serve the soup warm, garnishing each serving with a dollop of ricotta, or chilled, with a sprinkling of chives.

# Chapter 3
## MOSTLY GRAINS and VEGETABLES

Introduced by Arab occupiers, rice failed miserably as a crop in southern Italy. Growing conditions were more suitable in northern Italy where, by the fifteenth century, authorities were relying on this "new" food to feed the peasant classes. *Panissa*, combining rice with beans and sausage, began as a one-bowl meal for laborers—and today's somewhat richer versions are served in Piedmont restaurants as a main course, not a *primo*.

It's been said that cheese is milk's leap to greatness, and risotto relates to rice in a similar way. I've sometimes wondered what brilliant soul hit upon the idea of sautéing rice grains in fat, then dousing them repeatedly with hot flavorful broth. More likely, the technique evolved gradually, and I'm grateful for that advance each time I make risotto with vegetables, meat, or seafood.

Several dishes make use of the Italian delight in stuffing vegetables of all kinds: baby artichokes, bell peppers, and summer squash, to name a few. Usually the filling is based on bread crumbs, but cooked farro is featured in a zucchini recipe. It is no accident that the Garfagnana, historically among the poorest zones of Tuscany, is known for growing farro and for its many *cucina povera* recipes using the grain. Barley is used in similar ways, especially in central and northern Italy. In addition to their uses in soups and salads, both grains can be cooked like risotto.

In its earliest forms, polenta was a porridge made with ground whole grains such as rye and buckwheat. Modern polenta, from field corn varieties brought from the New World, was embraced as a staple by peasants in northern Italy, its popularity spreading as cooks discovered how happily polenta pairs with condiments and sauces, whether a meat *ragu*, *baccala*, a good cheese, or sautéed mushrooms. A blend of cornmeal and buckwheat is called *polenta taragna*—prepared simply and studded with chunks of melting cheese, it tastes sublime.

In regional Italian cookbooks, including one called *La Grande Cucina Piemontese*, polenta dishes are sometimes categorized as *piatti unici*. Perhaps that's because of their history as sustenance for hard-working folks, but it also recognizes the rib-sticking qualities of these dishes. As my friend Meme Amosso Irwin observes, "After eating a big plate of polenta with *ragu*, how can you think of eating anything else?"

Also in this chapter are recipes for vegetables that take center stage as light but sustaining one-dish meals, including gratinéed asparagus and a Piemontese specialty, raw vegetables with garlicky *bagna cauda* sauce.

# MOSTLY GRAINS and VEGETABLES

*Rice, Beans, and Sausage Simmered in Red Wine*

*Risotto with Baby Artichokes*

*Risotto with Winter Squash, Radicchio, and Ham*

*Risotto al Vin Santo*

*Buckwheat-Corn Polenta with Fontina*

*Polenta with Two Cheeses and Mushroom Medley*

*Potatoes, Onions, and Tomatoes al Forno*

*Zucchini with Farro, Goat Cheese,
   and Walnut Stuffing*

*Stuffed Baby Artichokes*

*Gratinéed Asparagus with Prosciutto*

*Crisp Vegetables with Anchovy-Garlic Dip*

# RICE, BEANS, and SAUSAGE SIMMERED in RED WINE

*Panissa*

MAKES 4 SERVINGS | PREP: 15 MINUTES *(plus up to 6 hours soaking time for the beans)* | COOK: ABOUT 1½ HOURS

I made the happy acquaintance of panissa *in the town of Vercelli, surrounded by golden fields of rice. Half an hour after asking for the cooked-to-order specialty, we dipped into deeply satisfying bowls of rice mingled with plump beans and sausage, tinted a delicate mauve after simmering in local Barbera wine.*

Panissa *originated as a nourishing one-dish affair eaten by rice-field workers, including the* mondine, *women brought from all over northern Italy for the tasks of planting and weeding. It hasn't traveled much beyond this area in the northwest corner of Italy, but it deserves a larger audience.*

1 cup dried cranberry beans *(borlotti)* or pinto beans (see Note)
Extra-virgin olive oil
1 cup chopped onion
1 cup Carnaroli or Arborio rice
1 clove garlic, finely chopped
1 cup Barbera or other fruity red wine
3 to 4 ounces *cacciatorini* or other dried Italian sausage, cut into
   small pieces (see Note)
1 teaspoon chopped fresh rosemary or ½ teaspoon dried
   rosemary
Sea salt or kosher salt
Freshly ground black pepper
½ cup grated Parmigiano Reggiano, Grana Padano, or
   Bra Duro cheese

1. Place the beans in a medium saucepan and cover with cold water; soak for 6 hours or as directed on the package. Drain and wash well under cold running water. Return the beans to the saucepan and cover with fresh water to a depth a couple of inches above the beans. Bring to a boil. Lower the heat and slowly simmer until the beans are tender, about 1 hour.

**2.** In a large, broad saucepan or deep skillet, heat enough olive oil to coat the bottom (about 2 tablespoons) over medium heat. Cook the onion until lightly browned, about 7 minutes. Stir in the rice and garlic and cook just until fragrant. Add ½ cup wine, simmering until the wine is almost evaporated.

**3.** Add the beans with 3 cups of their cooking liquid. Stir in the sausage, rosemary, and remaining ½ cup of wine. Bring to a boil. Taste the broth and season with salt and pepper. Reduce the heat and simmer, partially covered, until the rice is cooked through, about 15 minutes.

**4.** Spoon the *panissa* into shallow soup bowls, sprinkling each serving with grated cheese.

### NOTES

For the record, *saluggia* beans—a kind of *borlotti*—are the variety preferred for this dish in the Piedmont, while the sausage typically used is put up in jars, *sott'olio* (under oil). Neither is readily available in the U.S.

Look for dried sausages in the deli department of supermarkets or Italian specialty stores.

### VARIATIONS

No time to cook beans from scratch? Substitute 2 cups canned beans; drain and rinse them and add to the dish toward the end of cooking. Simmer the sausage by itself in a mixture of half beef or chicken broth and half water. If using prepared broth, which tends to be salty, season the dish at the end, only after tasting.

When in season, fresh cranberry beans (or another variety) are a treat. Just shell them and simmer in the broth and/or water until tender, about 20 minutes.

# RISOTTO with BABY ARTICHOKES

*Risotto ai carciofi*

MAKES 3 SERVINGS | PREP: 20 MINUTES | COOK: 20 MINUTES

*I'd never seen artichokes growing until we arrived in Tuscany's Arno Valley in early May to tend a farmhouse for friends. Pieraldo, the gardener, clipped long-tailed, purple-edged artichokes shaped like tulip buds from the centers of the leggy plants and brought them to our kitchen door. Until well into June, this routine continued, as I worked my way through every artichoke dish I could dream up.*

*I began with risotto, made with generous quantities of artichokes. This recipe follows the inclination of many Italian cooks to feature just one—or, at most, two—seasonal vegetables in a risotto or pasta.*

½ lemon
4 to 6 baby artichokes (about 3 ounces each)
2 tablespoons unsalted butter
2 tablespoons extra-virgin olive oil
1 small leek, washed well (see Note, page 40), or large spring
   onion, thinly sliced
Sea salt or kosher salt
Freshly ground black pepper
4 to 5 cups easy meat broth (recipe follows) or prepared chicken broth
1 cup Carnaroli or Arborio rice
⅔ cup grated Parmigiano Reggiano, Grana Padano, or aged
   Montasio cheese

1. To prepare the artichokes: Fill a bowl with cold water and squeeze the lemon juice into it. Trim and discard the pointed ends of the artichoke and most of the stems; peel and chop the trimmed stems, placing them in the water. Break off the outer leaves until you reach the pale, edible leaves on the interior. As you finish each artichoke, drop it in the water. When all are prepped, remove them one at a time and cut into thin slices.

2. In a large skillet or broad-bottom saucepan over medium heat, melt 1 tablespoon of the butter with 1 tablespoon olive oil. Sauté the leek until it softens. Stir in the artichokes and chopped stems and continue to cook, stirring often, until the vegetables are lightly browned, about 10 minutes. Add ½ cup water and simmer for a few minutes, reducing the heat if necessary, until the artichokes are tender. Season with salt and pepper to taste, and transfer to a bowl.

**3.** In a small saucepan, bring the broth to a simmer; keep it warm over low heat.

**4.** Meanwhile, in the same skillet used for the artichokes, melt the remaining 1 tablespoon butter with 1 tablespoon olive oil over medium heat. Stir in the rice and cook for a minute or so, until the grains are coated and smell toasty. Ladle on enough of the hot broth to cover the rice. Simmer, stirring occasionally and adding more broth as the liquid is absorbed, until rice is al dente, about 15 minutes.

**5.** Add the artichoke mixture. Cook a few minutes longer, remove from heat, and stir in half of the cheese and a final ladleful of broth.

**6.** Serve immediately: Spoon the risotto into shallow bowls and sprinkle with the remaining cheese.

## Easy Meat Broth

MAKES ABOUT 2 QUARTS | PREP: 5 MINUTES | COOK: 1 HOUR

3 or 4 chicken wings or bone-in chicken thighs
1 or 2 beef bones
1 medium carrot, cut into 1-inch pieces
1 medium stalk celery, cut into 1-inch pieces
1 small onion, thickly sliced
1 bay leaf
Sea salt or kosher salt
Freshly ground black pepper

**1.** Combine the chicken wings, beef bones, carrot, celery, onion, and bay leaf in a medium saucepan. Cover with cold water to a depth several inches above the ingredients. Bring to a boil. Lower the heat and simmer slowly, skimming off any scum that rises to the top during the first few minutes. Continue to cook at a slow simmer, partially covered, for 1 hour or longer, until the broth looks rich and golden. Season to taste with salt and pepper.

**2.** Cool the broth until warm, and strain into a bowl or another saucepan. The broth can be used immediately or, if time permits, chilled; afterwards, scoop off any fat that has solidified on top. The broth will keep, refrigerated, for up to a week, or freeze it in 1- or 2-cup containers.

## *Tilting Toward Grains and Veggies*

I never have trouble including enough cheese in my diet. That wedge of Taleggio or fresh pecorino in the refrigerator begs to be eaten and I'm more than willing to comply. Grains and fresh vegetables ask more of the cook—preparation and skill in making the most of their goodness. Fortunately, Italian traditions emphasize these foods and offer help in the perpetual challenge of bringing balance to the meal. A few suggestions:

*Keep a ready supply of the grains habitually used in the Italian kitchen:* short-grain rice such as Arborio, Carnaroli, and *vialone nano*; farro and barley; and stone-ground cornmeal. Check the label for production dates; grains from the latest growing season are preferable. Increasingly, grains are vacuum packed, extending their shelf life; once opened, they keep well in the pantry when tightly sealed, and even longer when stored in the freezer.

*Give glamorous grains a try: polenta taragna* (a traditional cornmeal-buckwheat blend) or polenta flavored with truffles, for instance. They're likely to have such an interesting flavor that little enhancement is needed.

*Farro and barley take time to cook*, so when you do, consider making more than needed for one meal. Use the cooked grain over several days in various ways: sautéed with a little onion as a side dish, added to a soup toward the end of cooking, or sprinkled into a hearty *insalatone*.

*With vegetables, take your cue from the season*. Summer squash look good? Sautéed or grilled, it's a side for meat or fish, a frittata filling, or an easy pasta sauce with an olive oil or tomato base. In winter, your choice might shift to a big bunch of chard or kale—simmered or braised, these greens are equally versatile.

*Master the basic techniques* of making a risotto or polenta and then improvise, using whatever vegetables you please as a component or topper.

> *"Keep a ready supply of the grains habitually used in the Italian kitchen: short-grain rice such as Arborio, Carnaroli, and vialone nano; farro and barley; and stone-ground cornmeal."*

*Add meat and seafood in small quantities* to vegetable and grain dishes to boost protein and add flavor.

*Season grains and vegetables in alluring ways*. Kale leaves, for instance, could be shredded, blanched, and dressed in olive oil infused with hot red pepper—or turned in a little melted butter and brightened with a splash of lemon juice. Or, follow the lead of one Italian chef I know, and sprinkle Himalayan pink salt on an otherwise unadorned bowl of steaming polenta made with stone-ground grain. ✎

# RISOTTO with WINTER SQUASH, RADICCHIO, and HAM

*Risotto con zucca, radicchio e prosciutto cotto*

MAKES 3 SERVINGS | PREP: 20 MINUTES | COOK: 20 MINUTES

*I love the warm autumnal colors and flavors in this risotto, which is hearty enough to serve on its own.*

2 pinches saffron threads
Half of a small butternut or other winter squash (about 8
　ounces) (see Note)
Extra-virgin olive oil
4 to 5 cups vegetable or chicken broth, or a mixture of broth and water
1 tablespoon unsalted butter
¼ cup finely chopped shallot or onion
1 cup Carnaroli or Arborio rice
⅓ cup white wine
1 cup firmly packed shredded radicchio
1 small thick-cut (¼-inch) slice Italian *prosciutto cotto* or any
　baked or smoked ham, diced into small cubes (about ⅓ cup)
Sea salt or kosher salt
Freshly ground black pepper
½ cup grated Grana Padano or other aged cheese
¼ cup snipped chives or flat-leaf parsley, for garnish (optional)

1. Preheat the oven to 400°F. In a small bowl, crumble the saffron into ¼ cup water. Peel the squash with a vegetable peeler and dice into ½-inch cubes (about 2 cups). Place on a baking sheet and drizzle with 1 tablespoon olive oil, stirring to coat the pieces. Roast until tender and lightly browned on several sides, about 20 minutes. Stir halfway through the cooking.

2. Bring the broth to a boil and adjust the heat to a slow simmer.

3. Meanwhile, in a large sauté pan or wide-bottom saucepan, melt the butter with 1 tablespoon olive oil over medium heat. Add the shallot and cook until golden. Stir in the rice and cook for a minute or so, until the grains are coated and smell toasty. Add the wine, stirring until it is absorbed.

*continued*

**4.** Ladle on enough of the hot broth to cover the rice. Simmer, stirring occasionally and adding more broth as the liquid is absorbed. After about 10 minutes, stir in the roasted squash, the radicchio, and the ham. Cook until heated through and the radicchio softens but does not lose its color and crunch, 5 to 10 minutes longer.

**5.** Remove from heat. Season to taste with salt and pepper and stir in the cheese, saffron and water, and a final ladleful of broth (you may not need it all); allow the risotto to collect itself for about 5 minutes.

**6.** Serve in shallow soup bowls, garnishing with chives or parsley if you wish.

### NOTE

As a convenience, buy the peeled winter squash chunks available in some produce departments.

### VARIATIONS

To make this dish vegetarian, use vegetable broth and omit the ham.

Substitute sliced white or crimini mushrooms for the radicchio, stirring them into the risotto at the same point in the recipe.

# RISOTTO al VIN SANTO

*Risotto al vin santo*

MAKES 4 TO 6 SERVINGS | PREP: 20 MINUTES | COOK: 25 MINUTES

*As a student at the Cordon Bleu in Paris, Massimo Zetti wrote his thesis on vin santo. His passion for Tuscany's great dessert wine remains strong—as any visitor can tell from the impressive display on the shelves of Osteria de L'Ortolano, the Florence gastronomia owned by Massimo and his wife Marta.*

*Vin santo is mostly for sipping, alone or with biscotti, but Massimo also employs its sweet resonance in certain savory dishes. Toward the end of a spring vacation, he and friends invented a risotto from the scarce provisions on hand. My version strays from Massimo's vegetarian original but, as in his, the distinctive taste of vin santo comes through.*

6 to 7 cups chicken or vegetable broth, or a mixture of broth
   and water
1 small onion
1 small stalk celery
1 small carrot
4 ounces green beans (preferably small and thin)
1 medium tomato (optional)
1 or 2 skinless, boneless chicken breast fillets or thighs (4 to 6
   ounces total)
3 tablespoons extra-virgin olive oil
2 cups Carnaroli, Arborio, or other short-grained Italian rice
¼ cup *vin santo* (see Note)
1 or 2 pinches hot red pepper flakes
1 tablespoon unsalted butter
½ cup grated Parmigiano Reggiano or aged pecorino cheese

1. In a medium saucepan, bring the chicken broth to a simmer; keep hot. Finely chop the onion and cut the celery and carrot into ¼-inch dice. Remove the ends from the green beans and cut into short lengths. If using, peel, seed, and cut the tomato into small dice. Cut the chicken into small pieces.

*continued*

**2.** Meanwhile, in a medium skillet or broad-bottom saucepan, sauté the onion in the olive oil over medium heat until tender, about 5 minutes. Stir in the rice and cook 1 to 2 minutes longer, until well coated and toasty smelling. Add half of the *vin santo*, stirring to moisten the rice.

**3.** Add the celery and carrot. Ladle on enough hot broth to cover the ingredients. Simmer for 5 minutes. Stir in the green beans, cubed chicken, and red pepper flakes. Continue to cook, stirring in more broth as needed, until the rice is tender, about 10 minutes longer.

**4.** Give the risotto a final ladleful of broth just before removing the saucepan from the heat. Stir in the tomato, remaining *vin santo*, butter, and cheese. Cover and let stand for 5 minutes before serving.

**NOTE**

*Vin santo* is distributed more widely in the U.S. now than in the past, but if you cannot find it, substitute Marsala, white vermouth, or Riesling; the flavor will be different but pleasant.

# BUCKWHEAT-CORN POLENTA with FONTINA

*Polenta taragna con Fontina*

**MAKES 4 TO 6 SERVINGS | PREP: 5 MINUTES | COOK: 25 TO 30 MINUTES**

*Visiting the Piedmont one fall, we decided to stay overnight in Cuneo and quickly discovered that a festival celebrating the fat chestnuts called* marrone *was in full swing. Shirtless, sweating men in the center of town were roasting chestnuts, while others stirred* polenta taragna *in vast cast iron cauldrons—all of this taking place over open fires. I decided to buy a bowlful of polenta—just one, because we had dinner plans—and the three of us stood in the street, dipping our spoons into the steaming, utterly delicious porridge, laced with melting chunks of local toma cheese.*

*Later that night, following a less than memorable dinner, I regretted that I hadn't eaten my fill of that remarkable polenta. Making it at home doesn't quite replicate that experience, but when stone-ground meal is used, it comes close.*

2 cups buckwheat-corn polenta (see Note) or coarse cornmeal,
   preferably stone-ground
Sea salt or kosher salt
Freshly ground black pepper (optional)
4 ounces fontina cheese (preferably from Valle d'Aosta), cut into
   small cubes (see Note)

1. Combine the polenta with 6½ cups water and 1 teaspoon salt in a large, heavy-bottom saucepan. Over medium heat, bring to a boil, stirring once or twice.

2. Adjust the heat to a gentle simmer. Stir often to keep the polenta from sticking, and break up any incipient lumps; start with a whisk and switch to a wooden spoon as the mixture thickens. Cook until the polenta reaches the consistency of runny cooked oatmeal and tastes fully cooked, 15 to 25 minutes, depending on the coarseness of the cornmeal. Taste and stir in additional salt if needed; season to taste with pepper, if using.

3. Just before serving, stir in the cheese. Once it is softened but not melted, dish the polenta into small, deep bowls or soup crocks.

*continued*

## NOTES

*Polenta taragna*, a blend of coarsely ground cornmeal and buckwheat, is typical of northern Italy. It turns a Dijon mustard color when cooked and has a wonderfully earthy flavor, with a slightly bitter edge from the buckwheat. If you are able to find *polenta taragna* online or at a market, buy it!

Any good melting cheese with a slightly nutty flavor, such as a young Asiago or Gruyère, will taste good here.

I find this polenta wonderfully comforting on its own, but if you want to pair it with a green vegetable, steam broccoli rabe or broccoli crowns and dress them with olive oil, lemon juice, and hot red pepper flakes.

## VARIATION

To make this dish even more substantial, stir in quartered, sautéed white or crimini mushrooms or cooked Italian sausage chunks just before adding the cheese.

# POLENTA with TWO CHEESES and MUSHROOM MEDLEY

*Polenta ai due formaggi con funghi misti*

MAKES 4 TO 6 SERVINGS | PREP: 20 MINUTES | COOK: 25 MINUTES

*I find this duo of rich, creamy polenta and earthy sautéed mushrooms very satisfying on its own, but it's also delicious with pan-grilled steak (page 169) or roast pork tenderloin (page 181).*

2 cups coarse cornmeal, preferably stone-ground
Sea salt or kosher salt
1½ pounds mixed fresh mushrooms, such as white, crimini, hen of
   the woods, and/or king oyster, cut into thick slices
Extra-virgin olive oil
2 cloves garlic, finely chopped
½ cup dry red wine or a sweeter wine such as Marsala
Freshly ground black pepper
½ cup mascarpone cheese, at room temperature (see Note)
2 to 4 ounces Gorgonzola cheese, crumbled

1. Combine the cornmeal with 6½ cups water and 1 teaspoon salt in a large, heavy-bottom saucepan. Over medium heat, bring to a boil, stirring once or twice.

2. Adjust the heat to simmer at a gentle pace. Cook, stirring often to keep the polenta from sticking and to break up any incipient lumps (start with a whisk and switch to a wooden spoon as the mixture thickens).

3. Meanwhile, heat a large skillet (cast iron works well) over medium-high heat. Add the mushrooms; sprinkle with salt and drizzle with 2 to 3 tablespoons olive oil. Let them sizzle for a few minutes, stirring occasionally, until they soften and begin to release their juices.

4. Add the garlic, stirring for a few seconds until fragrant, and then the wine and ½ cup water. Reduce the heat and simmer briskly until the mushrooms are soft and glossy and most of the liquid has evaporated. Season to taste with pepper.

*continued*

**5.** When the polenta reaches the consistency of runny cooked oatmeal and tastes fully cooked, after 15 to 25 minutes (depending on the coarseness of the cornmeal), fold in the mascarpone and Gorgonzola. Stir until they are completely incorporated and season to taste with salt and pepper.

**6.** To serve: Spoon a mound of polenta onto each plate. Spoon the mushrooms on top, letting them cascade onto the plate.

### NOTE

This recipe uses the so-called "slurry" method of making polenta rather than the traditional one, which requires adding handfuls of polenta in a slow, steady stream and is more susceptible to lump formation. As long as you stir often, especially toward the end, polenta made with the slurry method will be flawless.

### VARIATIONS

If you are fortunate enough to have access to fresh porcini mushrooms, by all means use them. Other wild mushroom varieties, such as chanterelles and morels, would also be wonderful in this dish.

In place of mascarpone, substitute ½ cup heavy cream. Add it at the beginning, reducing the amount of water to 6 cups.

# POTATOES, ONIONS, and TOMATOES al FORNO

*Patate, cipolle e pomodori al forno*

MAKES 4 SERVINGS | PREP: 25 MINUTES | COOK: 1 HOUR, OR A LITTLE MORE

*Elena Cecchi, an expert Tuscan cook with a curious mind, often adds dishes to her repertoire that she has discovered while traveling. She describes this casserole from Puglia as "a wonderful dish for a rustic and frugal meal." Southern Italy, known for especially flavorful produce, is home to many dishes that let vegetables stand on their own. These traditions have their roots in poverty, but now these dishes appeal for other reasons. And, by the way, this piatto unico isn't all that frugal when served in generous portions, as here.*

Extra-virgin olive oil
6 large ripe plum tomatoes or 3 medium round tomatoes
6 medium boiling potatoes
1 large yellow or purple onion
1 tablespoon dried oregano
2 teaspoons sea salt or kosher salt
Freshly ground black pepper, to taste (optional)
2/3 cup grated pecorino cheese

1. Preheat the oven to 375°F. Rub the bottom and sides of a large terracotta dish or other baking dish (about 9x14") with olive oil. Cut out the tomato stems and cut the tomatoes into medium dice. Peel the potatoes, placing each one as you finish in a bowl of cold water. Halve the onion, pole to pole, and cut the onion and potatoes crosswise into thin (1/8-inch) slices (see Note).

2. In a large bowl, combine the potatoes, onion, tomatoes, 1/4 cup olive oil, oregano, salt, pepper (if using), and half of the cheese. Mix with your hands and transfer to the baking dish, smoothing the top. Sprinkle with the rest of the pecorino. Drizzle 1 cup water around the edges into the dish.

3. Cover the vegetables with aluminum foil. Bake for 40 minutes. The tomatoes will have released their juices; spoon some over the top and bake in the upper third of the oven, uncovered, until the potatoes are quite tender and the top is golden, 20 minutes or more.

*continued*

**4.** Spoon vegetables into shallow soup bowls and drizzle some of the cooking juices over them.

## NOTE

A mandoline, if you have one, will rapidly produce uniformly thin slices of potato (and fennel, if you are doing that variation); it does not work well for onions.

## VARIATIONS

### Fish Fillets with Potatoes, Onions, and Tomatoes

Prepare the vegetables as instructed in the recipe and place in the oven. Coat 4 medium-thick fillets such as mackerel, sea bass, halibut, or tilapia with olive oil. Season with salt and, if you like, black pepper. About 10 minutes before the end of cooking, arrange the fillets on top of the vegetables. Spoon some of the tomato juices on top and bake until just tender.

### Potatoes, Fennel, and Onions al Forno

Substitute 1 small, thinly sliced fennel bulb for the tomatoes. Combine it with the potatoes, onions, and other ingredients. Add a little extra water to compensate for the liquid given off by the tomatoes. Proceed as directed in the recipe.

# ZUCCHINI with FARRO, GOAT CHEESE, and WALNUT STUFFING

*Zucchine ripiene di farro, caprino e noci*

MAKES 4 SERVINGS | PREP: 20 MINUTES | COOK: 45 MINUTES

*In Italian cookbooks and cooking magazines, I've seen recipes for stuffing virtually every vegetable: bell peppers, eggplant, cabbage, tomatoes, escarole, artichokes, and summer squash, including round patty pans and zucchini. Usually the stuffing is based on bread crumbs or rice, but this time farro fills in. Walnuts echo the nutty wholesomeness of the grain, while goat cheese adds tangy richness.*

Sea salt or kosher salt
3/4 cup farro (see Note, page 77)
4 large zucchini
1 tablespoon unsalted butter
2 tablespoons extra-virgin olive oil
2 shallots or half a small onion, finely chopped
1/4 cup walnuts, toasted and broken into pieces
1 tablespoon fresh thyme or 1/2 teaspoon dried thyme
Freshly ground black pepper
2 to 3 ounces goat cheese or semisoft sheep's milk cheese (feta is fine)
2 cups prepared or homemade marinara sauce (see step five, page 153)

1. Combine 1½ cups water and ½ teaspoon salt in a small saucepan and bring it to a boil. Add the farro, adjust the heat to a simmer, and cook until tender, about 20 minutes.

2. While the farro is cooking, cut off and discard both ends of the zucchini; halve the zucchini lengthwise. Fill a large, broad saucepan with 1 inch water and bring to a simmer; lay the zucchini halves flat in a steamer insert and place over the simmering water; cover and steam until a knife penetrates easily, about 10 minutes. Transfer to a cutting board or other work surface. Cool until they can be handled.

3. Preheat the oven to 350°F. With a spoon, scoop out the zucchini pulp, leaving shells about ½ inch thick. Sprinkle the shells lightly with salt. Roughly chop the pulp.

*continued*

**4.** Melt the butter with the olive oil in a medium skillet over medium heat. Sauté the shallots until golden. Add the zucchini pulp and cook briefly. Add the farro, walnuts, and thyme. Season with more salt, if needed, and pepper. Fold in the goat cheese.

**5.** Spread the marinara sauce over the bottom of a large rectangular casserole dish. Spoon some of the farro-goat cheese mixture into a zucchini shell, pressing lightly so that more can be mounded on top. Place it in the casserole dish and repeat with the other shells.

**6.** Bake the stuffed zucchini until heated through and lightly browned on top. Spoon some of the marinara sauce onto dinner plates or shallow soup bowls, tilting to spread it out; lay 2 zucchini on top of each. Serve with crusty whole-grain bread, if you like.

# STUFFED BABY ARTICHOKES

*Carciofini ripieni*

MAKES 3 OR 4 SERVINGS | PREP: 30 MINUTES | COOK: 30 MINUTES

*A country cook like Maria Gambini could probably prep and stuff baby artichokes in her sleep, so familiar are the techniques to her. Knowing this, I was hoping for a show-and-tell session. Alas, Maria was too busy with her grandchildren and housekeeping duties, but she did give me a blow-by-blow account of her method. With only minor tweaks, it worked quite well. I think you'll be equally pleased with this classic way to enjoy a seasonal delicacy.*

½ lemon
12 to 15 baby artichokes (2 to 3 ounces each)
1 thick-cut (¼-inch) slice pancetta, cut into small cubes (about ⅓ cup)
Extra-virgin olive oil
2 cloves garlic, finely chopped
1½ cups fresh white bread crumbs
⅓ cup finely chopped flat-leaf parsley
¼ cup grated Parmigiano Reggiano or aged pecorino cheese
2 tablespoons pine nuts, lightly toasted
Sea salt or kosher salt
Freshly ground black pepper

1. Fill a bowl with cold water and squeeze lemon juice into it. Trim and discard the pointed ends of the artichokes. Cut off the stems at the base (so that the artichokes sit flat); peel and chop the stems, placing them in the water. Break off the outer leaves until you reach the pale, edible leaves on the interior; complete the trimming at the stem end with a knife. As you finish each artichoke, drop it in the water.

2. In a medium saucepan over medium heat, cook the pancetta and the drained, chopped stems with 2 tablespoons olive oil until lightly browned, 5 to 10 minutes. Add the garlic, cooking just until fragrant. Add the bread crumbs and stir until moistened. Remove from heat and add the parsley, cheese, and pine nuts. Season to taste with salt and pepper.

3. Gently spread the leaves of each artichoke. Spoon some of the filling into each one, tamping it down; press the leaves around the filling. Drizzle a little olive oil (about 2 tablespoons) into a saucepan just large enough to hold all the artichokes in an upright position. Arrange the artichokes so they are supporting each other.

**4.** Add about an inch of water to the saucepan and bring it to a boil. Adjust the heat to a simmer, cover, and cook for about 20 minutes, or until the artichokes are tender (to test, pull off an outer leaf). Transfer with tongs to a platter. Serve warm or at room temperature.

### NOTE

Four large artichokes could be substituted for the baby artichokes. Filling the artichokes will take less time—because there are fewer of them—but they'll need to be steamed a little longer, about 30 minutes.

### VARIATION

**Stuffed Bell Peppers** (SERVES 2)

Halve 2 medium bell peppers and remove the seeds and veins. Reserving the Parmigiano Reggiano, use the same bread crumb filling as for the artichokes (minus the artichoke stems) to fill the bell pepper halves. Position in a baking pan, pouring about ½ cup of water around the peppers. Bake at 350°F, covered, until the peppers are tender and the filling is hot, about 30 minutes; uncover, sprinkle with the reserved cheese, and cook until lightly browned on top, about 5 minutes.

# GRATINÉED ASPARAGUS with PROSCIUTTO

*Gratinato d'asparagi con prosciutto*

MAKES 2 OR 3 SERVINGS | PREP: 10 MINUTES | COOK: 10 MINUTES

*A large helping of cheese-crusted asparagus, resting on a bed of prosciutto, makes a satisfying meal. Alternatively, try the poached egg variation. Be sure to serve with plenty of crusty bread to soak up the juices.*

½ cup fresh white bread crumbs
½ cup grated Parmigiano Reggiano, Piave, or other flavorful
  aged cheese
1 tablespoon unsalted butter, melted
1 pound asparagus, ends trimmed (see Note)
2 tablespoons extra-virgin olive oil
Sea salt or kosher salt
Freshly ground black pepper
4 to 6 slices prosciutto di Parma or other high-quality prosciutto

1. In a small bowl, mix together the bread crumbs, cheese, and melted butter.

2. Fill a medium skillet with enough cold water to cover the asparagus; bring to a boil. Cook the asparagus in a single layer until crisp-tender, about 2 minutes; drain.

3. Preheat the broiler. Line each dinner plate with 2 prosciutto slices. Place them in a warming drawer or, if the plates are reasonably heatproof, on a lower rack in the oven.

4. Place the cooked asparagus in an ovenproof dish and coat with the olive oil and season with salt and pepper. Sprinkle the bread crumb mixture on top. Place the pan in the top third of the oven. Cook until the topping is crisped and lightly browned, about 2 minutes. Place the gratinéed asparagus on top of the prosciutto.

**NOTES**

You can break off the asparagus ends, but I don't like the jagged look, reflecting an uncertain border between tough and tender. Instead, I line up several stalks and test with my knife to find the point at which it glides easily through. Fat asparagus look even nicer when the lower ends are peeled with a vegetable peeler.

The same method could be followed to prepare gratinéed broccoli rabe.

**VARIATION**

*Asparagus with Poached Eggs*

Simmer the asparagus as described above; drain, coat with olive oil, and season. Meanwhile, bring a medium saucepan or skillet two-thirds full of water to a very gentle simmer. Break each egg, one at a time, into a small dish and slide into the water. Poach the eggs until the whites are opaque and the yolks firm up slightly but are still soft, about 2 to 2½ minutes. Using a skimmer or slotted spatula, transfer each egg onto a clump of asparagus. Omitting the bread crumbs, drizzle with the melted butter and sprinkle with cheese. Place under the broiler just long enough for the cheese to melt, 30 seconds or less.

# CRISP VEGETABLES with ANCHOVY-GARLIC DIP

*Crudité alla bagna cauda*

MAKES 3 OR 4 SERVINGS | PREP: 15 MINUTES | COOK: 20 MINUTES

*My long-time neighbor Ernie Ferraro, who grew up in Brooklyn, recalls his Italian-born father preparing his favorite Friday night meal: an array of raw vegetables dipped in vinaigrette, a modification of the stronger-tasting bagna cauda sauce typical of his native Piedmont. Just about any combination of raw, blanched, or roasted vegetables can be used: cauliflower, radishes, baby turnips, and cardoons, for example. A dish like this would normally be eaten as an appetizer—except when you're in the mood, like Ernie's father, for a light meal of delicious vegetables with a warm, hearty dip.*

12 spears asparagus
1 small head radicchio
2 medium yellow or red bell peppers
1 medium fennel bulb or 3 celery ribs
1 cup extra-virgin olive oil
2 cloves garlic, cut into paper-thin slivers
¼ teaspoon sea salt or kosher salt, or to taste
8 anchovy fillets, pinched in small pieces
Warm country-style bread

1. Trim the asparagus ends. Trim the radicchio and separate the leaves, saving the inner part of the head for a salad; cut or tear the leaves in scoop-sized pieces. Trim the peppers and cut into strips. Cut off the fronds of the fennel and halve the bulb lengthwise; cut out and discard most of the core; cut lengthwise into thin wedges (if using celery, cut crosswise in half, and then lengthwise into strips).

2. In a small, heavy-bottom saucepan, heat the olive oil, garlic, and salt over medium-low heat at a very slow simmer, with an occasional bubble cracking the surface, until the garlic is tender and pale golden, about 15 minutes.

3. Meanwhile, fill a medium skillet with enough cold water to cover the asparagus; bring to a boil. Cook the asparagus in a single layer until crisp-tender, about 2 minutes; drain and cool under running water. Arrange the asparagus, radicchio, bell peppers, and fennel around the perimeter of 4 dinner plates.

**4.** Warm small bowls or ramekins in a warming drawer or slow oven, set at 250°F. Stir the anchovies into the olive oil and continue to simmer for a few minutes, pressing the anchovies against the bottom until they semi-dissolve (the mixture will remain somewhat cloudy, with visible bits of garlic and anchovy).

**5.** To serve: Spoon some of the garlic and anchovies that have sunk to the bottom of the pan into the warm bowls and pour the seasoned olive oil on top; place one in the center of each plate. Serve immediately with chunks of warm bread.

### VARIATIONS

For a cleaner-looking *bagna cauda*, use 3 garlic cloves and 12 anchovy fillets; strain the sauce before serving.

To lighten the sauce, add fresh lemon juice or a small amount of boiling water.

In the Piedmont, this anchovy-garlic dip is sometimes served with cooked vegetables, especially the region's meaty, succulent bell peppers. To do this, allow ½ large bell pepper per person. Roast the peppers and remove the blackened skin. Arrange on an ovenproof platter or casserole and spoon the *bagna cauda* over it. Return the platter to the oven just long enough to heat through.

Though not traditional with *bagna cauda*, poached or grilled shrimp would be delicious.

*Bagna cauda* also makes a great pasta sauce. Toss the pasta with the sauce until well coated, adding whatever other ingredients you like—cooked shrimp and roasted pepper strips, for example. You could also use it, strained and combined with fresh lemon juice or white wine vinegar, as a gutsy salad dressing for escarole or mixed greens.

# Chapter 4
## BRAISES and STEWS

Maria Gambini is telling me about the stewed pigeons with olives she often makes for her family's Sunday dinner. She has already cautioned against allowing the celery to lose its crisp greenness when the *soffritto*, a flavor base that also includes onion and garlic, is sautéed. Now the nicely browned pigeons are nestled in a big pot with wine and broth. *"Piano, piano!"* says Maria, tamping the air with her hands to emphasize that the pigeons must simmer slowly, slowly, until tender enough to please the pickiest grandchild.

Slow, moist cooking that begins with the right foundation—that's the unifying theme of this chapter's recipes. This technique transforms muscular cuts such as beef chuck and veal shanks into mouthwateringly tender, savory dishes. Birds, too, tend to fare well with such treatment. That's especially true of free-range chickens and other fowl in the habit of working out each day—the flesh of these robust animals benefits from lengthier cooking.

The Italian taste for hunting and eating game is worth mentioning in this context. In the countryside, you might hear shotgun blasts (even out of season)

as hunters pursue local deer, pheasant, boar, and other game. Once dressed and in the kitchen, this meat often calls for gentle cooking. In recognition of that tradition, this chapter includes a braised quail dish with juniper berries and bay leaves, seasonings meant to balance the assertive flavor of the game.

In a classic *bollito misto*, meats share their flavors, forming a rich broth. Despite the name, the meats are not really boiled, but simmered. A *gran bollito*, Piedmont style, calls for seven kinds of meat, while the considerably more modest but still delicious version given here combines just three.

Sometimes *slow* applies only to the heat level. Fish takes swimmingly to braising and stewing, but unless it's really large, the cooking time is short—and the same is true of meatballs simmered in a tomato pan sauce. If you need recipes that cook in a relatively short time, those are the ones.

Vegetables are incorporated into most of these braised or stewed dishes and, if not, a side is suggested to complete the *piatto unico*.

# BRAISES and STEWS

*Chicken Braised with Sweet Bell Peppers*

*Slow-Simmered Chicken with Olives,
    over Couscous*

*Quail al Vin Santo with Sweet-Sour Cabbage*

*Braised Veal Shanks with Saffron Risotto*

*Veal Stew with Mushrooms and Peas, on Toast*

*Bollito Misto with Fresh Parsley Sauce*

*Pot Roast with Porcini and Root Vegetables*

*Short Ribs Braised with Dried Figs and
    Balsamic Vinegar*

*Meatballs with Tomato Pan Sauce and
    Parsleyed Potatoes*

*Celery Bundles with Meat Stuffing
    and Tomato Sauce*

*Alberto's Streamlined Five-Fish Stew*

# CHICKEN BRAISED with SWEET BELL PEPPERS

*Pollo con peperonata*

MAKES 4 TO 6 SERVINGS | PREP: 25 MINUTES | COOK: ABOUT 1½ HOURS
*(including broth making)*

*Walking along country roads during a stay in the Arno Valley, I've often seen chickens scuttling here and there in the vineyards, pecking for insects. Smaller russet hens predominate, usually in the company of a few imposingly large white chickens that take the name of the area—pollo valdarno—and are justly prized for their flesh as well as their eggs. Wherever you live, seeking out a truly cage-free chicken, regardless of the breed, will make a tremendous difference in the taste of this dish.*

*Peperonata is usually served as a vegetable side, but here the bell peppers and other ingredients are integrated into the dish. A simple broth made from chicken trimmings contributes to the complex flavor of the sauce.*

1 chicken, preferably free-range (3 to 4 pounds) with neck,
   etc., cut into serving pieces and washed well (see Note)
1 medium onion
2 or 3 parsley sprigs
Sea salt or kosher salt
Extra-virgin olive oil
½ cup red or white wine
2 small red and/or yellow bell peppers, cut into small squares
2 cloves garlic, finely chopped
3 to 4 anchovy fillets, pinched into small pieces
½ cup strained tomatoes (such as Pomì) or chopped canned
   plum tomatoes
Freshly ground black pepper

1. To make the broth: Combine the wing ends, neck, and cleaned gizzard in a medium saucepan; if the chicken was sold with head and feet, throw them in too. Trim and peel the onion, adding the ends and skin to the saucepan; chop and reserve the onion. Cut off the parsley stems; add to the saucepan; coarsely chop and reserve the leaves. Cover the contents of the saucepan with water, add 1 teaspoon salt, and bring to a boil; reduce the heat and simmer, skimming off any frothy scum and fat that rise to the top, for 20 minutes to 1 hour.

*continued*

**2.** With paper towels, blot the chicken pieces dry and sprinkle with salt. Over medium-high heat, heat enough oil to coat the bottom of a large skillet. Cook the chicken, turning with tongs, until well browned on all sides. Lower the heat and add the wine and about the same amount of broth (dip it out of the saucepan and pour through a small strainer into the skillet); stir and cook until the liquid is reduced, 5 to 10 minutes. Transfer the chicken to a platter, pouring any pan juices over it.

**3.** Add a little more olive oil to the same skillet. Over medium heat, sauté the chopped onion until golden brown; add the bell peppers and garlic and sauté 1 to 2 minutes longer. Stir in the anchovies, pressing them into the sauce with a wooden spoon until they semi-dissolve. Add the strained tomatoes and an equal amount of the broth.

**4.** Return the chicken pieces to the skillet and stir to combine with the *peperonata* (pepper mixture). Simmer, partially covered, for about 30 minutes or until the chicken is tender. Taste and add more salt (if needed) and pepper. Garnish with the chopped parsley leaves.

**NOTES**

In Italian markets, free-range chickens are sold more or less intact to authenticate their origins. The scuffed feet point to a lifetime of foraging outdoors for food, while a healthy-looking head and yellow skin testify to the chicken's high quality. Your chicken may not come with these attributes, but at least try to buy one with neck and gizzard; otherwise, get a few extra wings for making the broth.

If you're short of time, buy prepared chicken broth rather than making it—choose an organic one with reduced sodium and a minimum of additives. Use any leftover broth to make steamed couscous or rice to go with the chicken.

# SLOW-SIMMERED CHICKEN with OLIVES, OVER COUSCOUS

*Pollo in umido con olivi neri*

MAKES 8 SERVINGS | PREP: 20 MINUTES | COOK: 1½ HOURS

*Even if you don't keep pigeons yourself, as Maria Gambini and her husband do, it's easy enough to buy them at the butcher or supermarket in Italy. Not so in the U.S., and so I've substituted chicken for the squab (otherwise known as pigeon) in Maria's Sunday dinner recipe.*

1 large chicken, preferably free-range (about 4 pounds),
   cut into serving pieces
Sea salt or kosher salt
Freshly ground black pepper
1 tablespoon unsalted butter
Extra-virgin olive oil
1 medium onion, chopped
1 large stalk celery, diced small
2 cloves garlic, finely chopped
2/3 cup white wine
3½ cups broth made from the chicken trimmings (see Note),
   or prepared chicken broth, or a mixture of broth and water
6 ounces Mediterranean black olives such as Gaeta or Kalamata,
   pitted and halved or cut into slivers (about 1 cup)
2½ cups instant couscous

1. Blot the chicken pieces dry with paper towels. Sprinkle all over with salt and pepper. Heat 1 very large skillet (or 2 smaller ones) over medium heat. Melt the butter with 2 tablespoons olive oil. Fry the chicken, turning it to brown well on all sides; remove to a platter.

2. If using 2 skillets, transfer the oil remaining in one to the other; add a little more olive oil if necessary and cook the onion, stirring often, until it turns a deep golden with some browned edges, about 10 minutes. Stir in the celery and cook for a few minutes (not so long that the celery loses its fresh green color). Add the garlic, cooking just until fragrant, and then the wine, using a heatproof spatula to loosen any browned bits on the bottom of the skillet.

*continued*

**3.** Arrange the chicken on top of the aromatic vegetables; if the pieces don't fit in one layer, place the breast pieces on top. Add ¾ cup chicken broth; when the liquid comes to a boil, reduce the heat and simmer slowly, partially covered, until the chicken is very tender, about 1 hour.

**4.** Using tongs, transfer the chicken to a platter. Raise the heat under the skillet so that the pan juices simmer briskly. Once they are reduced and begin to thicken, stir in the olives and lower the heat; simmer a few minutes longer.

**5.** While the sauce is simmering, bring the remaining 2¾ cups chicken broth to a boil in a small saucepan or microwaveable cup. Place the couscous in a bowl; pour the hot broth over it, cover, and let stand until absorbed, about 5 minutes.

**6.** Fluff the couscous and spoon onto a platter; arrange the chicken pieces on top and ladle the sauce and olives over it.

### NOTE

I prefer to buy a whole chicken, cut it in eight to twelve serving pieces, and use the trimmings (neck, wing ends, gizzard, etc.) to make a simple broth to use both in braising the chicken and steaming the couscous. Place the trimmings in a medium saucepan, cover with water, and add an onion end and bay leaf; bring to a boil and skim off any frothy scum that rises to the top. Reduce the heat and simmer for at least 20 minutes; season lightly with salt and pepper, keeping in mind the olives that will be added to the chicken.

### VARIATION

Sardinian *fregola* or Israeli couscous can be substituted for the instant couscous. You'll need a higher proportion of broth. Sauté the grains briefly in a little olive oil (about 2 tablespoons) before adding 3½ cups hot broth; reduce the heat and simmer for 10 to 15 minutes, or until the broth has been absorbed.

# QUAIL al VIN SANTO with SWEET-SOUR CABBAGE

*Quaglie al vin santo con cavolo agrodolce*

MAKES 3 OR 4 SERVINGS | PREP: 20 MINUTES | COOK: 1 TO 1½ HOURS

*This* piatto unico, *which juxtaposes the tart pungency of juniper berries with the sweetness of* vin santo, *conjures up images of a fall or winter feast following a country hunt. But I ate a similar dish on a balmy June Sunday at Da Delfina, a hillside restaurant near Florence, and did not regret it.*

6 to 8 quail (about 2 pounds) or 1 baby chicken (*poussin*)
Sea salt or kosher salt
6 to 8 bay leaves
1 teaspoon juniper berries
Extra-virgin olive oil
⅓ cup finely chopped shallot or onion
1 ounce pancetta or prosciutto end, diced small (about 2 tablespoons)
½ cup *vin santo* or another semisweet wine (see Note)
Freshly ground black pepper
1 cup unsalted or reduced-sodium chicken broth or water
Sweet-sour cabbage with apple and currants (recipe follows)

1. Preheat the oven to 350°F. Truss the quail (see Note) or cut *poussin* in serving-size pieces, if using. Lightly sprinkle the quail with salt inside and out. Tuck a small bay leaf (or piece of a larger one) inside each quail. Pulverize the juniper berries using a mortar and pestle; if you don't have one, crush by pressing them with the side of a cook's knife against a cutting board and then chop coarsely.

2. Over medium-high heat, heat enough olive oil (about 2 tablespoons) to cover the bottom of an ovenproof skillet large enough to hold the quail in a single layer. Once the pan is hot, place the quail on their sides in the skillet; if it's a fairly cozy fit, that's fine. Sear the birds, turning them until all sides are lightly browned.

*continued*

**3.** Add the shallot and pancetta to the spaces between the quail. Cook, stirring with a spatula, until the onion is tender and both are golden brown, about 2 minutes. Add the *vin santo*, juniper berries, and several grindings of black pepper, letting the wine sizzle for a minute or so.

**4.** Add the broth (the liquid should come about one-third of the way up the sides of the quail) and bring to a simmer. Place the skillet on the middle rack of the oven. Cook, partially covered, until the quail are so tender the drumsticks wiggle loosely in the sockets, 1 to 1½ hours. Check often to make sure the liquid remains at a gentle simmer (adjusting the temperature as necessary) and to baste with the braising liquid.

**5.** By this time the braising liquid may have thickened. If not, pour most of it into a small skillet and cook briskly over medium-high heat until it thickens.

**6.** Spoon the cabbage over the bottom of dinner plates or shallow soup bowls. Place 2 quail on top of each serving and spoon the sauce over them.

**NOTES**

Nothing tastes quite like *vin santo*, a wine made with Tuscan grapes and aged in wood, but alternatives that work well in this recipe include Spanish port and Marsala.

To truss each quail: Cross the feet and loop a piece of butcher's string (about 2 feet long) a couple times around them; form a knot, leaving both ends dangling. Push the quail legs toward the body so that the legs bend at the "knees" and are nestled on either side of the breast. Loop the string ends a couple of times around the length of the bird and tie to hold it in a compact shape.

# Sweet-Sour Cabbage with Apple and Currants

MAKES 3 OR 4 SERVINGS | PREP: 15 MINUTES | COOK: 25 MINUTES

1 small head purple or green cabbage
1 medium apple, quartered and cored
1 tablespoon currants or raisins
1/2 cup white or red vermouth
2 tablespoons unsalted butter
Sea salt or kosher salt
Freshly ground black pepper

1. Halve the cabbage; remove the core and thinly shred the cabbage crosswise (makes about 8 cups). Dice the apple in medium cubes (it's fine to leave the skin on). Combine the currants and vermouth in a small bowl.

2. Melt the butter in a large skillet over medium-high heat. Sauté the cabbage, stirring often, until it softens, about 10 minutes. Sprinkle with 1/2 teaspoon salt and continue to cook until the cabbage edges begin to turn golden brown. Add the apple, currants and vermouth, and 1/2 cup water; season with several grindings of black pepper.

3. When the liquid comes to a simmer, reduce the heat to medium-low and cook a few minutes longer, until the apple is tender. Taste and add more salt or pepper if needed.

## ✏ *Italian Market Strategies*

Eating in restaurants and trattorias is one of the pleasures of Italian travel, but there are other ways to experience the country's rich food culture, including visits to farms, participation in local food festivals, and exploring the multitiered system of markets.

Agri-tourism is huge in Italy, driven as much by the desire of Italians to remain in touch with their agricultural heritage as by motives related to tourism. Some *agriturismi* (farms that offer accommodations and meals) are merely inns with a few olive trees as window dressing, but others are full-fledged agricultural enterprises that raise farm animals, harvest produce, make cheese and wine, and press olive oil. On request, the proprietors of such establishments will give a customized tour of the grounds and kitchen, and cooking classes might be available as well.

Regardless of where you are staying, it is often possible to learn about a local specialty at close hand—whether a balsamic-making *acetaia* in Modena, an anchovy processing plant in Sicily, or a pasta maker in Umbria. And just about every town, it seems, boasts a food celebration. It needn't be the white truffle festival in Alba, drawing a high-flying international crowd, to be worth seeking out. One of the most fun I've attended is *Bucine in Fiore* ("in flower"), a progressive dinner of ten specialties consumed at outdoor stands scattered in parks and piazzas throughout the town of Bucine. We strolled down back streets from one to another, sampling local specialties such as stuffed chicken and fried frogs legs, each prepared with pride by cooks from Bucine or one of its outlying villages. Around our necks dangled *calici* (wine glasses), within easy reach for sampling wines displayed on stands throughout town. Whether we were sampling a super-Tuscan or the obscure *sangiovese* standing next to it, our filled glasses were included in the modest price of the dinner. As the festival gathered steam and the music got under way, no one bothered to check tickets anymore.

Markets merit a visit, if only to gather the makings of a gourmet picnic, but even more so if you have access to a kitchen (and plan to stay long enough to make use of it). There's no better way to gain intimacy with Italian ingredients and cooking techniques than to gather some of the bounty and get to work in the kitchen.

> *"Just about every locale has a market, usually outdoors, where vendors congregate to sell everything from doorknobs and underwear to porchetta sandwiches and produce."*

Italian supermarkets, reassuringly familiar but different enough to be illuminating, are a good place to start. Take the opportunity to eyeball foods and labels at your leisure before making selections. The dried pasta section might be three times the size of one in an American supermarket, for instance, and a larger supermarket may also have a counter devoted to fresh pasta. Because food regulations are stricter in Italy (and in Europe in general), labeling is likely to be quite precise. The label on a frozen packet of fish, for instance, may tell you not only whether it is wild or farmed, but exactly where it was caught and by what method. The word *nostrale* on labels and signs means "ours" and refers to local or regional products. *Biologico* (or just *bio*) designates organic products.

Produce selection is usually self-service, but touching the goods is frowned on. Instead, you are expected to don disposable plastic gloves from dispensers and to weigh and price your selection on a self-service machine.

Like us, Italians appreciate the convenience and competitive pricing of supermarkets, but they also frequent traditional shops, and so should you. Most neighborhoods with a residential population offer the following within easy walking distance of one another: butcher (*macelleria*), poultry vendor (*polleria*),

*continued*

fishmonger (*pescevendolo*), dairy store (*latteria*), bread bakery (*fornaio*), pastry shop (*pasticceria*), deli (*salumeria*), and all-purpose corner grocery (*alimentari*). To foreigners, these small shops can seem more intimidating than an impersonal supermarket setting. Customers tend to mill around rather than form orderly queues, but one learns over time to relax and accept that cultural difference. Like everyone else, I do edge toward the counter and try to make eye contact, but I trust that the counter person has seen me and will wait on me in turn—and, by and large, that's the case.

Just about every locale has a market, usually outdoors, where vendors congregate to sell everything from doorknobs and underwear to *porchetta* sandwiches and produce. The frequency varies, depending on the size of the place—every day for the Campo dei Fiori in Rome or Mercato Centrale in Florence, but just once a week in a small town. Usually the wares are not limited to local products; in fact, larger markets might give space to vendors from other parts of Italy or even other European countries: herbs from Provence, salmon from Norway, Serrano ham from Spain. But there may also be markets that carry only local goods. For instance, in Montevarchi, a town in the Arno Valley, Thursday is the regular market day. But there is also an indoor market, open most days, with more limited offerings, where you can be sure the eggs, legumes, cheeses, fish, and wines are strictly regional.

Shopping at both kinds of markets can lead to interesting insights. I was thrilled to find porcini at the outdoor market in June, for instance. When I asked a vendor at the indoor market why none were for sale there, he explained that Tuscan porcini were only plentiful enough in fall to show up in the market; any harvested in early summer would be consumed privately. He speculated that my porcini were from Albania. (No matter; they were delicious!)

Regardless of the venue, it's helpful to have a grasp of common metric sizes when shopping for food. A kilo of fruit or vegetables weighs slightly more than two pounds, and a *mezzo* kilo will get you half of that. *Etto*, meaning 100 grams of something (or about four ounces), is a useful word to have in one's vocabulary, especially when ordering cheese, cured meats, or other deli items. You can often get *la metà* (half) of a small wheel of cheese, large loaf of bread, or free-range chicken if you ask. Negotiations with a butcher or pasta vendor might also focus on how many servings you need to make (though of course his or her ideas on that may differ from yours!) And, if language fails, sign language and volunteer translators will almost certainly come to the rescue. ᱬ

# BRAISED VEAL SHANKS with SAFFRON RISOTTO

*Ossobuchi alla milanese*

**MAKES 6 SERVINGS | PREP: 20 MINUTES | COOK: 2 HOURS**

*Tradition calls for serving this classic risotto from Milan not as a first course—the traditional position for risotti in an Italian meal—but as a side to braised veal shanks. A finely chopped gremolata of parsley, lemon peel, and garlic, added in the final moments of cooking, brightens the sauce.*

*Add buttered Brussels sprouts or another green vegetable to the plate, or serve a tossed green salad on the side.*

6 cross-cut sections (about 2 inches thick) veal shank
  (4 to 6 pounds total)
Sea salt or kosher salt
Freshly ground black pepper
½ cup all-purpose flour, or as needed
Extra-virgin olive oil
1 small onion, chopped
1 medium carrot, diced small
1 large stalk celery, diced small
1½ cups homemade meat broth (page 99) or store-bought
  reduced-salt or unsalted chicken broth
1 cup chopped canned plum tomatoes, including some of the purée
1 cup red or white wine
½ cup flat-leaf parsley leaves
1 large clove garlic
1 large strip lemon zest (yellow part only; use a vegetable peeler)
Saffron risotto (recipe follows)

1. Preheat the oven to 400°F. Blot the veal shanks dry with a paper towel. Sprinkle generously with salt and pepper. Coat the veal shanks on all surfaces with the flour, patting off any excess.

2. In a large, straight-sided ovenproof skillet just large enough for the shanks to fit in one layer, heat enough oil to coat the bottom (about 2 tablespoons) over medium-high heat. Brown the shanks on both sides and on the edges, using tongs to turn them, about 15 minutes total. Transfer to a plate.

*continued*

3. Reduce the heat to medium and add 1 to 2 more tablespoons olive oil. Cook the onion, carrot, and celery, stirring often, until tender and lightly browned. Add the meat broth, tomatoes, and wine, scraping the bottom of the pan to loosen any browned-on bits.

4. Return the browned veal shanks to the pan. The liquid should come about halfway up the sides; if not, add a little water. Bring to a simmer and season to taste with salt and pepper. Slide the pan onto a middle rack in the oven and cook, covered, until fork-tender, about 1½ hours. Check frequently to make sure the liquid remains at a slow simmer; reduce the heat if it is bubbling furiously. (At this point, the veal shanks can be kept warm for up to 2 hours, or cooled and refrigerated for up to 1 day; if the latter, reheat the shanks in their sauce before proceeding.)

5. While the shanks are cooking, finely chop the parsley, garlic, and lemon zest together.

6. Transfer the tender veal shanks to a platter. Over medium heat, briskly simmer the pan liquid until it reduces and thickens. Stir in the chopped parsley mixture and cook for 1 to 2 minutes; taste and add more salt and pepper if needed. Return the shanks to the pan and spoon the sauce over them.

7. To serve: Spoon the risotto onto 6 plates; prop a veal shank against each mound, and spoon some of the sauce over it.

## Saffron Risotto

MAKES 6 SERVINGS | PREP: 15 MINUTES | COOK: 20 MINUTES

1 large pinch saffron threads
2½ cups homemade meat broth (page 99) or store-bought
   reduced-salt or unsalted chicken broth
Sea salt or kosher salt
2 tablespoons unsalted butter
1 tablespoon extra-virgin olive oil
⅓ cup finely chopped onion or shallot
2 cups Carnaroli or Arborio rice
½ cup dry white wine
⅔ cup grated Grana Padano or other aged cheese

1. Crumble the saffron into a small bowl. Cover with ¼ cup tepid water; set aside to steep.

2. Combine the broth with 2½ cups water in a medium saucepan; bring to a boil; adjust the heat to a slow simmer. Season to taste with salt.

3. In a medium saucepan, melt the butter with the olive oil over medium heat. Cook the onion, stirring often, until tender and golden, about 10 minutes. Stir in the rice and cook for a minute or so, until the grains are coated and smell toasty. Add the wine, stirring until most is absorbed. Ladle on enough of the hot broth to cover the rice. Simmer, stirring occasionally and adding more broth as the liquid is absorbed (you may not need it all), until the rice is cooked but still a bit firm in the center, about 20 minutes. Remove from heat; add the saffron water and a final ladleful of broth; cover and allow the risotto to collect itself for about 5 minutes. Stir in half of the cheese.

4. Divide the risotto among plates and sprinkle the remaining cheese on top.

# VEAL STEW with MUSHROOMS and PEAS, on TOAST

*Spezzatino di vitella con funghi e piselli, su crostini*

MAKES 4 OR 5 SERVINGS | PREP: 20 MINUTES | COOK: ABOUT 2 HOURS

*This delectable stew, with just a touch of cream, is Italian comfort food at its best.*

2 pounds bone-in veal shoulder steaks or 1¾ pounds boneless
　veal stew meat
Extra-virgin olive oil
½ cup chopped shallot or onion
1 thick-cut (¼-inch) slice pancetta, cut into small cubes (about ⅓ cup)
10 ounces crimini or white mushrooms, halved, thinly sliced
Sea salt or kosher salt
Freshly ground black pepper
2 tablespoons unbleached all-purpose flour
½ cup white wine
⅓ cup heavy cream
1½ cups frozen baby peas
4 large slices white or whole-grain country-style bread

1. Blot the veal shoulder dry with paper towels. Trim it, discarding the fat but reserving the bones. Cut the lean meat into ½-inch cubes.

2. Over medium heat, heat enough oil (about 2 tablespoons) to coat the bottom of a large, straight-sided sauté pan. Cook the shallot and pancetta, stirring often, until the fat is rendered and the shallot and pancetta are lightly browned, about 5 minutes. Stir in the mushrooms, cooking until they soften and release some of their liquid, about 8 minutes. Add salt and pepper to taste. Scoop the contents of the pan into a bowl.

3. Heat a little more olive oil (about 1 tablespoon) over medium-high heat in the same pan. Cook half of the cubed veal until lightly browned; season with salt and pepper. Stir and continue cooking until browned all over. Remove the veal to a bowl and brown the remaining meat in the same way.

*continued*

**4.** Return the first batch of veal to the pan. Lower the heat to medium. Sprinkle with the flour; stir for 1 to 2 minutes. Add the wine, letting it sizzle while loosening any browned bits with a spatula.

**5.** Return the reserved veal bones and mushroom mixture to the pan and add ½ cup water. When it comes to a simmer, reduce the heat to low and cook, partially covered, until very tender, about 1½ hours; add a little water from time to time if needed.

**6.** When the veal is tender, remove and discard the bones. Stir in the cream and peas and cook a few minutes longer until the peas are heated through and the sauce thickens slightly.

**7.** Toast the bread until crisp but not browned; slice in half diagonally. To serve: Arrange two toast halves in the center of each plate. Spoon the stew on top, letting it cascade over the sides of the toast.

## VARIATIONS

This savory braise could also be made with any beef or lamb cuts suitable for stew. The vegetables could be varied as well—why not baby limas, for instance?

# BOLLITO MISTO with FRESH PARSLEY SAUCE

*Bollito misto con salsa verde*

MAKES 8 SERVINGS | PREP: 15 MINUTES | TIME: ABOUT 2½ HOURS

*In Emilia-Romagna the boiled meat and vegetable dinner called* bollito misto *is taken seriously. The waiter typically wheels a cart to the table and dishes up the boiled meats and vegetables from covered containers according to each diner's preferences. Dining at I Cocchi, a Parma restaurant, I overheard a large party enter into vigorous negotiations once their carello rolled up. "No chicken breast!" decreed one man, leaping out of his chair to better supervise the waiter's work. He said yes to boiled beef, tongue, and cotechino sausage, however, and to the creamed spinach and whipped potatoes that were also on offer.*

*At home, a* bollito misto *can be a simpler affair, tailored to your preferences and the number of people. The idea of dining on boiled meats may not sound appealing, but I urge you to give this dish a chance. It is extremely simple to prepare, and the flavors of the meats and vegetables, each simmered according to its needs, are deeply satisfying. I adore this* piccolo bollito *with a deliciously piquant green sauce.*

1 onion, halved
8 whole cloves
4 large carrots
1 stalk celery
2 sprigs flat-leaf parsley
Sea salt or kosher salt
1 teaspoon black peppercorns
2 pounds beef brisket
4 large red-skinned potatoes or other boiling potatoes
8 small bone-in chicken thighs (about 2 pounds), skin removed
1 pound sweet Italian sausage, cut into 8 pieces
Fresh parsley sauce (recipe follows)
*Mostarda di Cremona* from a jar (optional) (see Note)

1. Stud the onion with the cloves. Cut 1 carrot and the celery stalk crosswise in half and combine in a large saucepan with the onion, parsley, 2 teaspoons salt, and the peppercorns.

*continued*

**2.** Fill the saucepan two-thirds full of water (about 4 quarts) and bring to a boil. Lower the brisket into the saucepan, and when the water returns to a boil, adjust the heat to a gentle simmer. Skim off any scum that rises to the top during the first few minutes of cooking. Cook, partially covered, until the meat is tender, about 2 hours.

**3.** Meanwhile, quarter the potatoes and cut the remaining carrots into equal chunks. Add the chicken thighs to the saucepan and simmer about 10 minutes; fish out and discard the cooked carrot, celery, and onion. Add the freshly cut potatoes and carrots and cook about 20 minutes longer, until tender.

**4.** At the same time, fill a small saucepan with enough water to cover the sausage. Bring to a boil. Add the sausage and simmer until cooked through, about 20 minutes.

**5.** Remove the brisket, chicken, and vegetables from the larger saucepan. Strain the broth into a bowl and return to the saucepan; season to taste with salt. Add the brisket, chicken, vegetables, and sausage. (At this point, the *bollito* can be cooled and refrigerated overnight; remove any solidified fat before proceeding.)

**6.** Shortly before serving, heat the contents of the saucepan over low heat. Skim off any fat shimmering on top.

**7.** To serve: Transfer the brisket to a cutting board and carve across the grain into slices. Arrange on a deep platter with the chicken, sausage, carrots, and potatoes. Spoon a little of the broth over the meats and vegetables. Serve immediately with fresh parsley sauce and, if using, the *mostarda di Cremona*.

## Fresh Parsley Sauce

MAKES 1 CUP | PREP: 10 MINUTES

1 tablespoon capers, preferably salt-cured
2 cups firmly packed flat-leaf parsley leaves
1 cup extra-virgin olive oil
1 clove garlic, roughly chopped (optional)
2 anchovy fillets, halved
Fresh lemon juice
Sea salt or kosher salt

1. Place the capers in a small bowl and cover with water. Soak for 5 minutes; drain. Combine the capers with the parsley, olive oil, garlic (if using), and anchovy fillets in a food processor bowl. Pulse until the mixture is puréed but still has some texture, pausing once or twice to scrape the sides of the bowl.

2. Scrape the sauce into a small serving bowl. Season to taste with fresh lemon juice and salt.

### NOTES

*Mostarda di Cremona* is a sweet-spicy condiment of translucent, jewel-like fruits preserved in a syrup containing mustard oil. The town of Cremona is justly proud of its *mostarda*, but there are other versions typical of Mantua or Milan. Buy these products in an Italian specialty store or from an online vendor.

The making of *bollito misto* generates a potful of meat broth to be used in other ways. Traditionally, a full-scale *bollito misto* dinner leads off with *anolini* or another kind of small pasta simmered in the lovely *brodo*. This works in a restaurant setting, but I prefer to leave the meats and vegetables immersed in the broth until just before serving, for maximum moistness. If there are leftover meats, return them to the broth; reheat the next day and you have another meal. Otherwise, use the broth in other ways: soups, risotto, sauces, and so on.

### VARIATION

To make *lesso di manzo*, a streamlined version of what is already a very simple preparation, skip the chicken and sausage. Instead, simmer a brisket weighing four to five pounds. Serve with the parsley sauce.

# POT ROAST with PORCINI and ROOT VEGETABLES

*Brasato di manzo con porcini, patate e carote*

MAKES 6 SERVINGS | PREP: 20 MINUTES | COOK: ABOUT 3 HOURS

*In some parts of Italy, this dish is called* brasato, *referring to the braising method, and in others,* stracotto, *meaning "overcooked." When cooked in a moist environment at a barely perceptible simmer, the roast will not taste overcooked but meltingly tender and savory. The porcini speak softly or more forcefully, depending on the quantity you use.*

3 pounds well-marbled beef chuck roast, tied with string (see Note)
Sea salt or kosher salt
Freshly ground black pepper
Extra-virgin olive oil
1 medium onion, finely chopped
2 cloves garlic, finely chopped
2 tablespoons all-purpose flour
1 cup Chianti or other red wine
1 cup chopped canned plum tomatoes with some of the purée
2 sprigs rosemary or sage
½ to 1 ounce dried porcini mushrooms
4 medium Yukon Gold or other boiling potatoes, or turnips, or a
   mix of the two, peeled and cut into chunks
4 medium carrots, cut into chunks

1. Preheat the oven to 300°F. Sprinkle the beef all over with plenty of salt and a more frugal amount of pepper. Over medium-high heat, heat an ovenproof Dutch oven or broad saucepan large enough to hold the beef with room for vegetables around the edges. Add just enough olive oil to film the bottom of the pan, tilting it to reach the corners. Sear the beef, turning it with tongs, until well browned on all sides and ends. Transfer to a plate.

2. The roast will have given off a little of its own fat, but if it doesn't seem adequate, add a little more olive oil to the skillet before cooking the onion, stirring until golden brown, about 10 minutes. Add the garlic, cooking just until fragrant. Sprinkle the flour over the top and cook, stirring constantly, for 1 to 2 minutes. Add the wine, tomatoes, rosemary, and enough water to come one-third of the way up the sides of the roast. Bring the liquid to a boil.

3. Remove from heat and return the beef to the pan; spoon some of the liquid over it; cover. Place the pan on a rack in the lower third of the oven and cook until the beef is fairly tender but a fork plunged into it meets some resistance, about 2 hours. Check periodically to make sure the liquid remains at a bare simmer, and baste the roast with the braising liquid; about halfway through the cooking, turn the roast.

4. While the beef is in the oven, place the porcini in a small bowl and cover with warm water. Let stand for about 15 minutes. Remove the porcini pieces from the bowl, rinse off any grit, and roughly chop. Line a small strainer with a double thickness of paper towel or cheesecloth, and strain the porcini liquid into another small bowl.

5. Remove the pan from the oven; using a serving spoon or small ladle, skim off some of the fat floating on the surface of the beef braising liquid (see Note). Add the porcini pieces and filtered liquid. Surround the beef with the potatoes and carrots, spooning the liquid over them; they need not be fully immersed. Cook in the oven about 1 hour longer, partially covered, basting often, until the beef and vegetables are fork-tender and the sauce is dense (see Note). Remove the rosemary sprigs.

6. Transfer the beef to a cutting board and remove string. Slice across the grain in thick slabs and arrange with the vegetables on a platter or in broad, shallow bowls. Spoon the sauce over and around the meat and vegetables.

### NOTES

Choose what my butcher calls a "first-cut" chuck roast with visible marbling and connective tissue. Top-blade pot roast and chuck-eye roast are other cuts that will yield good results when cooked this way.

If you are making the pot roast a day in advance, don't bother to skim the surface fat when the roast is tender. Instead, cool and refrigerate the meat. When ready to proceed, remove and discard the solidified fat. Reheat in a 300°F oven before adding the porcini and vegetables and completing the cooking.

If the sauce doesn't seem thick enough at the end of cooking, boil it down for 1 to 2 minutes after removing the beef. Too thick? Dilute with a little hot water.

# SHORT RIBS BRAISED with DRIED FIGS and BALSAMIC VINEGAR

*Brasato di manzo con salsa ai fichi e aceto balsamico*

MAKES 6 SERVINGS | PREP: 20 MINUTES | COOK: 4½ HOURS

*Short ribs deliver a rich and luxurious dining experience that is unrelated to cost. These muscular hunks of beef qualify as cheap cuts, but subjected to the alchemy of a slow oven, they turn meltingly tender and succulent. Serve these short ribs with soft polenta or rice to capture some of the sauce, and braised greens.*

1½ cups Chianti or other fruity red wine
2 oranges, zested, juiced, shells quartered
⅓ cup balsamic vinegar
Sea salt or kosher salt
Freshly ground black pepper
½ teaspoon sugar
½ teaspoon dried thyme
2 bay leaves
5 pounds beef short ribs
1 cup stemmed, halved dried figs, preferably Mission (see Note)
1 tablespoon unsalted butter
¼ cup finely chopped shallot or onion

**1.** Preheat the oven to 275°F. In a small bowl, combine the wine, orange juice and zest, balsamic vinegar, 1 teaspoon salt, ½ teaspoon pepper, the sugar, thyme, and bay leaves.

**2.** Place the ribs and squeezed orange quarters in a roasting pan. Pour the wine-orange juice mixture over them. Cover the pan tightly with foil and place on a middle rack in the oven to cook for 2 hours. Check the ribs a few times, replenishing evaporated liquid with more wine or water as needed.

**3.** Turn the short ribs with tongs. Remove and discard the orange sections. Drop the figs into the liquid surrounding the ribs. Continue to braise the ribs, covered, until fork-tender, about 2 hours longer. Remove from the oven and cool, covered, for 15 minutes.

4. Transfer the figs and meat to a bowl; leave the bones attached, if you wish, or pull them away from the meat and discard. Strain the warm liquid in the roasting pan into a liquid measuring cup and discard solids; you should have about 2 cups of liquid. Skim and discard the fat that rises to the top or, even better, chill the liquid and scrape off the fat once it solidifies (see Note).

5. To finish the sauce: In a medium saucepan, melt the butter over medium heat. Sauté the shallot, stirring, until soft and fragrant, about 5 minutes. Add the skimmed braising liquid and simmer briskly until it is reduced by about half and thickens slightly. Taste and correct the seasoning. Return the short ribs and figs to the roasting pan, pour the sauce over them, cover, and heat in a 275°F oven.

6. To serve: Prop the ribs against the polenta or rice. Spoon some of the figs and sauce over each serving.

## NOTES

Mission figs are stocked in the same section as raisins and other dried fruits; Sunkist is one brand that packages them.

To quickly congeal the fat on top of the braising liquid, place the measuring cup in the freezer to chill. After about an hour, there will be a layer of white fat on top; scoop it off and discard. Or, if you are preparing this recipe well in advance, chill the liquid and meat separately in the refrigerator; scrape off and discard congealed fat before reheating the liquid and meat together.

# MEATBALLS with TOMATO PAN SAUCE and PARSLEYED POTATOES

*Polpette al pomodoro con patate al prezzemolo*

MAKES 3 OR 4 SERVINGS *(12 meatballs)* | PREP: 20 MINUTES | COOK: 25 MINUTES

*A freight train had overturned on the tracks, causing massive delays in commuter schedules all over central Italy. After commiserating with the woman sitting next to me over what seemed an endless journey from Florence to Parma, we turned to conversation about cooking—specifically, one-course piatti unici. Before long the woman across from us chimed in: "Polpette!" It turned out she was on her way home to Reggio Emilia, a province known for fine cuisine, so her meatball recipe merited attention. She serves hers with peperonata—a stew of bell peppers and other vegetables—but agreed that potatoes would taste good, too.*

*As I jotted down the last instruction, our train pulled into the station. After bidding my companions goodbye and stepping onto the platform, I found myself wishing the ride had lasted just a little longer.*

1 pound meatloaf mix (1 part each ground beef, veal, and pork)
  (see Note)
½ cup unseasoned dry bread crumbs
⅓ cup grated Parmigiano Reggiano cheese
2 tablespoons pine nuts
⅓ cup finely chopped flat-leaf parsley or chives
1 clove garlic, finely chopped
Sea salt or kosher salt
Freshly ground black pepper
1 egg, beaten
Vegetable oil
6 small boiling potatoes, cut into chunks
Extra-virgin olive oil
½ cup dry white wine
1½ cups strained tomatoes (such as Pomì) or chopped canned
  plum tomatoes with some of the purée

1. Place the meatloaf mix in a medium bowl, kneading with one hand to combine the meats. Add the bread crumbs, cheese, pine nuts, half of the parsley, garlic, ½ teaspoon salt, and ¼ teaspoon pepper; mix until the ingredients are incorporated. Add the egg and knead gently until the mixture is moistened.

2. Check the seasoning by breaking off a small glob of the meatball mix and frying in a little vegetable oil in a small pan until cooked through. Taste and add more salt and pepper to the entire mixture if needed.

3. With a spoon, scoop up a golf ball–size piece of the meatball mixture. Gently roll to make a ball (about 2 ounces); flatten slightly with your hand. Place on a piece of waxed paper and repeat with the rest of the meatball mixture.

4. Place the potatoes in a medium saucepan and cover with water. Bring to a boil. Reduce the heat and simmer until tender, about 15 minutes. Drain and return to the pan. Drizzle with a little olive oil, season with salt and pepper, and stir in the remaining parsley; keep warm over the lowest setting.

5. In a large skillet, heat a generous quantity of vegetable oil (about 1/3 cup) over medium heat. Fry the meatballs, turning with tongs or a wooden spoon, until well browned on both sides but not cooked through, about 10 minutes. Remove to a plate.

6. Drain and discard all but a film of crusty oil on the bottom of the skillet. Add the wine, letting it bubble and reduce a little as you scrape up any brown bits clinging to the bottom of the pan. Stir in the tomatoes and add a pinch of salt. Return the meatballs to the pan, spooning the sauce over them. Simmer slowly, covered, until the meatballs are cooked and the sauce is fairly dense, about 15 minutes; during the cooking, turn the meatballs once or twice to coat with the sauce.

7. Serve the meatballs and potatoes alone or with a steamed green vegetable such as broccoli.

## NOTE

After messing around with meatballs for a while, I figured out a couple of secrets to getting them to turn out consistently tender and succulent. The first is not to overdo it with bread crumbs. The second, and more important, rule is to use the best ground meat you can get. Ask your butcher to grind a top-drawer meatloaf mixture. Alternatively, grind top-quality beef chuck at home in a food processor. For this, you'll still need help from the butcher or meat manager. Here's what to do: Buy 12 ounces of beef chuck in one piece plus a couple of ounces of solid beef or pork rib fat (most likely this will be free). Cut the meat into 1-inch pieces and the fat into 1/2-inch pieces. Place one third of each in a food processor, and pulse about 20 times until chopped medium fine. Remove the ground meat to a bowl and process the other two batches. Use in the recipe as instructed.

# CELERY BUNDLES with MEAT STUFFING and TOMATO SAUCE

*Sedani ripieni*

MAKES 8 SERVINGS | PREP: 1 HOUR | COOK: 1½ HOURS

*Elena Cecchi taught me how to make this dish from her hometown, Prato. Celery rarely lands a starring role, but here it is stuffed, fried, and then baked with a sauce! Like* lasagne, sedani ripieni *call for a rather intricate preparation of components, which are then assembled and cooked together. Give the project the time it deserves, and you'll be well rewarded.*

*Elena, a virtuoso cook, serves stuffed celery as one among several courses. But I find that this substantial dish stands on its own as a piatto unico.*

2 large bunches celery

Sea salt or kosher salt

⅓ cup dried porcini mushrooms (about ⅛ ounce)

1 medium onion, finely chopped

Extra-virgin olive oil

¼ pound ground beef

¼ pound chicken livers, chopped to a paste

¼ pound deli ham, chopped fine

¼ pound prosciutto, chopped fine (see Note)

½ cup white wine

1 cup plus 1 tablespoon unbleached all-purpose flour

½ cup plus 2 tablespoons freshly grated Parmigiano Reggiano cheese

Freshly ground black pepper

⅛ teaspoon nutmeg

½ cup milk

1 (28- or 35-ounce) can Italian plum tomatoes with purée or juice

Leaves from 2 sprigs fresh basil or parsley

2 eggs

1 cup fine unseasoned bread crumbs

Vegetable oil

1. Preheat the oven to 350°F. Break off the large outer stalks of the celery bunches. You will need 12 to 16 stalks. (Save the tender inner stalks for other uses such as salads and *soffritto*.) Trim the ends, remove the strings, and cut each stalk crosswise into 2 or 3 pieces (about 4 inches long).

2. Fill a large saucepan with enough water to cover the celery. Add 1 heaping tablespoon salt and bring to a boil. Slide the celery into the water and when it returns to a boil, reduce the heat and simmer until tender (test with the point of a knife), but still green and firm enough to hold its shape, 10 to 15 minutes. Drain the celery and cool under running water (this prevents further cooking and preserves the celery's color).

3. To prepare the filling: Place the porcini in a small bowl and cover with 2/3 cup warm water; let stand for about 15 minutes. Meanwhile, in a skillet over medium heat, sauté the onion in about 1 tablespoon olive oil until tender. Add the ground beef and stir briefly just until it loses its raw look. Add the livers and do the same. Stir in the ham and prosciutto.

4. Remove the mushrooms from the liquid and rinse gently to remove any grit. Chop and add to the contents of the skillet. Strain the mushroom liquid through a small strainer, lined with a double thickness of paper towel or cheesecloth, into the skillet. Add the wine and simmer, reducing the heat if necessary, until the liquid has mostly evaporated. Sprinkle 1 tablespoon flour over the mixture and cook, stirring often, for 2 to 3 minutes. Add 2 tablespoons Parmigiano Reggiano, pepper, and nutmeg. Taste before adding salt; given the sodium in the deli meats and cheese, you may need little or none. Stir in the milk and simmer until thick, about 15 minutes longer.

5. To make a simple tomato sauce: Place the tomatoes and purée in a medium saucepan; break up the tomatoes with a wooden spoon or by squishing them between your fingers. Add 1 to 2 tablespoons olive oil and the basil leaves. Bring to a boil over medium-high heat; reduce the heat and simmer for about 15 minutes until the sauce is dense. Season to taste with salt and pepper. Cool slightly and transfer to a food processor. Using the pulse button, process briefly until puréed but still a bit chunky.

6. To assemble the celery bundles: Gently flatten a celery section, splitting it a bit in the middle if necessary. Fill the concave side with the meat filling. Cover with a celery section of about the same dimensions, pressing the edges together (the seal need not be airtight, for the breading will help hold the bundles together as they fry). Save leftover filling for another use (see Note).

*continued*

7. Place 1 cup flour, the eggs, and the bread crumbs in separate bowls. Beat the eggs with ¼ teaspoon salt. Coat each celery bundle on all sides with flour, then egg, then bread crumbs.

8. Fill a frying pan or wide saucepan with vegetable oil to a depth of 1½ inches. Heat over medium-high heat until the surface shimmers. Working in batches as necessary, fry the celery bundles until browned on all sides; drain on paper towels.

9. Spread some of the tomato sauce on the bottom of a ceramic or Pyrex casserole large enough to hold the celery in a single layer. Arrange the celery bundles on top. Sprinkle with ¼ cup grated Parmigiano Reggiano. Cover with more tomato sauce (you may not need it all) and sprinkle the remaining ¼ cup cheese on top.

10. Cover the casserole dish with aluminum foil. Bake the celery bundles until heated through, 10 to 15 minutes. Uncover and cook a few minutes longer, until the cheese is lightly browned.

## NOTES

Elena's recipe calls for ham, both cooked and *crudo*, and for the sake of authenticity that is the recipe given here. But when in a thrifty frame of mind I use double the quantity of the deli ham and no prosciutto—once cooked in the dish, the difference between the two is subtle. To simplify the recipe still more, skip the chicken livers and use more ground beef.

You will end up with more meat filling than needed for this recipe, but cutting back on the proportions will make it cook too quickly, failing to achieve the proper texture. In any case, this filling is useful to have around (or to freeze for later). Use it as a crostini topping or filling for crêpes—or combine with any remaining tomato sauce to make a pasta sauce.

# ALBERTO'S STREAMLINED FIVE-FISH STEW

*Cacciucco veloce all' Alberto*

MAKES 6 SERVINGS | PREP: 30 MINUTES | COOK: 15 MINUTES

*Pasta is usually the ticket when Alberto Recca is cooking for two adolescent sons with healthy appetites. Eager for a break from that menu, he decided to make a festive seafood soup, similar to cacciucco (the five-fish Tuscan soup), but free of complicated or messy preparations or the need to fit all the seafood into one pot. The sons approved of the seafood feast, and Alberto was pleased with his two-pot solution. "Spectacular and fast!" he said, snapping his fingers.*

*Serve this dish with a tossed green salad and don't stint on thick slices of country-style bread, necessary to fare la scarpetta (chase sauce around the bowl with a shoe-shaped piece of bread).*

1¼ pounds little-neck clams or Manila clams
1¼ pounds mussels (preferably the small farm-raised variety)
½ pound cleaned squid, including tentacles
18 large shrimp or 9 halved sea scallops
1 cup pinot bianco or other dry white wine
1 quart spicy tomato sauce (recipe follows)
1 to 2 tablespoons extra-virgin olive oil
1½ pounds lemon sole fillets or other mild-tasting fish (6 small
   fillets or 3 larger ones, cut in half diagonally)
Sea salt or kosher salt
Hot red pepper flakes
½ cup roughly chopped flat-leaf parsley leaves

1. Under running water, give the clams and mussels a quick scrub with a hard brush (see Note). Cut the squid bodies crosswise in rings; cut tentacles in smaller clumps. Peel the shrimp, leaving the tails attached.

2. Place the clams and mussels in a large saucepan. Add half of the wine and turn the heat to medium-high. After several minutes, the shellfish will start to open (the mussels first). Add half of the spicy tomato sauce. When all of the shellfish have opened (remove any that fail to do so), reduce the heat to low and cover to keep warm.

*continued*

3. In a large skillet over medium heat, heat the olive oil. Sauté the squid until it firms up, about 3 minutes. Unless the squid are "dry" (untreated with preservatives), they will give off some liquid. When most has evaporated, stir in the shrimp and lay the fish fillets on top. Pour in the rest of the sauce. When it comes to a simmer, reduce the heat and cook, partially covered, until the shrimp and fish are cooked through, about 10 minutes. Taste the sauce and add salt and red pepper flakes to taste.

4. To serve: Using a ladle or large spoon, spoon the clams and mussels into shallow soup bowls; capture some of the tomato chunks but leave most of the liquid (which may contain sand) undisturbed. Transfer the shrimp and squid to the bowls, with some of the brothy sauce. Lay the fish fillets on top, spooning more broth over them. Sprinkle parsley on each serving.

**NOTE**

Alberto's speedy method calls for dishing up the shellfish while leaving behind potentially sandy broth. Alternatively, you could use the broth, though the procedure is a bit more time-consuming. First, encourage the cleaned clams (and mussels, too, if not farm-raised) to expel sand by covering with a mixture of six parts water to one part salt; soak for one to two hours. Cook the shellfish as described in the recipe; remove the shellfish to a bowl. Strain the broth and add to the skillet with the squid, shrimp, and fish.

## Quick Spicy Tomato Sauce

MAKES ABOUT 1 QUART | PREP: 10 MINUTES | COOK: 15 MINUTES

2 or 3 cloves garlic, peeled, cut into thin slivers
Extra-virgin olive oil
1 (28- or 35-ounce) can plum tomatoes with purée or
   1 similar-size container strained tomatoes (such as Pomì)
1 teaspoon sea salt or kosher salt, or to taste
1/2 to 1 teaspoon hot red pepper flakes

1. In a large, broad-bottom saucepan over medium heat, sizzle the garlic in enough olive oil to coat the bottom of the pan (about 2 tablespoons) until golden and fragrant, but not browned, about 2 minutes.

**2.** Add the tomatoes and 1 cup water. Break up the tomatoes with a wooden spoon (or, easier yet, squish them with one hand before they heat up). Bring to a slow boil; adjust the heat and simmer until slightly reduced but still chunky, about 10 minutes. Season with salt and hot pepper flakes.

### VARIATION

Fresh hot red peppers can be substituted for the red pepper flakes; if so, sauté one or two with the garlic when making the tomato sauce; discard when the sauce is done.

# Chapter 5
# ROASTED, GRILLED, or SAUTÉED

When my young family of three lived in Florence at the beginning of the '80s, we ate at least once a week at a local *rosticceria* near the Porta Romana. On the way in, we always took a close look at what was rotating on a spit over the open fire—birds of some kind, generally, or pork, or lamb—knowing that was most likely our dinner in this limited-menu place.

Our budget was limited, too, and we could relax, knowing the meal would cost scarcely more than cooking for ourselves. The waiter brought us a hot dinner with a half-liter of red wine. The baby laughed or cried, depending on her mood, and no one was fazed. It felt like home.

For me, meals cooked by fire still trigger the same feeling of comfortable ease. In that category I'd include roast pork tenderloin, grilled lamb chops, fish seared in a hot skillet—all dishes that turn succulent following a relatively brief blast of heat. Also in this roundup are pork ribs, finished in a flash on the grill or under a broiler, but first tenderized by hours of ultra-slow cooking. In most cases, I've matched these proteins with sides that are ready at more or less the same time.

Around the world, fire renders foods edible. What makes these recipes Italian are characteristic seasonings, such as the rosemary-sage-fennel blend in the classic pork roast called *arista*. Or, perhaps a technique—for example, the practice of butterflying and weighting a chicken with bricks to speed the grilling. Steaks, veal chops, and the like are tender cuts fit for any celebratory meal, and with a price tag to match. But we could take a lesson from watching Italian cooks at the butcher's counter just before a holiday or weekend. Typically, at least part of their purchase could be categorized as a splurge—or, from another point of view, as a sensible investment in living well.

# ROASTED, GRILLED, or SAUTÉED

*Chicken Cutlets alla Milanese with Arugula Salad*

*Butterflied Grilled Chicken with Lightly Pickled Vegetables*

*Duck Breasts all' Arancia*

*Pan-Grilled Steak with Fried Turnips and their Greens*

*Veal Chops with Sage and Carrot-Leek Farro*

*Grilled Lamb Chops with Peas alla Fiorentina*

*Aromatic Leg of Lamb Roasted with Potatoes*

*Herbed Roast Pork Tenderloin with Parsnip Purée*

*Tuscan-Texan Barbecued Ribs with Marinated Cucumbers*

*Porgies with Saucy Spaghetti*

*Braided Sole Fillets with Fennel-Orange Salad*

*Fish Fillets with Cherry Tomatoes, Olives, and Capers*

# CHICKEN CUTLETS alla MILANESE with ARUGULA SALAD

*Cotolette di pollo alla milanese con insalata di rucola*

MAKES 4 SERVINGS | PREP: 15 MINUTES | COOK: ABOUT 3 MINUTES

*On several occasions my husband and I have stayed in Gallarotta, a pleasant town conveniently close to Milan's Malpensa airport, before an early morning flight to the U.S. As a result, I've come to associate* cotolette alla milanese, *my usual last-night dinner choice, with the bittersweet anticipation of leaving Italy. This version is topped with tangy arugula and tomatoes, with roasted potatoes as an optional addition.*

1 pound thin (about ¼ inch) chicken cutlets (preferably naturally
  raised) cut from the top round or leg
Sea salt or kosher salt
Freshly ground black pepper
2 or 3 large eggs
2 cups unseasoned finely ground bread crumbs, or as needed
Safflower oil or other vegetable oil
4 cups torn arugula or baby arugula
Extra-virgin olive oil
Balsamic vinegar or a *vincotto* wine vinegar blend
2 medium tomatoes, cut into wedges
Roasted potatoes (page 180) (optional)

1. Blot the cutlets dry with paper towels. With a smooth meat pounder or the bottom of a small, heavy saucepan, pound the cutlets (using a firm, gliding motion) to a uniform thickness. Sprinkle with salt and pepper on both sides. Break the eggs into a small, shallow bowl; beat with a fork or whisk. Place the bread crumbs in another bowl.

2. Dip each cutlet first in the eggs, letting any excess drip off. Coat well with the bread crumbs (you will probably not need all of the egg or crumbs). Placed on a platter and covered, the cutlets can be held at this point for up to 30 minutes or, refrigerated, up to an hour.

3. Pour vegetable oil into a large, heavy-bottom skillet to a depth of ¼ inch. Heat over medium-high heat until it shimmers (test with a pinch of bread crumbs to see if they sizzle). Working in batches, fry the cutlets until well browned on both sides, about 3 minutes. Because the cutlets are so thin, they will be cooked through by the time the outside is crusty. Assuming you have used enough oil and it is hot enough, most of the oil will remain behind in the skillet. Drain the cutlets on a plate lined with paper towels.

4. Place the arugula in a shallow bowl. Drizzle with a little olive oil (1 to 2 tablespoons) and an equal amount of balsamic vinegar. Season lightly with salt and pepper. Toss well.

5. Using tongs or a spatula, lay the warm cutlets on dinner plates. Top with the dressed arugula. Garnish with tomato wedges and, if serving, the roasted potatoes.

### NOTES

Any kind of thin cutlet, such as veal, turkey, or pork, can be substituted for the chicken. Thinly sliced eggplant or angle-cut zucchini could also be battered and fried in the same way.

In lieu of the arugula salad, consider serving the cutlets with saffron risotto (page 138).

# BUTTERFLIED GRILLED CHICKEN with LIGHTLY PICKLED VEGETABLES

*Pollo al mattone, con giardiniera*

MAKES 4 SERVINGS | PREP: 15 MINUTES | COOK: 20 TO 25 MINUTES

*To butterfly (or spatchcock) a chicken means to cut it open and remove the backbone as well as a piece of cartilage on the breast side—all in pursuit of making a bone-in chicken lie flat on a grill. Wrapped bricks or tile, laid on top of the bird, flatten it even more. This brilliant technique solves the problem of producing grilled bone-in chicken that is browned and crisp on the outside and cooked through on the inside.*

*I like the notion of preserving garden vegetables in seasoned vinegar, but I've never loved the usual mouth-puckering reality of giardiniera. So I decided to tone down the acid, diluting wine vinegar with water, and was much happier with the mild sweet-sourness of the pickled vegetables, a refreshing side for the chicken. When making this meal, be sure to allow 2 hours marinating time for the giardiniera.*

1 medium chicken (about 3 pounds), preferably free-range
1 clove garlic, crushed
Sea salt or kosher salt
Freshly ground black pepper
Hot red pepper flakes (optional)
Extra-virgin olive oil
6 lemon wedges
Pickled vegetables (recipe follows)

1. Position the chicken on a cutting surface with the backbone facing up. Using very sharp kitchen shears or a knife, cut along one side of the backbone; cut along the other side to detach the backbone; discard or reserve for another use, such as broth. Turn the chicken over and make a small cut at the upper end of the breast; twist the breast apart, which should make the white cartilage (called the keelbone) pop up; detach it. At this point, the chicken should lie more or less flat. Rinse it and pat dry with paper towels.

2. Place the chicken on a platter or Pyrex dish. Rub it all over with the garlic. Sprinkle generously with salt (about 1 teaspoon), pepper (about 1/2 teaspoon), and hot red pepper flakes (about 1/2 teaspoon), if using. Rub lightly with olive oil and spritz with 2 of the lemon wedges. Arrange the chicken so the drumsticks are rotated inward (they'll have a knock-kneed look).

**3.** Allow the chicken to marinate at room temperature while preparing a medium-hot fire on a charcoal or gas grill. Wrap 2 bricks (or 2 pairs of quarry tiles) in aluminum foil.

**4.** Lay the chicken on the grate, skin side down. Place the bricks on top. Grill the chicken, adjusting the heat and moving the chicken as necessary, so that the skin browns well but does not burn, 10 to 15 minutes. Remove the bricks and, using long tongs, turn the chicken; drizzle with any remaining marinade; reposition the bricks on top. Continue to grill until the chicken is browned and cooked through (turn down the heat or cover if the fire seems too hot), about 10 minutes longer.

**5.** Transfer the chicken to a clean platter. Carve into quarters and surround with the remaining lemon wedges. Serve with a bowl of the pickled vegetables.

# Lightly Pickled Vegetables

MAKES 4 SERVINGS | PREP: 15 MINUTES | COOK: 2 MINUTES *(plus at least 2 hours for marinating)*

½ **small head cauliflower**
1 **medium red, yellow, or green bell pepper, trimmed and seeded**
2 **medium carrots, peeled**
1 **small fennel bulb**
1 **cup white wine vinegar**
3 **tablespoons sugar**
2 **tablespoons extra-virgin olive oil**
2 **teaspoons sea salt or kosher salt**
½ **teaspoon freshly ground black pepper**
2 **bay leaves**
4 **cloves garlic, halved**
1 **small fresh hot red pepper, seeded and quartered lengthwise (optional)**

**1.** Cut the cauliflower into florets and small pieces; cut the bell pepper into squares about the same size. Cut the carrots into thin slices on an angle. Cut the fennel into thin wedges.

*continued*

**2.** Combine the vinegar with 3 cups water, the sugar, olive oil, salt, pepper, and bay leaves in a medium saucepan. Bring to a boil; stir, making sure the sugar and salt have dissolved. Add the cauliflower, bell pepper, carrots, fennel, garlic, and (if using) hot red pepper; when the liquid returns to a boil, adjust the heat to a brisk simmer. Cook the vegetables until crisp-tender, about 2 minutes. Remove from the heat and cool in the saucepan, uncovered.

**3.** Marinate the vegetables for at least 2 hours or, refrigerated in the liquid, for up to 2 days. When ready to serve, drain the vegetables, discarding the bay leaves, and transfer to a serving bowl.

# DUCK BREASTS all' ARANCIA

*Petti d'anatra all' arancia*

MAKES 4 SERVINGS | PREP: 10 MINUTES | COOK: 12 TO 15 MINUTES

*I've never much relished the spattering fat and general mess involved in cooking whole ducks. But, when a duck farmer started showing up at my farmers' market, I decided to give these birds another try—and found duck breasts to be much more manageable. The citrus and sweet vermouth featured in the pan sauce balance the richness of the duck. Sweet-sour cabbage (page 133) or parsnip purée (page 182) would make a good side for this dish.*

2 breasts (about 2 pounds) from Muscovy or Moulard (not Pekin)
  ducks, at room temperature
Sea salt or kosher salt
Freshly ground black pepper
½ cup off-dry white vermouth (such as Martini)
Grated zest and juice of 1 tangerine or juice orange (about ½ cup)
½ cup chicken broth
2 tablespoons finely chopped shallot

1. Preheat the oven to 400°F. With a knife, score the skin side of the duck breasts by cutting parallel diagonals, about 1 inch apart, down through the skin and thick layer of fat to the flesh; cut diagonals in the opposite direction to make a diamond pattern. Season the fleshy side of the breasts with salt and pepper.

2. Combine the vermouth, tangerine zest and juice, and chicken broth in a liquid measuring cup or bowl.

3. Heat a large, heavy ovenproof skillet (cast iron works great) over medium-low heat. Place the duck breasts skin side down in the pan and cook until most of the fat has been rendered and the surface is well browned, about 8 minutes (if the duck is not browning properly, raise the heat to medium). Turn and brown the other side.

4. The duck will have generated a good deal of fat; pour off and discard most of it and place the skillet in the oven. Cook the duck until medium rare, about 5 minutes longer. Using tongs, transfer the duck to a cutting board. Pour off and discard nearly all the fat, leaving a thin film in the skillet.

*continued*

**5.** Over medium heat, cook the shallot in the skillet, stirring, until tender and lightly browned, about 5 minutes. Add the vermouth mixture and simmer rapidly for a few minutes, until it reduces and thickens; season to taste with salt and pepper.

**6.** Cut the duck breasts at an angle into thin slices and arrange on plates or a platter. Drizzle the pan sauce over them.

# PAN-GRILLED STEAK with FRIED TURNIPS and their GREENS

*Tagliata alla griglia con rape fritte e foglie di rapa*

MAKES 3 SERVINGS | PREP: 5 MINUTES | COOK: 4 TO 6 MINUTES

*This recipe adheres to the Tuscan tradition of grilling* steak al sangue, *while offering an alternative to those who prefer that it be cooked a little past rare. Salt is typically added only after grilling (I've heard theories about the proteins escaping if salt is added in advance), and quite often black pepper is not in the picture. Accustomed to presalting steaks, I had my doubts, but I found that the Tuscan method works perfectly well.*

*Sweet young turnips are delightful when deep-fried to serve with steak; they, too, are salted after cooking. Their leafy tops, braised, complete the meal.*

Vegetable oil
2 or 3 boneless (1-inch-thick) ribeye or shell steaks
  (1¼ to 1½ pounds total), at room temperature
Coarse sea salt, pink Himalayan salt, or kosher salt
Freshly ground black pepper (optional)
Fried turnip fingers and their greens (recipe follows)
Good-quality balsamic vinegar, for drizzling (optional)

1. Heat a large, heavy skillet or grill pan (preferably cast iron) over medium-high heat. Add just enough vegetable oil to coat the bottom. Lay the steaks in the skillet and reduce the heat to medium. Sear them, undisturbed, until well browned (to check, lift a corner with tongs), about 2 minutes. Turn and cook on the other side until well browned, about 2 minutes longer. Transfer to a platter, season generously with salt and (if using) pepper, and let them stand for several minutes.

2. Slice the steaks at an angle to make long slices about ½ inch thick. The steak will be rare at this point; if that's what you have in mind, arrange the slices on plates. If you prefer the beef to be cooked longer, reheat the skillet over medium heat, add a little more oil if needed, and turn the steak slices in the pan for just a little longer.

*continued*

3. Serve with fried turnip fingers and greens. Pass the balsamic vinegar (if using) in a container fitted with a small metal spout, or in a small bowl with a small spoon. Just a thread on the steak—not a splash—is enough.

## NOTE

If you happen to be making this recipe in Italy, the butcher should know that *tagliata* is what you need. The term refers to tender beef cuts (often boneless) that take well to grilling—*entrecote di manzo* is one option but certainly not the only one.

## VARIATION

You could grill the steaks outdoors when the weather cooperates. Build a medium-hot fire and grill the steaks to the desired doneness (no olive oil). Sprinkle on both sides with salt and serve on a bed of arugula tossed with a balsamic dressing and garnished with cherry tomatoes and Parmigiano Reggiano shards.

# Fried Turnip Fingers and their Greens

MAKES 3 SERVINGS | PREP: 15 MINUTES | COOK: 5 MINUTES (PER BATCH)

3 medium turnips (preferably young and sweet) from a bunch
  with the leafy tops attached (see Note)
Sea salt or kosher salt
2 to 3 tablespoons unsalted butter or a mixture of butter and
  extra-virgin olive oil
Freshly ground black pepper
½ cup unbleached all-purpose flour, or as needed
Vegetable oil

1. Preheat the oven to 250°F. Cut off the turnip tops at the stem end of the turnips. If they are young, no need to peel; cut them into fingers about 2½ inches long.

2. Cut off and discard the stems attached to the greens; tear or cut off the leaves to separate from the thick stems (discard the latter). Cut the greens crosswise into ½-inch ribbons; place in a salad spinner colander and immerse in water, changing the water until no grit remains.

**3.** Fill a large saucepan with water and 1 tablespoon salt. Bring to a boil. Add the greens, cooking until wilted and some of the bitterness has dissipated, about 5 minutes. Drain.

**4.** Melt the butter in a skillet over medium heat; add the greens and stir until coated and hot; season to taste with salt and pepper; keep warm.

**5.** Coat the turnip fingers with flour, dusting off any excess. Pour ½ inch of oil (about 2 cups) into a medium, broad-bottom saucepan or straight-sided skillet. Heat over medium-high heat until the oil shimmers and begins to make popping noises. Add some of the turnip fingers to the pan; don't crowd them or add so many that the oil stops bubbling. Fry until lightly browned on the surface and darker brown on the edges, about 5 minutes. Drain on paper towels; blot and sprinkle with salt while still hot; keep warm in the oven while frying the rest.

### NOTE

When the turnips come with their tops, as they often do at farmers' markets, it seems like a natural to cook both (if the greens are not attached, of course, they can be purchased separately). This means a bit of last-minute multitasking at the stove as you sauté the steak, fry the fingers, and finish the greens in butter. If you're not comfortable with that, cook only the turnips or greens as a side, not both.

# VEAL CHOPS with SAGE and CARROT-LEEK FARRO

*Lombatine di vitella con salvia e farro alle carote e porri*

MAKES 4 SERVINGS | PREP: 5 MINUTES | COOK: 7 TO 8 MINUTES

*I feel more comfortable entrusting precious veal chops to a skillet, where the temperature can be controlled more readily, than to a grill. They cook quickly, so it's best to cook the farro first.*

4 veal chops (about 2½ pounds), preferably naturally raised
Sea salt or kosher salt
Freshly ground black pepper
3 large sage sprigs
Extra-virgin olive oil
½ cup dry white or red wine
Carrot-leek farro (recipe follows)

1. Blot the veal chops with paper towels; season generously with salt and sparingly with pepper. Remove leaves from 2 of the sage sprigs.

2. In a skillet large enough to hold the chops, heat enough olive oil to coat the pan (about 2 tablespoons) over medium heat. Sauté the sage leaves briefly until slightly crisped but still green; using tongs, remove to a plate.

3. Raise the heat to medium-high. Add a little more olive oil if needed to coat the bottom of the pan. Sauté the chops with the remaining sage sprig until browned; turn and brown on the other side, about 4 minutes. Add the wine, scraping with a heatproof spatula to loosen any browned bits on the pan. Reduce the heat to medium-low and cook a couple of minutes longer, turning the chops once, until tender but still pink at the center. Transfer to a platter. If necessary, reduce the sauce until thickened and pour over the chops, discarding the sage.

4. To serve: Spoon the carrot-leek farro onto 4 plates, off center. Prop a chop against each mound; drizzle some of the pan sauce over it; arrange the sage leaves on top.

**VARIATION**

Pork chops could be substituted for the veal chops. Care must be taken to avoid overcooking the lean pork so prevalent now; chops from an old-fashioned breed that produces well-marbled pork will be more forgiving.

## Carrot-Leek Farro

MAKES 4 SERVINGS | PREP: 10 MINUTES | COOK: 30 MINUTES

2 tablespoons unsalted butter
1 tablespoon extra-virgin olive oil
½ cup halved, thinly sliced leek (see Note, page 40) or scallions,
   including some of the tender green parts
1 medium carrot, diced small (about ½ cup)
Up to 2½ cups easy meat broth (page 99) or chicken broth,
   or a mixture of broth and water
1 cup farro (see Note, page 77) or barley
Sea salt or kosher salt
Freshly ground black pepper

**1.** In a medium saucepan, melt the butter with the olive oil over medium heat. Sauté the leek and carrot, stirring often, until the leek softens, about 5 minutes.

**2.** Meanwhile, bring the broth to a simmer in a small pan (or microwave in a measuring cup).

**3.** Stir the farro into the leek-carrot mixture, cooking for 1 to 2 minutes until it is well coated and smells toasty. Add 2 cups of the hot broth. Bring to a boil and adjust the heat so that the farro simmers slowly, partially covered. Cook until the farro is done (it will have a firm, chewy consistency), about 20 to 30 minutes, adding the remaining ½ cup of the broth if needed. Season to taste with pepper and, if needed, additional salt.

**VARIATION**

Think about throwing in some sliced mushrooms while sautéing the leek and carrot.

# GRILLED LAMB CHOPS
## with PEAS alla FIORENTINA

*Costolette d'agnello con piselli alla fiorentina*

MAKES 6 SERVINGS | PREP: 10 MINUTES | COOK: 6 MINUTES

*This is a dish to make in spring, when lamb and peas are both in their prime and it's time to fire up the grill again.*

12 lamb loin chops (about 3 pounds), at room temperature
1 or 2 cloves garlic, crushed and peeled
Extra-virgin olive oil
Sea salt or kosher salt
Freshly ground black pepper
1 large lemon, cut in 6 wedges
Peas *alla fiorentina* (recipe follows)

1. Prepare a medium-hot fire on a charcoal or gas grill. Blot the chops dry with paper towels. Rub them all over with the garlic and moisten with olive oil (don't be too lavish or there may be flare-ups once the chops go to the grill). Sprinkle with salt and pepper.

2. Grill the chops on both sides until browned on the outside and cooked to a rosy pink inside, 4 to 5 minutes.

3. Serve the chops on a platter garnished with lemon wedges; serve the peas in a bowl, or plate the chops and peas together.

### VARIATION

If you prefer, sauté the chops rather than grilling them. To do so, rub with garlic and sprinkle with salt and pepper. Instead of rubbing the olive oil on the chops, heat it in a large skillet over medium-high heat (throw in what's left of the garlic, to flavor the oil). Working in batches as necessary, brown the chops on both sides. Lower the heat and cook a few minutes longer to the desired doneness.

# Peas alla Fiorentina

MAKES 6 SERVINGS | PREP: 30 MINUTES | COOK: 20 MINUTES

2 slices prosciutto di Parma or other good-quality prosciutto
  (about 1 ounce)
Sea salt or kosher salt
2 pounds fresh peas, shelled (about 3 cups)
Extra-virgin olive oil
1/2 cup chopped spring onion or yellow onion

1. Trim and reserve the fat from the prosciutto slices. With a knife or kitchen shears, cut the lean part into small, thin strips.

2. Fill a large saucepan with enough cold water to cover the peas. Add 2 teaspoons salt and bring to a boil. Add the peas and when the water returns to a boil, reduce the heat and simmer for 5 to 10 minutes, until tender. Drain.

3. Meanwhile, in a medium skillet, heat 2 tablespoons olive oil with the prosciutto fat over medium-low heat for several minutes, until the prosciutto fat has mostly liquefied (if there is very little fat, you may need a little more olive oil); discard any solid remnants of the fat.

4. Sauté the onion in the fat until tender, about 5 minutes. Stir in the peas and heat through. Just before serving, stir in the prosciutto strips, and season to taste with salt and pepper.

## VARIATIONS

When fresh peas are out of season, this dish can be made with frozen baby peas. Just add to the sautéed onion in the skillet; unless thawed, they may take a little longer to heat up than the blanched fresh peas.

Pancetta, cut into small cubes and cooked in the olive oil until fairly crisp, can be substituted for the prosciutto.

## ∽ At the Butcher, Fishmonger, and Deli Counter

At the old-fashioned Tuscan *macelleria* I frequented years ago, we looked up to the butcher, literally as well as figuratively. Salvatore presided at a counter set high above the customers, deftly carving chops and cutlets with an enormous knife while joking with customers and dispensing advice. He might steer you toward a beef cut less costly and, in his view, just as tender as the *filetto* (beef tenderloin) that you intended to buy, or, hearing of your plans to make a lamb stew, share his aunt's recipe. His brother owned a butcher shop right next door, but I never shopped there, betting that my loyalty to Salvatore would be repaid in sound advice. For the same reason, I found a fishmonger I liked and never strayed, hoping to be in the valued-customer category, worthy of inside info on which fish was the freshest and best that day.

Whether I'm cooking in Italy or the U.S., I still like to have those kinds of conversations and, with luck, build a relationship. Shopping contributes more than almost anything else to the quality of an Italian meal. Though we make most of our purchase decisions in silence, meat, fish, and cut-to-order deli purchases sometimes deserve meaningful interaction. The supermarket where I often buy meat has knowledgeable counter staff who are proud to share their knowledge. If the veal shanks for making osso buco *alla milanese* are thicker or thinner than I want, they'll cut more to order. Which kind of chuck is best for my Italian-style pot roast? Do the steaks labeled "organic" come from grass-fed cattle? Quite often the butcher or meat manager knows or can find out.

In choosing where to buy fish, I trust my senses above all. I want a place that is free of the fishy odors that signal over-the-hill seafood, where the fish has a healthy-looking luster. Some vendors post information about the origin of a particular species as well as pros and cons relating to sustainability and health but, if not, the counter person should be able to answer my questions.

Deli and cheese counters offer a great opportunity to compare the merits of various products. Ask for a taste to see if the sweet Gorgonzola or the sharper (*piccante*) one is more to your taste. If there's a choice, cheeses should be cut to order for maximum freshness. And, again, questions about the origins of deli or cheese counter items are in order.

> "In choosing where to buy fish, I trust my senses above all. I want a place that is free of the fishy odors that signal over-the-hill seafood, where the fish has a healthy-looking luster. "

How cured meats are sliced is another issue. Pancetta is most useful when cut into thicker slices (about 1/4 inch) that are easily cut into small cubes for sauces and sautés. The big, paper-thin slices of prosciutto that I plan to serve with fresh melon and figs need to be cut from the center section of the ham, not the narrower ends—and I make sure the deli person knows this before the slicing begins. For flavoring soups, on the other hand I might inquire about buying a prosciutto end (which should be sold for less than the rest of the ham).

Farmers' markets are promising places to buy all of these products—and to conduct informative conversations with people who are passionate about the foods they grow and make. Grass-fed beef and true free-range chicken might be on hand, or a locally made duck salami could be the centerpiece of an antipasto platter. With fish, there can be a freshness advantage if you're buying from a vendor who operates or buys directly from fishing boats. And, when I'm in the mood for fried pecorino (page 239), a local semisoft sheep's milk cheese can stand in for hard-to-get Tuscan pecorino. ◌

# AROMATIC LEG of LAMB ROASTED with POTATOES

*Cosciotto d'agnello con patate arrosto*

**MAKES 6 SERVINGS | PREP: 20 MINUTES | COOK: 1 HOUR 10 MINUTES**

*Medium-rare has always been my mantra for lamb, but I've noticed that it's usually cooked medium in Italy. So I asked our guests whether they'd prefer the baby lamb leg already roasting in the oven to be cooked "al sangue o più cotto." With horrified looks on their faces, they replied in unison, "Più cotto!" The lamb stayed put a few minutes longer and, to my surprise, emerged deliciously moist and fragrant. Despite that experience, I stick with medium-rare when roasting lamb in the U.S., where the animals tend to be larger.*

2 or 3 cloves garlic, peeled
1 thick-cut (¼-inch) slice pancetta
Several sprigs rosemary or thyme
Extra-virgin olive oil
½ bone-in leg of lamb (preferably the shank end), with a layer of
   external fat (4 to 6 pounds), at room temperature (see Note)
Sea salt or kosher salt
Freshly ground black pepper
½ cup red or white wine
Roasted potatoes (recipe follows)

1. Cut the garlic into thin slices, and then lengthwise into slivers. Cut the pancetta into thin strips about the same size. Clip the rosemary with kitchen shears to make spriglets of a similar length. Place the garlic, pancetta, and rosemary in separate small bowls.

2. Preheat the oven to 375°F. Lightly oil a roasting pan. Sprinkle the lamb generously with salt and more sparingly with pepper. Positioning the leg fat side up, slide a paring knife into the fat at an oblique angle to make a long but shallow slit (avoid cutting into the meat). Gather a garlic sliver, pancetta strip, and rosemary spriglet to make a small clump and stuff it into the slit; it should be nearly hidden in the fat, with just the tip peeking out. Repeat these cuts all over the fat-covered part of the leg, stuffing them with the trio of aromatic ingredients. Place the lamb on a rack in the roasting pan.

**3.** For rosy-pink slices of lamb—in other words, medium-rare—roast the lamb on a middle rack to an internal temperature of 125°F (test with an instant-read thermometer, stuck in the deepest part of the flesh without touching the bone), for about an hour and 10 minutes. For medium (cooked through but still juicy), cook a few minutes longer to an internal temperature of 135°F. (The potatoes can roast with the lamb during the final 40 minutes of cooking.)

**4.** When the lamb is beautifully browned on top and cooked to your preferred doneness, transfer it to a platter and allow to rest for a few minutes. Meanwhile, pour almost all of the roasting pan fat and juices into a small liquid measuring cup or bowl. After 1 to 2 minutes, pour or spoon off and discard the fat floating above the denser juices. Add the pan juices, wine, 1 cup water, and any pink juices in the platter to the roasting pan, scraping up any browned bits on the bottom; taste and season with salt and pepper if needed. Return the roasting pan to the oven to heat up and reduce the sauce.

**5.** To serve: Carve the lamb into thin slices (see Note), arranging them on a platter. Drizzle with the pan sauce and surround with the roasted potatoes.

**NOTES**

Opinions vary on whether the butt or shank end is more tender, but for sure the shank end of the leg has more meat in proportion to bone and is easier to carve. American lamb is at the upper end of the weight range; New Zealand and Australian lambs tend to be smaller. If you're able to get baby lamb, it can be cooked in the same way, with proportionately less of the seasonings.

To carve the shank end: Turn the leg on its side with the shank bone facing away from you. With a sharp knife, carve off a couple of thin slices on the side facing you. Turn the leg so that the shank bone is pointing up. Starting by the shank bone, cut downwards and across the grain to make uniform thin slices. Once you reach the other end of the roast, cut along the leg bone to release the slices.

**VARIATION**

A boned leg of lamb can be seasoned and cooked in a similar way: Chop the garlic, rosemary, and pancetta together in roughly equal proportions and spread on the boned side of the lamb. Sprinkle lightly with salt and pepper. Alternatively, season the interior and outside of the boned lamb with rosemary-sage salt (page 186). Starting at one of the long ends, tightly roll up the meat and truss with string (see step two, page 181). If most of the fat has been trimmed, rub the meat lightly with olive oil and, in any case, sprinkle with salt and pepper. Roasting times will be somewhat shorter for boned lamb; start testing the temperature after 45 minutes.

*continued*

# Roasted Potatoes

MAKES 6 SERVINGS | PREP: 10 MINUTES | COOK: 30 MINUTES
*(can be cooked with the lamb)*

6 medium Yukon Gold or other yellow-fleshed potatoes
 (2½ to 3 pounds)
Extra-virgin olive oil
Sea salt or kosher salt

1. Preheat the oven to 400°F. Cut the potatoes crosswise into ½-inch slices or similar-sized wedges and pile them on a rimmed baking sheet. Drizzle with the olive oil (about ¼ cup) and sprinkle with salt, turning the potatoes with your hands to coat them. Spread out in a single layer.

2. Roast the potatoes on a center rack until lightly browned and cooked through, about 30 minutes.

**VARIATION**
Peeled sweet potatoes or rutabagas could be roasted the same way.

# HERBED ROAST PORK TENDERLOIN with PARSNIP PURÉE

*Arista con puré di pastinaca*

**MAKES 6 SERVINGS | PREP: 15 MINUTES | COOK: 20 MINUTES**

*In Italy, pork loin is the usual choice for roasting, but pigs there haven't been bred to be super lean, as many of ours have. Unless you can get an old-fashioned pork loin with a substantial amount of fat, you'll get moister, juicier results from pork tenderloins. They cook more quickly, too.*

Leaves from 1 large sprig rosemary
Leaves from 1 large sprig sage
1 large clove garlic
1 teaspoon fennel seed
1 strip lemon zest (peeled with a vegetable peeler)
Sea salt or kosher salt
Freshly ground black pepper
2 pork tenderloins (about 2½ pounds total), at room temperature
Extra-virgin olive oil
½ cup white or red wine
Parsnip purée (recipe follows) or roasted potatoes (page 180)

1. Preheat the oven to 350°F. Combine the rosemary and sage leaves, garlic, fennel seed, and lemon zest on a cutting board. Chop until very fine (alternatively, chop in a mini food processor.) Transfer the seasoning blend to a small bowl. Stir in ½ teaspoon salt and ¼ teaspoon pepper.

2. Cut lengthwise down the center of 1 tenderloin, stopping about 1 inch short of the other side. Open and flatten it like a book. Repeat with the other tenderloin. Rub the seasoning blend over the surface (facing up). Close each tenderloin and tie with butcher's string (alternatively, use small metal skewers to secure). Lightly sprinkle the outside with salt and pepper. (The tenderloins can be covered and refrigerated for up to 12 hours at this point.)

*continued*

**3.** Heat a large skillet over medium-high heat, adding enough olive oil to coat the bottom (about 2 tablespoons). Sear the tenderloins, turning with tongs, until browned on all sides. Transfer them to a roasting pan. Roast to an internal temperature of 135°F, or until the tenderloins are cooked but still slightly pink on the inside, about 15 minutes.

**4.** Transfer the tenderloins to a cutting board and allow them to rest for 5 minutes. Meanwhile, add the wine and ½ cup water to the hot roasting pan, scraping up any savory browned bits. Reheat briefly in the oven. Cut the tenderloins into thick slices, arrange on plates, and drizzle the cooking juices over them. Serve with the parsnip purée or roasted potatoes.

### VARIATION

Instead of serving the parsnip purée with the roast pork, try an idea I spotted in a collection of Slow Food recipes from Florence and the Chianti: Drizzle half of the deglazed cooking juices over the sliced tenderloin and keep warm. Add 3 cups cooked white beans with some of the cooking liquid (page 72) to the juices that remain in the roasting pan. Stir to coat well and heat in the oven; serve alongside the roast pork.

## Parsnip Purée

MAKES 6 SERVINGS | PREP: 15 MINUTES | COOK: 20 MINUTES

10 medium parsnips (about 2½ pounds),
    peeled and cut into chunks
2 medium boiling potatoes, peeled and cut into chunks
Sea salt or kosher salt
Freshly ground black pepper
⅛ teaspoon nutmeg
2 tablespoons unsalted butter, cut into bits
Up to ½ cup heavy cream or half-and-half

**1.** Combine the parsnips and potatoes in a medium saucepan. Barely cover with water and add 1 teaspoon salt. Bring to a boil. Reduce the heat and simmer, partially covered, until very tender, about 15 minutes.

**2.** Drain the vegetables, reserving the liquid, and transfer them to a food processor bowl; process until smooth, adding some of the cooking liquid through the funnel (take care not to overdo it—the purée shouldn't be too soupy to hold its shape on a plate). Season to taste with the salt and pepper and add the nutmeg; process briefly to blend in the seasonings.

**3.** Fill the bottom of a double boiler with about an inch of water (you can improvise a double boiler by fitting a bowl or smaller saucepan into a larger one). Scrape the contents of the food processor bowl into the top of the double boiler. Over low heat, mix in bits of the butter until incorporated. Taste and add as much of the cream as you please.

# TUSCAN-TEXAN BARBECUED RIBS with MARINATED CUCUMBERS

*Rostinciana alla Toscana con cetrioli marinati*

MAKES 6 SERVINGS | PREP: 15 MINUTES | COOK: 2 TO 3 HOURS

*"So, do you grill at home?" I asked Paolo and Leda, our neighbors in Tuscany, disingenuously. And then I casually mentioned that, although the area is famous for grilled meats, I'd only eaten them in restaurants.*

*After shamelessly laying that groundwork, I was not surprised to find Paolo beaming over a grill filled with bistecca and pork ribs when we arrived for a summer dinner on their terrace. What did astonish me was Leda's bountiful spread of vegetable dishes from their garden: tiny marinated cucumbers, zucchini soup, shredded cabbage salad, even ratatouille. Different from barbecue sides in Texas, where I grew up, and just as good.*

*When it was time to cook barbecued ribs myself, though, I resorted to a reliable Texan method for slow-cooking tough cuts in foil before finishing them on the grill. Even so, I can promise that the seasoning is true Tuscan. Serve these ribs with the marinated cucumbers (provide a slotted spoon) and, if you like, white beans mixed with fresh chopped tomatoes, olive oil, and sea salt.*

5 to 6 pounds baby-back pork ribs
4 to 5 tablespoons rosemary-sage salt (recipe follows)
3 large cucumbers (regular or seedless)
1½ teaspoons sea salt or kosher salt, or to taste
¼ cup white wine vinegar
2 tablespoons extra-virgin olive oil
1½ teaspoons sugar
Up to ¼ cup snipped chives or dill

1. Rub the ribs with the rosemary-sage salt (you'll have some left over). Wrap each rack in heavy-duty aluminum foil securely but not tightly—a little room allows steam to circulate. Place the ribs on a roasting pan, slide it in the oven, and set the heat at 275°F. Slow-cook the ribs until fork-tender, about 2 hours.

2. Peel the cucumbers only if the skins are tough. Halve them lengthwise and scoop out the seeds with a spoon; slice the halves crosswise into ½-inch slices (if using seedless cucumbers, merely slice them). Place the cucumbers in a colander and toss with the salt. Let them stand in the sink for 20 to 30 minutes, until they soften and give up some of their liquid.

*continued*

3. Meanwhile, in a small bowl, combine the vinegar, olive oil, and sugar. Transfer the cucumbers to a serving bowl. Add the vinaigrette and chives and mix well.

4. Once the ribs are tender, let them cool a bit while you prepare a medium-hot fire on a charcoal or gas grill or preheat the broiler.

5. Carefully unwrap the ribs; drain off and discard the fat and foil. Grill or broil the ribs on both sides until well browned, 5 minutes or less. Let rest for 5 minutes.

6. To serve: Cut between each rib or pair of ribs. Arrange on a platter and serve with the cucumbers.

## Rosemary-Sage Salt

MAKES A SCANT 1/2 CUP | PREP: 10 MINUTES

*This seasoned salt can be held at room temperature for several weeks. Greenish and damp to begin with, it will dry and turn a darker color over time, but the flavor will remain intact.*

1/2 **cup sea salt or kosher salt**
**Leaves from 1 small sprig rosemary**
**Leaves from 1 small sprig sage**
1 **clove garlic, halved**
1/2 **teaspoon black peppercorns**

Combine the salt, rosemary, sage, garlic, and peppercorns in a mini food processor; process until finely chopped. (Alternatively, finely chop the rosemary, sage, garlic, and peppercorns together on a cutting board and combine with the salt.)

### NOTE

Rosemary-sage salt has many applications. For example, use it as a dry rub for pork and chicken cutlets before sautéing or, combined with olive oil, as a seasoning for vegetables or mushrooms that you plan to roast.

# PORGIES with SAUCY SPAGHETTI

*Pagelli con spaghetti al pomodoro*

MAKES 2 SERVINGS | PREP: 15 MINUTES | COOK: 10 TO 12 MINUTES

*During a lazy stay in Camogli, a small seaside town in Liguria, we dined the first night at Da Paolo, a family-owned place. The next day, I spotted the chef-owner selecting seafood at the harbor. Among his choices were scorpion fish, a bony, red-skinned fish with a hideous face. Curious to see what he would do with them, we returned to the restaurant that evening.*

*Full of flavor but bony, scorpion fish normally go into a soup, but instead, our chef sautéed them. Also unusual was the fact that he served spaghetti with a highly spiced tomato sauce on the same plate, not as a first course. He pointed to a couple at another table who, when attending Genoa's boat show each year, make a point of ordering this dish. Naturally, we did too, and were not disappointed. Scorpion fish isn't available in the U.S., but I find that porgies (an inexpensive variety of sea bream) work admirably.*

Sea salt or kosher salt

2 porgies (about 12 ounces each), scaled and gutted, heads and
   tails intact (see Note)

6 or more sprigs flat-leaf parsley

Extra-virgin olive oil

1 to 1½ cups quick spicy tomato sauce (page 156), or good-
   quality jarred marinara sauce spiked with hot red pepper flakes
   and extra garlic

⅓ cup dry, fruity white wine

6 to 8 ounces spaghetti

1. Preheat the oven to 250°F. Add a generous pinch of salt to the cavity of each porgy; tuck a parsley sprig inside.

2. In a skillet large enough to hold both porgies (preferably nonstick), heat enough olive oil to coat the bottom of the pan (about 2 tablespoons) over medium-high heat. Lay the porgies, facing opposite directions, in the skillet; fry until nicely browned (lift one side with a spatula to check). Turn and brown on the other side. Reduce the heat to medium-low and continue to cook several minutes longer until cooked through.

*continued*

**3.** Using 2 spatulas, transfer each porgy to a platter. Sprinkle with salt on both sides, ending with the nicer-looking side facing up; keep warm in the oven.

**4.** Fill a large saucepan about two-thirds full with cold water and place over high heat to bring to a boil. Meanwhile, in a skillet large enough to hold the cooked pasta, heat the tomato sauce over medium heat. Stir in the wine and simmer for a few minutes.

**5.** When the pasta water comes to a boil, add a small handful of salt. Add the spaghetti, bending as it softens until completely immersed. Stir well and boil until al dente, 8 to 12 minutes.

**6.** Drain the pasta and immediately turn it into the skillet with the tomato sauce. Mix well. Tear the leaves from the remaining parsley sprigs into small pieces and stir into the pasta.

**7.** To serve: Using tongs, place half of the pasta on each plate. Lift each fish with 2 spatulas and slide it onto the other half of the plate, snuggled against the spaghetti.

### NOTES

In place of the porgies, you could use Mediterranean sea bream (*orata*) or any small white fish with a simple bone structure.

The first time out, it's probably best to serve this dish—which would be categorized as rustic, not elegant—to a family member rather than a guest. I'm content to eat the fish off the bone, alternating bites with a bite of spaghetti, and moving the bones to the discard plate. My husband prefers a less messy approach, serving the fish and pasta on a large platter, placing filleted pieces and pasta onto his plate. Either way, it's delectable.

If you'd prefer not to cope with a whole fish on your plate, have the fish filleted by the vendor. Fry it as described in the recipe; the cooking time will be somewhat shorter. To serve: Mound the pasta on plates or broad, shallow bowls and place a fillet (nice side up) on top of each one.

# BRAIDED SOLE FILLETS with FENNEL-ORANGE SALAD

*Filetti di sogliola con insalatina di finocchio e arancia*

**MAKES 4 SERVINGS | PREP: 15 MINUTES | COOK: 10 MINUTES**

*I first braided fish fillets in a cooking class taught by chef Roberto Carcaghi at the Accademia Barilla cooking school in Parma. The technique initially seemed a bit fussy—just a pretty way to present fish—but I changed my mind after discovering that it also consolidates a fillet such as sole or flounder (which may taper to almost nothing at the edges) into a uniform shape that facilitates even cooking. Plus, what's wrong with pretty?*

1/3 cup fine dry unseasoned bread crumbs
1/3 cup finely ground cornmeal
1/2 teaspoon dried oregano or thyme
8 small fillets (or 4 larger ones no more than 1/2-inch thick) cut from
   sole, flounder, turbot, or other thin white fish (11/2 pounds total)
Sea salt or kosher salt
Freshly ground black pepper
1/3 cup safflower or other vegetable oil
Lemon wedges
Fennel-orange salad (recipe follows)

1. In a small, shallow bowl, combine the bread crumbs, cornmeal, and oregano.

2. Rinse the fish fillets and blot dry with paper towels. Season with salt and pepper. Lay each fillet on a cutting surface; cut lengthwise to make 3 strips, stopping about 1 inch short of one end so that they remain attached. Braid the strips without twisting them; tuck the ends under or around the braided fish. Flatten each fillet with the palm of your hand and press the ends in place (use toothpicks to secure them if you like). Coat both sides of the fillets with the crumb mixture.

3. Heat the oil over medium heat until it shimmers in a sauté pan just large enough to hold the fillets (or, if using a smaller pan, work in batches). Supporting each fillet with a wide spatula or two smaller ones, slide it into the pan. Fry until nicely browned; turn it carefully with the spatula and cook until browned and cooked through. The total cooking time should be 8 to 10 minutes. Drain on paper towels. Serve with lemon wedges and the fennel-orange salad.

*continued*

# Fennel-Orange Salad

MAKES 4 SERVINGS | PREP: 15 MINUTES

4 thin red onion wedges
¼ cup extra-virgin olive oil
1 tablespoon white wine vinegar or white balsamic vinegar, or to taste
2 medium navel oranges
Sea salt or kosher salt
Freshly ground black pepper
4 cups baby spinach or other microgreens
½ small fennel bulb, cored and cut into thin slivers

1. If the onions are sharp tasting, soak them in water while preparing the rest of the salad. In a small jar or bowl, combine the olive oil and vinegar.

2. With a sharp knife, peel the oranges, removing and discarding all of the peel and white pith. Cut between the membranes to free the segments; reserve segments. Squeeze juice from the orange remains into the jar; season to taste with salt and pepper; shake or whisk well.

3. Combine the baby spinach, fennel, and drained onion in a large bowl. Toss with the dressing.

4. Using tongs, heap the salad onto plates. Strew the orange segments on top.

# FISH FILLETS with CHERRY TOMATOES, OLIVES, and CAPERS

*Pesce con pomodorini, olivi e capperi*

MAKES 4 SERVINGS | PREP: 20 MINUTES | COOK: 12 TO 15 MINUTES

*This lovely recipe comes from Luisa Moscucci Neri, a small blonde dynamo who has taught cooking to foreigners at the Dante Alighieri School, in the center of Siena, for more than twenty years.*

*Serve this fish with country-style bread and, if you like, dressed arugula or other greens on the side.*

1 to 2 tablespoons capers, preferably salt cured
1¼ cups whole cherry tomatoes
⅓ cup whole Gaeta olives or other black Mediterranean olives
⅓ cup flat-leaf parsley leaves
Extra-virgin olive oil
4 medium-thick white fish fillets such as porgies, sea bass (wild or
  farm-raised *branzino*), *orata*, or perch (about 1½ pounds total)
Sea salt or kosher salt
Freshly ground black pepper
½ cup white wine

1. Preheat the oven to 400°F. Place the capers in a small bowl and cover with water. Soak 5 minutes. Drain. Halve or quarter the cherry tomatoes. Pit the olives and cut them into slivers. Snip the parsley into small pieces.

2. Drizzle a little olive oil over the bottom of a roasting pan and smear it around with your hand. Rinse the fillets and run your fingers over them to find any pin bones; pull them out with fish tweezers or your fingers.

3. Sprinkle the fillets with salt and pepper and place them in the roasting pan, skin side down. Scatter the cherry tomatoes, olives, drained capers, and half of the parsley over and around the fish. Drizzle generously with olive oil (2 to 3 tablespoons) and the wine.

4. Bake until the fillets are just done, 10 to 15 minutes, depending on their thickness. Sprinkle with the rest of the parsley.

5. To serve: Transfer the fillets to shallow soup plates. Spoon the toppings and juices on and around the fish.

# Chapter 6

## INSALATONE and
## OTHER COLD PLATES

In Italy, salads tend to be simple. An *insalata verde* dressed by diners to their own tastes is likely to consist of nothing but fresh greens. Choose an *insalata mista,* and a few other things show up in the mix—shredded carrots, generally, plus tomatoes and cucumbers if they happen to be in season.

When the ingredients are good, as happens more often than not in Italy, a basic salad like this can be incredible. The greens must be garden fresh and, if there are tomatoes, the right variety, ripened to the proper stage—not blood red, but still changing color, so that they will have the tang considered ideal. Above all, the taste of the salad depends on a dressing made with a good olive oil, usually in combination with an acid, typically vinegar or lemon juice, and a touch of sea salt.

This lesson—quality matters—applies also to the more substantial salads that are the subject of this chapter. They are meant to suffice as meals, both in quantity and in nutritional balance, so attention to detail is important. The idea of entrée salads, so familiar to us, was once alien to Italians, but now the line is not drawn so firmly. The meal-size salad, or *insalatone*, is making its way into Italian life, most noticeably in urban settings where customers might order one for lunch. Though substantial, they are characterized by restraint, bringing into play several well-matched ingredients rather than a multitude.

I've also included salads built on a base of grains rather than greens as well as meal-size antipasti such as platters of cured meats and cheeses that, when served with salad and bread, surely qualify as *piatti unici*.

# INSALATONE and OTHER COLD PLATES

*Spinach Salad with Pear, Pecorino, and Whole-Grain Croutons*

*Zucchini Carpaccio*

*Rice Salad with Roasted Peppers and Mozzarella*

*Farro, Baby Octopus, and Green Bean Salad*

*Tuscan Bread Salad with Tuna*

*Couscous Confetti Salad with Tuna*

*Escarole, Anchovy, and Cheese Salad*

*Mixed Greens with Asparagus and White Anchovies*

*Mountain Salad with Bacon, Fontina, and Sweet-Sour Onions*

*Bresaola Involtini with Herbed Goat Cheese Filling*

*Salumi, Cheese, and Salad Platters*

*Chopped Italian Deli Salad*

# SPINACH SALAD with PEAR, PECORINO, and WHOLE-GRAIN CROUTONS

*Insalatona di spinaci, pere e pecorino*

**MAKES 3 OR 4 SERVINGS | PREP: 15 MINUTES**

*Il Santo Bevitore belongs to a new breed of restaurants that offers piatti unici and piattini (small plates) as well as traditional courses. Diners at the popular spot in Florence's San Frediano quarter are encouraged to tailor meals to their appetites. Anticipating an afternoon of work followed by a big dinner, my friend Richard ordered this light but satisfying salad for lunch.*

¼ cup extra-virgin olive oil
2 tablespoons white balsamic vinegar or white wine vinegar
   sweetened with a touch of sugar or honey
Sea salt or kosher salt
Freshly ground black pepper
8 cups tender spinach leaves, torn into bite-size pieces,
   or baby spinach
1 large firm-ripe pear such as Comice, Anjou, or Bartlett
Pecorino or another flavorful aged cheese, such as Piave,
   in a wedge
2 cups whole-grain croutons (recipe follows)
1 heaping tablespoon pine nuts, lightly toasted

**1.** In a small bowl or jar, combine the olive oil, vinegar, and salt and pepper to taste; mix well. Place the spinach leaves in a large bowl.

**2.** Shortly before serving, cut the pear into quarters; peel the skin only if tough and trim the core. Cut into thin slices and add to the spinach. Toss with the dressing and, using tongs, arrange the spinach and pears on 4 dinner plates.

**3.** Using a vegetable peeler, cut shards from the cheese, letting them drop onto each salad. Sprinkle the croutons and pine nuts over the salads.

# Whole-Grain Croutons

MAKES 2 CUPS | PREP: 5 MINUTES | COOK: 10 MINUTES

2 or 3 slices whole-grain bread
2 tablespoons extra-virgin olive oil

1. Preheat an oven or toaster oven to 350°F. Trim the crusts from the bread or, for a more rustic look, leave them on; cut the bread into cubes.

2. Place the cubes on a rimmed baking sheet. Drizzle with the olive oil and turn the cubes with your hands to coat them. Spread out in a single layer.

3. Bake until crunchy but not completely dried out, about 10 minutes.

## VARIATIONS

Consider using any other interesting bread for the croutons. For instance, my favorite for this salad is a raisin-fennel semolina bread from an Italian bakery.

Another great cheese-fruit salad combo is thinly sliced apple (skin left on) with matchsticks of a hearty mountain cheese such as semisoft *Crucolo* from the Trentino; if you don't find that, Gruyère and Comté are good substitutes.

# ZUCCHINI CARPACCIO

*Carpaccio di zucchine*

MAKES 3 OR 4 SERVINGS | PREP: 40 MINUTES *(includes standing time for the zucchini)*

*This dish delighted my daughter Mary when we ate at Da Delfina, a wonderful restaurant with a view of a Medici villa—and I was equally delighted, on returning home, to figure out the kitchen's methods for slicing and wilting the zucchini.*

*To round out this light, no-cook meal, serve onion focaccia or rustic whole-wheat bread spread with a young goat cheese.*

6 tablespoons extra-virgin olive oil
1 to 2 teaspoons chives snipped with scissors, or fresh thyme leaves
3 to 4 small zucchini or yellow summer squash
Sea salt or kosher salt
2 cups microgreens
2 tablespoons balsamic vinegar reduction (recipe follows),
  *vincotto* wine vinegar blend, balsamic glaze, or 1 tablespoon
  balsamic vinegar (see page 19)
1 medium tomato, peeled, seeded, and cut into small dice
2 tablespoons pine nuts, lightly toasted

1. Combine the olive oil and chives in a small bowl. Let stand at room temperature.

2. Scrub the zucchini with a brush (no need to peel if the skins are thin). On a mandoline, insert the cutting blade with the ruffled edge showing; set the thickness to very thin, 1/16 to 1/8 inch. Slice the zucchini lengthwise; cut larger slices horizontally in half. (If you don't have a mandoline, use a sharp chef's knife to cut the zucchini in ultra-thin lengthwise slices.)

3. Place the zucchini slices in a colander. Sprinkle with 1 tablespoon salt and massage gently with your hands to coat the slices. Let stand in the sink until the zucchini wilts, about 30 minutes.

4. Rinse the excess salt off the zucchini and lay flat on paper toweling; blot dry. Arrange the zucchini on dinner plates like spokes of a wheel. Spoon 4 tablespoons of the chive oil over them.

5. Place the greens in a small bowl; toss with the remaining 2 tablespoons chive oil and salt to taste. With tongs, place a clump of microgreens at the center of each plate. Drizzle a little of the balsamic vinegar reduction over the greens, dotting the zucchini with the remainder. (If using balsamic vinegar rather than the thicker alternatives, drizzle only on the greens.)

6. Scatter the tomato and pine nuts over and around the zucchini.

## Balsamic Vinegar Reduction

MAKES 1/2 CUP | PREP: 2 MINUTES | COOK: 15 MINUTES

**1 cup balsamic vinegar (inexpensive is fine)**
**White or brown sugar (optional)**

1. In a small saucepan, bring the balsamic vinegar almost to a boil, whisking occasionally.

2. Adjust the heat so that the vinegar simmers slowly. Whisking often, cook until the volume is reduced by about half and the vinegar coats the back of a spoon, about 15 minutes (cooking time may vary depending on your stove and the dimensions of the pan). If the vinegar thickens too much, blend in a little water.

3. Cool slightly and taste. If the reduction tastes too sharp, stir in a little sugar. Finish cooling.

# RICE SALAD with ROASTED PEPPERS and MOZZARELLA

*Insalata di riso con peperoni arrostiti e mozzarella*

MAKES 4 TO 5 SERVINGS | PREP: 20 MINUTES | COOK: 10 MINUTES

*Balance is the key to making rice salad with contrasting colors, textures, and flavors. I always make sure to include something crunchy (in this case, the fennel), something soft and savory (the mozzarella), and something tangy (the olives). You can serve the salad immediately but it will taste even better if the flavors blend at room temperature for an hour or so, or up to a day, refrigerated.*

½ cup extra-virgin olive oil
Juice of 1 small lemon (3 to 4 tablespoons)
Sea salt or kosher salt
Freshly ground black pepper
2 cups Carnaroli or Arborio rice
2 small red and/or yellow bell peppers, roasted and cut into
   small squares
½ cup diced fennel bulb or celery
¼ cup black Mediterranean olives, pitted and halved or slivered
¼ cup snipped chives, basil, or flat-leaf parsley leaves
6 to 8 ounces fresh mozzarella, diced small
2 cups baby arugula (optional)

1. In a serving bowl large enough to hold the salad, whisk the olive oil and lemon juice. Season to taste with salt and pepper.

2. Fill a large saucepan about two-thirds full of water and add a small handful of salt. Bring to a boil. Add the rice, stirring well; when it returns to a boil, reduce the heat and simmer, uncovered, until just tender, about 10 minutes. Turn into a colander or strainer and cool under a gentle stream of running water; drain well. Transfer to the bowl with the dressing and stir gently.

3. Mix the bell peppers, fennel, olives, and chives into the rice. Taste and add more salt or pepper if needed. Let the flavors blend for up to an hour at room temperature (or longer, refrigerated).

4. Just before serving, fold in the mozzarella. Pass the serving bowl or serve in shallow bowls lined around the edges with baby arugula.

# FARRO, BABY OCTOPUS, and GREEN BEAN SALAD

*Insalata di farro, moscardini e fagiolini*

**MAKES 2 SERVINGS | PREP: 20 MINUTES | COOK: 30 MINUTES**

*In Tuscany's Arno Valley, where meat rules, Lo Schicchero—a restaurant in the village of Mercatale that specializes in seafood—is an anomaly. Among well-executed but standard offerings such as fried squid and seafood risotto, I found this intriguing salad. What's the story behind it? "Alla fantasia," said owner Fabrizio Tinta, summing up the salad's origin—his own imagination—in two words.*

Sea salt or kosher salt
1 cup farro or barley (see Note, page 77)
½ pound cleaned baby octopus (1 to 2 ounces each) or baby squid
4 ounces green beans (preferably the small, thin kind), trimmed,
  long ones cut in half
1 small red or yellow bell pepper, roasted and cut into thin strips
Extra-virgin olive oil
1 to 2 tablespoons fresh lemon juice
Freshly ground black pepper

1. Fill a saucepan with more than enough cold water to cover the farro, and add 2 teaspoons salt. Bring to a boil; add the farro and, when it returns to a boil, reduce the heat and simmer, partially covered, until the water has been absorbed and the farro is tender, 20 to 30 minutes.

2. Meanwhile, cut off and halve the octopus heads. Cut the tentacles into smaller, bite-size clumps. Rinse and drain well.

3. In a microwave-safe dish, microwave the baby octopus until it firms up and the tentacles curl, about 20 seconds (see Note).

*continued*

**4.** Fill a small saucepan with water; bring to a boil. Cook the green beans at a brisk simmer just until tender, 3 to 5 minutes. Drain and add to the octopus, along with the bell pepper.

**5.** When the farro is tender, drain it and add to the bowl. Drizzle with 3 tablespoons olive oil and 1 tablespoon lemon juice; gently mix the ingredients; season to taste with salt and pepper and add more olive oil and lemon juice if needed.

**6.** Serve the salad warm, at room temperature, or chilled.

### NOTES

Lo Schicchero's dish calls for barley, but I think farro tastes better and cooks a little faster, so that's my first choice.

The baby octopus could also be sautéed briefly in a little olive oil, or simmered in water for 5 to 10 minutes. I've found that the results are more or less the same with the three methods (microwave, sauté, simmer)—pleasantly chewy, just the way octopus should be. If baby octopuses larger than 3 ounces each are used, it's best to simmer them until tender.

# TUSCAN BREAD SALAD with TUNA

*Panzanella con il tonno*

**MAKES 2 OR 3 SERVINGS | PREP: 15 MINUTES** *(plus 1 hour soaking and standing time)*

*"There's no tomato in a classic panzanella!" insists Lina Romei. And no cucumbers, capers, or tuna either. Black pepper? Lina wrinkles her nose.*

*She's right. Bread, onion, olive oil, vinegar, and basil: These are the essentials of this refreshing salad from the cucina povera tradition. The ideal bread is the salt-free loaf soaking in a basin in Lina's sink. She tears off a sodden, unpromising handful, squeezes it, and rubs it between her fingers. The bread disintegrates into feathery crumbs en route to the bowl, where it will be anointed with good Tuscan oil.*

*Panzanella is so easy to make that in Tuscan slang the word is used figuratively to mean a no-brainer. I've made it Lina's way, successfully, but I must confess to a liking for some of the banned ingredients and perhaps you will, too.*

½ to ⅔ cup chopped red onion
4 to 5 cups cubed bread from a firm-textured whole-grain or
    white loaf, stale or oven-dried (see Note)
Up to ¼ cup extra-virgin olive oil
2 teaspoons white wine vinegar
1 small ripe tomato, diced small
½ small cucumber, peeled and seeded, diced small
Leaves from 1 sprig basil
Sea salt or kosher salt
Freshly ground black pepper (optional)
1 (6- to 7-ounce) can good-quality tuna packed in olive oil, drained

1. If the onion tastes sharp, place it in a small bowl and cover with water; let stand for at least 15 minutes; drain.

2. Meanwhile, place the bread in a bowl and cover with water; let stand until the bread is saturated, 5 to 10 minutes. Remove the bread, one handful at a time, and gently but thoroughly squeeze out the water; crumble into a serving bowl. While the bread is still moist, drizzle with olive oil, sprinkle with the vinegar, and toss with a fork.

3. Add the onion, tomato, and cucumber to the dressed bread. With scissors or a small knife, snip the basil leaves into ribbons, letting them fall into the bowl. Mix the ingredients. Add salt and (if using) pepper to taste.

*continued*

**4.** Allow the *panzanella* to stand at room temperature for at least an hour or, refrigerated, for several hours.

**5.** To serve: Break up the tuna, placing it in a small bowl. Pass the bowls of *panzanella* and tuna at the table. Diners can mix the tuna with the *panzanella* or, in Italian fashion, eat it separately.

**NOTES**

Unsalted Tuscan bread is difficult to find even in other parts of Italy and is unlikely to be among the options you'll find in the U.S. It can be hard to judge, on the basis of look and feel, whether a substitute loaf will hold up to the water treatment. I suggest soaking a slice in advance to find out whether it crumbles compliantly or turns into a gummy mess. I've had the best luck with sturdy whole-grain bread, homemade or purchased from a good baker.

To dry fresh bread: Spread the cubes on a rimmed baking sheet. Place in the oven, turn the heat to 275°F, and cook until dry to the touch but not browned, 10 to 15 minutes.

# COUSCOUS CONFETTI SALAD with TUNA

*Insalata di couscous con tonno*

MAKES 4 SERVINGS | PREP: 20 MINUTES

*Asked for a favorite main-course salad, Giuseppe Scarlata immediately proposed this appetizing combination from his couscous- and tuna-loving zone on the west coast of Sicily. I've also eaten couscous salads similar to this one during a restorative day of soaking in the mineral baths at Terme S. Giovanni in Rapolano. The salads served in the informal restaurant contain the healthful ingredients expected in a spa setting, but are substantial enough to keep hunger at bay.*

*Cutting the ingredients into small pieces gives them a confetti-like appearance, once combined with tiny couscous grains. Not only are the results pretty, but the diner can be certain that each bite will contain a little of everything.*

1½ cups instant couscous

1 heaping tablespoon capers, preferably salt cured

1¼ cups cherry tomatoes

4 scallions, including some of the tender green parts

⅓ cup Nocellara olives or other Mediterranean olives

½ cup extra-virgin olive oil

¼ cup fresh lemon juice

¾ teaspoon sea salt or kosher salt, or to taste

Hot red pepper flakes

1 (6½- to 7-ounce) can good-quality tuna packed in olive oil

6 cups firmly packed baby arugula or other microgreens

1. Bring 1½ cups water to a boil. Put the couscous in a medium bowl and pour the boiling water over it, making sure the grains are immersed. Cover and let stand for at least 5 minutes. Place the capers in a small bowl and cover with cold water; let stand for several minutes and drain. If the capers are large, coarsely chop them; if small, leave them whole. Quarter the tomatoes. Cut the scallions in half lengthwise and thinly slice them crosswise. Pit the olives and cut into slivers.

2. Combine the olive oil, lemon juice, salt, and red pepper flakes to taste in a small bowl or liquid measuring cup; add about a tablespoon of olive oil from the can of tuna. Whisk to form an emulsion.

*continued*

**3.** Fluff the couscous with a fork, gently breaking up clumps. Add the lemon dressing and mix gently but thoroughly. Flake the tuna into the bowl by rubbing the chunks between your fingers. Add the tomatoes, scallions, olives, and capers. Mix well.

**4.** To serve: Scatter the greens around the edges of broad, shallow bowls or dinner plates. Mound the couscous salad in the center.

### VARIATIONS

Colorful raw or roasted bell peppers, cut confetti style, would be good in this salad.

In place of the hot pepper flakes, finely chop a fresh hot pepper; spicy-sweet pickled peppers such as peppadews are another alternative.

Good-quality jarred or canned mackerel or diced roast chicken could be substituted for the tuna.

# ESCAROLE, ANCHOVY, and CHEESE SALAD

*Insalata di scarola, acciughe e formaggio*

**MAKES 2 SERVINGS | PREP: 15 MINUTES**

*This salad claims no pedigree but possesses so much lusty Italian brio it deserves to stand on its own, accompanied only by some delicious, coarse-textured bread.*

2 to 3 tablespoons extra-virgin olive oil
2 to 3 teaspoons fresh lemon juice
Sea salt or kosher salt
Freshly ground black pepper
1 large pinch sugar (optional)
4 cups firmly packed tender escarole leaves, torn (see Note)
6 anchovy fillets (see Note)
Aged pecorino or Parmigiano Reggiano cheese

**1.** In a small bowl, whisk together the olive oil, lemon juice, salt and pepper to taste, and, if using, sugar.

**2.** Place the escarole leaves in a bowl. Add the dressing and toss well. Divide between 2 dinner plates.

**3.** Pinch the anchovy fillets in half and scatter on the salads. Using a vegetable peeler, cut shards from the cheese wedge, allowing them to drop onto the salads in random fashion.

## NOTES

If the outer escarole leaves are tough, use only the tender inner leaves.

Use high-quality anchovies canned in olive oil or, even better, salt-cured anchovies, which can be refrigerated indefinitely for use as needed. To fillet the latter, run a nail down one edge to open, and lift out the backbone and tail; separate the fillets.

# MIXED GREENS with ASPARAGUS and WHITE ANCHOVIES

*Insalata mista con asparagi e alici marinate*

MAKES 4 SERVINGS | PREP: 15 MINUTES | COOK: 2 MINUTES

*This recipe is from Alberto Recca, whose Sicilian family is a leading processor of luscious Mediterranean anchovies.*

¼ cup extra-virgin olive oil
1 to 2 tablespoons white wine vinegar or sherry vinegar
Sea salt or kosher salt
Freshly ground black pepper
12 to 16 spears asparagus
8 cups microgreens or other mixed salad greens
1 cup halved grape tomatoes or quartered cherry tomatoes
2 marinated baby artichokes, cut into slivers (see Note)
16 white anchovies (see Note)

1. Combine the olive oil and vinegar in a large salad bowl. Season to taste with salt and pepper.

2. Trim the asparagus ends (see page 119). Angle-cut the asparagus into short lengths. Bring a small, broad saucepan or skillet filled about two-thirds full with water to a boil. Cook the asparagus until crisp-tender, about 2 minutes. Drain and cool under running water until just warm, but not cooled entirely. Turn the asparagus into the salad bowl and gently mix with the dressing.

3. Add the microgreens and tomatoes to the bowl. Toss with the dressed asparagus. Using tongs, mound the salad on dinner plates. Garnish with the slivered baby artichokes and white anchovies.

**NOTES**

I have in mind the whole baby artichokes found in a good deli. You could substitute jarred marinated artichoke hearts, but they are smaller and you will probably need six.

White anchovies marinated in citrus juice can be found in the refrigerated case of some Italian delis. Alternatively, you could marinate fresh anchovies yourself. To prepare them: Pull off the heads (the tiny entrails will follow) and split open the anchovy with a thumbnail. Pull off one fillet. Strip off the backbone and tail, leaving the other fillet behind. Rinse the fillets and marinate in fresh lemon juice for at least one hour or until they turn white; drain. If you don't find prepared white anchovies or fresh anchovies, sauté small shrimp instead.

# MOUNTAIN SALAD with BACON, FONTINA, and SWEET-SOUR ONIONS

*Insalatona di montagna con prosciutto affumicato,*
*Fontina e cipolline in agrodolce*

MAKES 4 SERVINGS | PREP: 15 MINUTES | COOK: 10 MINUTES

*I enjoyed this wonderfully hearty salad at the Rifugio Ristorante, on the way down after crossing the glacier between Courmayeur in Italy and Chamonix in France. The authority that operates the funicular also runs this excellent restaurant; I tried but failed to imagine Amtrak accomplishing an equivalent feat. Take note that, although the salad is quickly assembled, the sweet-sour onions require lengthy cooking. Make them anyway—you won't be sorry.*

4 strips bacon, cut crosswise into thirds
¼ cup extra-virgin olive oil
1 to 2 tablespoons red wine vinegar
Sea salt or kosher salt
Freshly ground black pepper
8 cups torn Boston lettuce or other soft greens
1 medium carrot
1 cup halved cherry tomatoes or 1 large ripe tomato, diced
4 ounces Fontina Valle d'Aosta or other flavorful mountain
    cheese (see Note, page 199), cubed (about 1 cup)
Whole-grain croutons (page 199)
12 sweet-sour onions (recipe follows), at room temperature

**1.** Lay the bacon pieces in a skillet; cook over medium-low heat until browned and crisp, turning once. Drain on paper towels.

**2.** In a small bowl, whisk the olive oil and vinegar with a fork; season to taste with salt and pepper.

**3.** Place the greens in a large bowl. Add half of the dressing and toss well. Transfer the greens to 4 dinner plates. Using a vegetable peeler, cut carrot shavings, letting them drop onto the salads.

*continued*

**4.** Scatter the cherry tomatoes, cheese, and croutons over the salads; drizzle with the remaining dressing. Arrange 3 sweet-sour onions on each plate. Lay the bacon pieces on top.

## Sweet-Sour Onions

MAKES ABOUT 24 ONIONS | PREP: 15 MINUTES | COOK: 1½ HOURS

2 pounds *cipolline* (small, flat onions), pearl onions, or shallots
1 tablespoon extra-virgin olive oil
1 tablespoon unsalted butter
2 tablespoons red wine vinegar
1 teaspoon sugar
¼ teaspoon sea salt or kosher salt

**1.** Fill a medium saucepan or skillet broad enough for the onions to fit in a single layer with water; bring to a boil. Add the onions (they will bob to the top) and let them cook for about 20 seconds; drain and cool slightly. Pull off the papery outer skin; trim any dangling roots or tips but leave the root ends intact (otherwise, the onions will come apart when cooked).

**2.** Return the onions to the saucepan; add water half way up the sides of the onions. Bring to a boil; reduce the heat and simmer the onions for about 20 minutes, stirring at least once, until tender and about half of the water has evaporated. Add the olive oil, butter, vinegar, sugar, and salt; continue to simmer slowly, partially covered, stirring often, until the liquid has mostly evaporated, about 40 minutes.

**3.** When the onions start to sizzle, pay close attention. This is when they begin to brown—a good thing, but you must be careful not to burn them. Add a little water and reduce the heat if they seem to be cooking too quickly. When they are a burnished golden brown, consider them done.

**NOTE**
You'll end up with more onions than needed for the salad—and that's deliberate, for it's not worth the trouble to make a smaller quantity. Serve the leftovers, reheated gently, with steak, pot roast, roast chicken—or make this *insalatona* again.

# BRESAOLA INVOLTINI with HERBED GOAT CHEESE FILLING

*Involtini di bresaola e caprino con rucola*

**MAKES 4 SERVINGS | PREP: 15 MINUTES**

*The night scene at Bevivino, I've heard, is young and raucous. It wouldn't be the place for me then, but a slow lunch in the cool, dark recesses of this Florence enoteca is precisely to my taste. Among the light dishes we ordered were these* involtini *("rolls"), savored with a bottle of Carmignano wine. Both were memorable.*

6 ounces goat cheese, at room temperature
2 teaspoons snipped chives
4 cups baby arugula or regular arugula torn into small pieces
1 to 2 tablespoons extra-virgin olive oil
Sea salt or kosher salt
4 ounces *bresaola* cut into paper-thin slices (see Note)
4 lemon wedges

1. In a small bowl, mash the goat cheese and chives together with a fork. Gradually add water as required to make it spreadable but not runny. (At this point, the spread can stand at room temperature for at least an hour, or longer if refrigerated.)

2. Place the arugula in a bowl. Drizzle with olive oil and season lightly with salt. Toss well.

3. Gently separate the *bresaola* slices from one another and pile them loosely. Scoop up a teaspoon of the goat cheese spread and, with a small spatula or the back of a teaspoon, smear it down the center of a slice of *bresaola*. Fold it loosely to make a cone-shaped *involtino*. Repeat with the rest of the *bresaola* slices and goat cheese, arranging them in a circular pattern on dinner plates (pointy ends facing the center, seam side down). You should have 5 or 6 slices per serving, depending on their size.

4. Using tongs, place a mound of dressed arugula at the center of each plate. Garnish with a lemon wedge.

*continued*

**NOTES**

The delicately flavored, air-cured beef called *bresaola* is a traditional product of Lombardy's Valtellina Valley. *Bresaola* imported to the U.S. is produced in Argentina or Uruguay, under the supervision of the Italian consortium, and is superior to the domestically made *bresaola* I've tasted.

*Friselle* (see page 268), bagel-shaped bread from Southern Italy that is oven-dried until rock hard, can be used to make delightful crouton-like crumbles for this arugula salad or any other salad. Just dip a *friselle* in water until soft enough to crumble. Crumble it into the bottom of the salad bowl, drizzle with a little olive oil and add the other ingredients.

# SALUMI, CHEESE, and SALAD PLATTERS

*Piatti di salumi, formaggi e insalata*

**MAKES 6 SERVINGS | PREP: 20 MINUTES**

*After a morning of museum hopping in Cortona, we passed up the chance to join other tourists at sidewalk cafés, eating what looked to be mediocre pizza, and instead ducked into Enoteca Etruria. At her hand-cranked slicer, an energetic middle-aged woman was filling one platter after another with affettati, featuring a sampling of local salami, one studded with black truffles and another with fennel. Before long we were acquainted with the gregarious Imola, who reserved room on her platters for billowy slices of truffled mortadella and for two kinds of pecorino cheese, one with truffles and one without. Without a wasted motion, she finished platters with a simply dressed salad and delivered them to tables with liters of local red wine and warm focaccia.*

*It didn't escape my notice that our wonderful lunch was all about shopping, not cooking. Back in the U.S., I set out to make a similar meal. Despite the more limited choices of Italian specialties at the local deli, the platters on our table were the very picture of abbondanza.*

4 to 6 ounces Italian prosciutto or speck (lightly smoked ham from Alto Adige), thinly sliced

4 to 6 ounces Genoa salami or spicy *soppressata*, thinly sliced

4 to 6 ounces mortadella, thinly sliced

2 cups mixed Mediterranean olives

12 ounces young pecorino cheese, whole or cut into thin wedges

12 ounces aged pecorino *pepato* (studded with peppercorns), in one piece or broken into chunks

1 large head Bibb lettuce or other soft-leafed lettuce

Extra-virgin olive oil

White or red wine vinegar

Sea salt or kosher salt

Freshly ground black pepper

6 whole marinated baby artichokes or 12 marinated artichoke hearts

3 fresh tomatoes, sliced (optional)

Sliced focaccia or any crusty country-style bread

*continued*

1. Arrange the slices of prosciutto and other cured meats on a large platter; turn the olives into a small pretty bowl and place it at the center. Arrange the 2 cheeses on another platter.

2. Tear the lettuce leaves, letting them drop into a large bowl. Add 2 tablespoons olive oil and 2 teaspoons vinegar; toss. Season to taste with salt and pepper; taste again, adding more olive oil or vinegar as needed. Quarter the baby artichokes and arrange on top, or serve them whole on a separate plate.

3. Arrange the tomato slices, if using, on a small platter. Drizzle with olive oil and sprinkle lightly with salt.

4. To serve: Pass the platters and bowl at the table or serve buffet style, accompanied by warm focaccia or another good bread.

**NOTES**

In choosing this recipe's assortment of cured meats, I went for contrasting flavors, textures, and looks. Another time, I might opt for exploring more subtle variations by, for example, offering a tasting of two-year prosciutto from Parma or San Daniele along with duck prosciutto from the Hudson Valley.

This recipe features two sheep's milk cheeses, but the semisoft fresh pecorino will taste milder compared to the peppery, sharper-tasting aged cheese. Alternatively, you could choose cheeses that differ more dramatically, pairing an intense-tasting Gorgonzola with creamy fontina, for instance.

# CHOPPED ITALIAN DELI SALAD

MAKES 4 SERVINGS | PREP: 20 MINUTES

*This salad can be varied in keeping with deli ingredients you might have on hand or want to try. For example, thin strips of mortadella and small cubes of semisoft Asiago or provolone could be substituted for the salami and mozzarella. Marinated artichokes or mushrooms could stand in for the peperoncini.*

¼ cup extra-virgin olive oil, plus more to taste
2 tablespoons red or white wine vinegar, plus more to taste
¼ cup snipped basil, dill, chives, or parsley leaves
Sea salt or kosher salt
Freshly ground black pepper
1 cup fresh mozzarella cubes or halved *bocconcini* (about 5 ounces)
2 to 3 ounces thick-cut Genoa salami, cut into small cubes
1 (19-ounce) can chickpeas, drained and rinsed
8 oil-cured black olives, pitted and halved
2 or 3 pickled Italian peppers (*peperoncini*)
3 cups shredded crisp greens such as romaine, escarole, or a mixture

1. Whisk together the olive oil, vinegar, basil, ½ teaspoon salt, and ¼ teaspoon pepper in a bowl large enough to hold the salad. Add the mozzarella, salami, chickpeas, olives, and peppers; stir until coated with the dressing. Place the greens on top. (At this point the salad can be refrigerated for several hours.)

2. Toss the greens with the ingredients at the bottom of the bowl. Taste and add more olive oil, vinegar, salt, or pepper if needed. Serve with warm focaccia or *grissini* (crisp Italian breadsticks).

## Aperitivo Time

The universe of before-dinner libations traditionally consumed by Italians is comfortingly small. A bitter-sweet *aperitivo* is considered appropriate: artichoke-flavored Cynar or Punt e Mes, anytime; or in warm weather, scarlet Campari with a splash of soda or a *spritz* made with orange Aperol. Vermouth, red or white, sweet or dry, also primes the appetite. Ice in your drink or a *scorza* (twist of lemon peel) is added only on request.

Sparklers like *prosecco* tickle the taste buds, and so do wines that might range from a fragrant Falanghina from Campania to Lagrein, an obscure Alto Adige red, depending on where you are. A wine bar could offer a dozen choices, an ordinary bar just one white and red by the glass. In Italian homes, a host might offer several of these choices, or only one, or none; if you've come for dinner, you may go directly to the table.

Similarly, the tidbits that accompany *aperitivi* tend to be a no-big-deal proposition. Our Tuscan friends bring out *salati* ("salted things") such as cracker-like *schiacciata* broken into pieces, savory *taralli*, pretzels, and nuts. From-the-deli items like olives (plain or marinated), anchovy-stuffed hot peppers, and pickled mushrooms could also show up. There might be a few cubes of mozzarella or fresh pecorino, though most cheeses are considered too filling for this pre-dinner interlude.

I've never much enjoyed making elaborate, appetite-destroying tidbits, so the idea of simplifying the options for *aperitivo* time really appeals. Most of the time I bring out an easy, no-prep array based on what I can easily get. For instance, for the *schiacciata* that was readily available in Tuscany but not here, I might substitute olive-oil crackers stocked by my supermarket.

Occasionally I take a tiny bit more trouble, as in these examples:

Toast some crostini (using a skinny baguette, follow directions in step two on page 276) and spread a thin layer of fig preserves on each one. Top it with a folded piece of thinly sliced prosciutto or some other delicious cured meat (such as the peppery Tuscan ham I found in a local deli).

*"I've never much enjoyed making elaborate, appetite-destroying tidbits, so the idea of simplifying the options for aperitivo time really appeals."*

Marinate mozzarella or *burrata* cubes in extra-virgin olive oil enlivened with sea salt, shredded fresh basil or mint, and lemon zest.

Sprinkle young sweet radishes, baby turnips, or thin fennel wedges with sea salt.

If I feel a surge of ambition, I might make a batch of *taralli*, plain or seasoned with black pepper and fennel seed (recipe follows). They're the perfect lead-in to just about any *piatto unico*. ᑫᕯ

# TARALLI with BLACK PEPPER and FENNEL SEED

*Taralli con pepe nero e semi di finocchio*

**MAKES ABOUT 3 DOZEN | PREP: 30 MINUTES | COOK: 1 HOUR** *(plus 2 hours rising time for the dough)*

*Small, crunchy, boldly seasoned taralli are a delightful treat for aperitivo time, followed by a piatto unico of your choice. When properly made, they are simmered in water before being baked. This method is shared with bagels, and the taralli made by baker Charlie Lalima at Madonia Bakery in the Bronx might be compared to "everything" bagels, bursting with flavor from salt, coarse black pepper, and fragrant seeds. Charlie spent part of a morning teaching me the fundamentals of taralli-making and, while they baked, we made good use of the time, devouring sausage heros built by Peter Madonia Sr. Then I headed home to wrestle Charlie's recipe down to home-cook dimensions.*

1 teaspoon active dry yeast
1 pound unbleached all-purpose flour (about 3½ cups), plus
   more as needed
⅓ cup extra-virgin olive oil, plus more as needed
⅓ cup dry white wine
1½ teaspoons sea salt or kosher salt
1 teaspoon freshly ground black pepper
1 tablespoon fennel seed or anise seed, or a combination of the
   two (see Note)

**1.** Combine the yeast with ½ cup warm water (110°F to 115°F) in a liquid measuring cup. Let stand for a few minutes, until a beige scum forms on top.

**2.** Meanwhile, combine the flour, olive oil, and wine in a mixing bowl. Using an electric mixer fitted with a paddle, mix over low speed until well blended. Add the salt, pepper, and fennel seed and mix briefly until blended.

**3.** Add the yeast mixture and, on low speed, mix until a dough forms. On a pastry board or other smooth surface dusted with flour, knead the dough briefly and form a ball. Coat a medium bowl lightly with olive oil; turn the dough to coat and let rest, covered, until more or less doubled in size, about 2 hours.

**4.** Preheat the oven to 400°F. Divide the dough in half. Flatten one piece to form a rectangle and roll from one long side to the other using both hands, working from the center outwards, to make a thick rope about 1½ inches in diameter and 12 inches long. With a dough scraper or knife, cut crosswise at ½-inch intervals. Roll each piece to make a skinny rope about 7 inches long. Loop it to make an oval shape with one end crossing the other. Press firmly with your thumb to make an indentation at the point where the ends intersect (see Note). Repeat with the rest of the dough, lining up the *taralli* on 2 trays or rimmed baking sheets.

**5.** Bring a medium saucepan about two-thirds full of water to a simmer. Drop in 8 *taralli*; line the space freed up on the baking sheet with a clean dish towel. Simmer *taralli* for a few seconds until they rise to the surface; scoop out with a slotted spoon and lay on the dish towel. Simmer the rest of the *taralli* in the same way, unfolding the dish towel into the freed-up space and returning the *taralli* to dry until moist but not slimy to the touch.

**6.** Lightly oil 2 baking sheets. Arrange the *taralli* about 1 inch apart. Bake on center racks for half an hour. Turn the *taralli* and return to the oven (switching the position of the pans). Bake 30 minutes longer; they may brown earlier than this, but need the full time for the insides to dry; cover with aluminum foil or parchment paper if they seem in danger of burning or browning too much.

**7.** Cool the *taralli* on racks and store at room temperature in sealed containers; they can also be frozen.

**NOTES**

Fennel and anise seed can be used whole, or crushed with mortar and pestle, or ground in a spice grinder or mini food processor. Dried rosemary would be an interesting alternative. Or, the *taralli* can be seasoned only with salt.

According to Charlie, the thumbprint indentation signifies that the *taralli* are handmade; machines can't duplicate this maneuver.

The dough can also be mixed and kneaded by hand. It is fairly "tight," in baker's terminology, and very easy to work. Rolling and forming *taralli* is just plain fun—a great project if children are on hand, both for their sakes and because many hands make light work. Catering to their tastes, you might cut back on the pepper and fennel, or leave them out altogether.

# Chapter 7
# EGGS and CHEESE

Eggs saturate the fresh pastas of central and northern Italy with their golden richness. A ricotta filling or white sauce is often enhanced with an egg or two. And, at Teatro del Sale in Florence, I watched chef Fabio Picchi whisk beaten egg into a tomato-based pasta sauce, thereby boosting its flavor and nutritional heft.

As the focus of a meal, however, eggs don't get much play in Italian cooking. It's true that *Il Cucchiao d'Argento* ("The Silver Spoon")—a cookbook on the shelves of many Italian homes—abounds in egg recipes, but quite a few of these, such as curried mushroom omelet and "American-style eggs" (fried eggs and bacon, for the record) are derivative of other cuisines or otherwise outside the mainstream of Italian eating.

Pellegrino Artusi's definitive *La Scienza in Cucina e l'Arte di Mangiare Bene,* ("The Science of Cooking and the Art of Eating Well") includes just fourteen egg recipes and, of those, eight are for frittatas. His emphasis isn't wrong because, as a technique for cooking eggs, frittatas are brilliant. The eggs cook, undisturbed, at a low temperature calculated to preserve their creamy texture. The cook's challenge, always, is to achieve a browned top without destroying the voluptuous softness that lies beneath. Among the endless possible fillings, my favorite is a trio of potatoes, onion, and pancetta.

Frittatas make terrific *piatti unici,* any time of day, and so do omelets (Italians make them, too), as well as savory deep-dish pies with names like *torta salata,* Easter pie, and pizza *rustica.* Typically, eggs are incorporated into the pastry used for the crust, and they are the constant in varied quiche-like fillings such as the asparagus and ham combination in this chapter. Also here is the Italian dish I eat most often, at least once a week—eggs cooked slowly, with repeated bastings of the best olive oil in the house.

Cheese, another glory of the Italian table, has already been sprinkled lavishly throughout this book. Many pastas, risottos, and soups would seem incomplete without it. But cheese also does a solo turn in some dishes. The best fresh local cheeses, whether one of the Sienese Crete's prized pecorinos or a *toma* in the Piedmont, are grilled, fried, baked, even microwaved to be enjoyed alone or with accompaniments. And it's no accident that the pinnacle of a delectable prosciutto and vege-table stack is reserved for a warm slice of mozzarella.

Rounding out this chapter are several dishes that combine eggs and cheese in the Italian equivalent of casseroles. The layered zucchini-ricotta *tian* adds up to a satisfying one-dish meal—and, yes, it can be made ahead—but the wonderful taste is the real reason I make it so often.

# EGGS and CHEESE

*Potato, Onion, and Pancetta Frittata*

*Goat Cheese, Tomato, and Marjoram Omelet*

*Eggs Basted in Fragrant Olive Oil, on Toast*

*Parmigiano Reggiano Baskets
    with Scrambled Eggs*

*Warm Mozzarella, Prosciutto, and Tomato Stack*

*Fried Pecorino with Spicy Eggplant and Peppers*

*Savory Baked Ricotta with Fig, Pine Nut,
    and Greens Toss*

*Layered Zucchini-Ricotta Casserole*

*Cabbage, Fontina, and Whole-Grain
    Bread Casserole*

# POTATO, ONION, and PANCETTA FRITTATA

*Frittata di patate, cipolla e pancetta*

MAKES 2 OR 3 SERVINGS | PREP: 15 MINUTES | COOK: 25 MINUTES

*Staying in a farmhouse in the Valdarno, we had easy access to luscious orange-yolked eggs from local free-range hens. My husband, Kent, fell into the habit of making frittatas with whatever we had on hand. Even when the larder was almost bare, we always seemed to have potatoes, onions, and pancetta—and a filling made from these quickly became my favorite.*

6 eggs, preferably from cage-free hens
2 tablespoons chopped flat-leaf parsley or baby spinach
½ teaspoon sea salt or kosher salt
Freshly ground black pepper
1 tablespoon butter
2 tablespoons olive oil
2 medium boiling potatoes, peeled, diced small
1 medium onion, halved lengthwise, cut into thin wedges
1 to 2 ounces pancetta, diced small
½ cup grated young Asiago, Montasio, or other mild-tasting cheese
Sliced tomatoes drizzled with balsamic vinegar (optional)

1. In a small bowl, whisk the eggs with ¼ cup water; add the parsley, salt, and several grindings of pepper.

2. Melt the butter with the olive oil in a medium (8-inch) nonstick skillet with sloping sides over medium heat; cook the potatoes, onions, and pancetta, stirring from time to time, until nicely browned and the potatoes are tender, about 15 minutes.

3. Add the eggs to the pan, tilting to spread evenly. Reduce the heat to medium-low; sprinkle with the cheese and cook until almost set, lifting the edge with a spatula to allow the liquid egg to run under. Cover the pan for a few minutes until the top is set.

4. Peek under the frittata. If not browned on the underside, raise the heat to medium and cook just long enough to brown it. Loosen the frittata with a spatula; place a platter upside down over the skillet and invert the frittata onto it, browned side up (see Note).

5. Serve warm or at room temperature, cut into wedges, alone or with sliced tomatoes drizzled with a little balsamic vinegar.

### NOTE

After browning the frittata on one side, you can slide it from the platter back into the skillet to brown on the other side. I prefer leaving the second side softly set but not browned.

# GOAT CHEESE, TOMATO, and MARJORAM OMELET

*Omelet con caprino, pomodori e maggiorana*

MAKES 2 SERVINGS | PREP: 10 MINUTES | COOK: 5 MINUTES

*Italians are better known for frittatas, but they also make omelets quite well. This one has everything I love in an omelet—cheese, tomato, a fresh herb—and no precooking!*

2 ounces goat cheese
Leaves from 2 sprigs marjoram or thyme (1 heaping tablespoon)
1 medium ripe tomato or a handful of grape tomatoes
4 large eggs, preferably from cage-free hens
Sea salt or kosher salt
Freshly ground black pepper
2 teaspoons unsalted butter
2 teaspoons extra-virgin olive oil

1. Preheat the oven or toaster oven to 200°F. Crumble the goat cheese into a small bowl. Add the marjoram and, using your fingers, toss the two together. With a serrated knife, cut the tomato into medium dice (or halve grape tomatoes).

2. Combine 2 eggs and 2 tablespoons water in a small bowl. Season with a generous pinch of salt and a sprinkling of black pepper, and whisk well.

3. Heat an omelet pan or small nonstick skillet with sloping sides over medium-high heat. Melt 1 teaspoon butter with 1 teaspoon olive oil, tilting the pan to coat well. Add the seasoned eggs and let them sizzle and bubble for a few seconds (counting slowly to 5 works for me). Swiftly mix the eggs by moving a heatproof spatula or fork in a side-to-side motion around the pan; tilt the pan to evenly distribute the coagulated clumps and liquid. Return to the burner and cook a few seconds longer until barely runny on top.

4. Off heat, distribute half of the herbed goat cheese and tomatoes down the center of the omelet. With the spatula, flip one side of the omelet toward the middle and overlap with the other. Turn onto a warm plate, seam side down. Keep warm in the oven or toaster oven while cooking the other omelet.

## VARIATIONS

To make a frittata instead, combine all the eggs, filling ingredients, and seasonings with ¼ cup water in a medium bowl. Heat the olive oil and butter over medium heat and cook the frittata as described on page 228.

For a tasty ham-and-eggs vibe, dice a little ham into small cubes or gently tear a slice of prosciutto into strips and add with the other fillings. Or, sizzle tiny cubes of pancetta in a small skillet until the fat is rendered and add to the omelet.

# EGGS BASTED *in* FRAGRANT OLIVE OIL, *on* TOAST

*Uova al tegamino*

MAKES 3 SERVINGS | PREP: 5 MINUTES | COOK: 3 TO 4 MINUTES

*In Italy, the new year brings not only cooler temperatures but newly bottled olive oil from the fall harvest. Natalia Ravidà, author of Seasons of Sicily, has a childhood memory of family gatherings around a wood-burning stove. While the adults sipped red wine and dipped bread in the season's new olive oil, she cooked her first meal: an egg basted with the same fragrant oil.*

*"My main concern was to make sure the oil would retain its aromas," Natalia remembers. Pampered with olive oil bastings at low heat, the whites cook to tender perfection, while the yolks remain soft and luscious.*

*Eggs prepared Natalia's way are wonderful at breakfast, but they also serve admirably as a simple lunch or dinner. If one egg doesn't seem generous enough you can, of course, make two eggs per serving, and more toast as well.*

¼ cup extra-virgin olive oil, preferably new season
3 large eggs, preferably from cage-free hens
Sea salt or kosher salt
Freshly ground black pepper (optional)
3 slices country-style white or whole-wheat bread

1. In a large skillet over medium-low heat, warm the olive oil for a few seconds. Break an egg into a small, shallow bowl and slide it into the pan; repeat with each remaining egg.

2. As the whites begin to firm up, tilt the pan and scoop up some of the warm oil with a spoon; drizzle it over the eggs. Repeat the scooping and drizzling until the whites are cooked through but the yolks are still soft, about 3 minutes. Season with salt and, if using, the pepper. (If the oil begins to sizzle, lift the pan for a moment and lower the heat.)

3. Meanwhile, toast the bread.

4. To serve: Place the toast on small plates. Top each with an egg and pour some oil from the skillet over it. Add an extra drizzle of olive oil if you like.

## VARIATIONS

### Italian-Style Ham and Eggs

Prepare the eggs and toast as directed above. Top each piece of toast with a thin slice of prosciutto or speck (smoked ham from northern Italy) before placing an egg on top.

### Asparagus and Eggs on Ciabatta

Arrange several spears of steamed asparagus on toasted ciabatta or other coarse-grained bread. Top with an egg basted in olive oil and a sprinkle of Parmigiano Reggiano or Grana Padano cheese.

### Roasted Vegetables with Eggs

Spoon any combination of roasted vegetables (such as the eggplant, bell pepper, and onion combo on page 239, for instance) onto plates. Top each with an egg basted in olive oil.

# PARMIGIANO REGGIANO BASKETS with SCRAMBLED EGGS

*Cestini di Parmigiano Reggiano con uova*

MAKES 6 SERVINGS | PREP: 20 MINUTES | COOK: 12 MINUTES

*Gary Radke is recognized for his achievements as an art historian specializing in the Italian Renaissance—and, at least by his family, for specialties such as this lovely dish. They eat it for brunch on Christmas Day, but it's also great as a light dinner.*

2 to 3 tablespoons unsalted butter, plus more for pans
1½ cups grated Parmigiano Reggiano cheese, preferably young
12 large eggs
½ cup milk
Sea salt or kosher salt
Freshly ground black pepper
2 or 3 cloves garlic, peeled, cut into paper-thin slivers
¼ cup extra-virgin olive oil
1 tablespoon balsamic vinegar or sherry vinegar
9 cups lightly packed microgreens or other mixed greens

**1.** Preheat the oven to 400°F. Streak 2 baking sheets with butter and line with parchment paper. Spoon the cheese onto the baking sheets in 12 small heaps; pat them to make disks about 3½ inches in diameter. Have a muffin tin ready for shaping the baskets (see Note).

**2.** Place the baking sheets on a middle rack in the oven. Watch through the window as the cheese begins to bubble and fuse and then flattens out and deepens in color, about 3 minutes. Remove from the oven and let stand for a few seconds. Gently slide a metal spatula under each disk (if it scrunches up, it's still too hot; let stand a little longer, then try again). Carefully fit it into a muffin cup, crimping as necessary. Cool the baskets thoroughly, uncovered. (The baskets can be prepared up to a day ahead and stored, in a single layer, in a sealed container.)

**3.** Whisk the eggs and milk in a large bowl until well blended. Add ½ teaspoon salt and season lightly with pepper.

**4.** Melt the butter over medium-low heat in a large skillet; add the garlic, stirring and cooking until translucent (not browned) and fragrant. Add the eggs and cook slowly, stirring often. At first nothing will appear to happen. Gradually soft lumps will form; continue to cook until all of the liquid is incorporated and the eggs form a soft mass. Remove from heat, taste, and add more salt and pepper if necessary.

**5.** While the eggs are cooking, whisk the olive oil and vinegar together in a large bowl; season with salt and pepper. Add the greens and toss well.

**6.** To serve: Spread the greens on 6 plates. Top each one with 2 baskets. Spoon the scrambled eggs into the baskets.

### NOTE

The first time you try this recipe, start by making just one or two of the *cestini* ("baskets") to get the hang of it. The goal is to cook them enough to be chewy-crisp once cooled, but not so long that they harden up and are difficult to shape. If the cheese crisps too much to be shaped, go to equally delicious Plan B: Crumble the crisps over the scrambled eggs. No muffin tin? Shape the baskets over upside-down glasses instead.

### VARIATIONS

Add a pinch or two of ground hot red pepper to the Parmigiano Reggiano if you like. You could also sprinkle finely chopped walnuts over the disks once they're on the baking sheet.

If you enjoy the taste of truffle oil, drizzle a drop or two over the scrambled eggs in each basket. Even better: If you're making this dish in Italy and it's the right season, shower them with shaved fresh truffles! A garnish of sautéed mushrooms such as chanterelles or morels would also be lovely.

# WARM MOZZARELLA, PROSCIUTTO, and TOMATO STACK

*Composizione di mozzarella, prosciutto e pomodoro*

MAKES 2 SERVINGS | PREP: 10 MINUTES | COOK: ABOUT 1 MINUTE

*This delectable pile-up of good things, created by chef Daniel Van Etten, is always on the menu at Mima, an Italian wine bar and restaurant in Irvington, New York.*

6 medium endive leaves
1 ripe medium tomato, thinly sliced
2 to 4 slices prosciutto di Parma or other good-quality prosciutto
½ medium red bell pepper, roasted and cut into strips
2 thick slices fresh mozzarella or *burrata* (about 2 ounces each)
Extra-virgin olive oil
Sea salt or kosher salt
Freshly ground black pepper
Basil oil (optional) (recipe follows)

1. Arrange the endive leaves side by side in 2 rows with the edges touching on a broiling pan.

2. Place the tomato slices on top of the endive leaves, but without completely covering them. Add the prosciutto slices, draping them to fit, and top with the bell pepper strips. Place a mozzarella slice on top of each stack.

3. Drizzle each stack generously with olive oil. Sprinkle the cheese lightly with salt and pepper.

4. Place the pan on the top rack of the oven and turn on the broiler. Leaving the door closed but peeking through the glass, broil the stacks until the cheese begins to soften and some edges of the endive char, no more than 1 minute.

5. With a spatula, transfer each stack to a dinner plate. If including the basil oil, use a squeeze bottle or spoon to drizzle some on the edge of each plate (you won't need it all).

# Basil Oil

MAKES ⅓ CUP | PREP: 10 MINUTES | COOK: 20 SECONDS

*Use this oil to garnish dishes; drizzle on fish, soup, or pasta; or, combined with white wine vinegar or lemon juice, as a salad dressing.*

½ cup firmly packed basil leaves
½ cup extra-virgin olive oil
Sea salt or kosher salt, to taste

1. In a small saucepan, bring 2 cups water to a boil. Blanch the basil for about 20 seconds. Drain and cool under running water. (This step helps preserve the fresh green color.)

2. In a blender, combine the basil and olive oil. Blend until very smooth, scraping down the sides. Strain through a fine-mesh strainer.

3. Transfer the oil to a squeeze bottle, if you have one, or a small bowl. This infused oil will keep for a couple of days, refrigerated.

# FRIED PECORINO with SPICY EGGPLANT and PEPPERS

*Pecorino fritto con melanzane e peperoni arrostiti*

**MAKES 3 SERVINGS | PREP: 20 MINUTES | COOK: 25 MINUTES**

*There's more than one way to crisp a young pecorino on the outside while rendering the inside meltingly delicious. A bout on the grill might give it a slight smokiness; some recipes call for broiling; and a server at a restaurant in Florence confessed that the pecorino on my plate had been "grilled" in a microwave. After trying all these techniques (and sometimes reducing the cheese to a puddle), I've settled on frying as the most reliable.*

3 or 4 small purple or lavender eggplants (about 1 pound), trimmed
1 large yellow or red bell pepper
1 large onion, trimmed
Extra-virgin olive oil
Sea salt or kosher salt
Hot red pepper flakes
1 ripe large tomato, diced
1 large egg
2/3 cup unflavored dried fine bread crumbs, or as needed
8 ounces young, flavorful cheese such as pecorino or Fontina
    Valle d'Aosta

1. Preheat the oven to 450°F. Peel the eggplants only if the skins are thick or tough; cut into 1/4-inch slices. Cut the pepper in short strips; slice the onion pole to pole in thin wedges.

2. Divide the vegetables between 2 rimmed baking sheets. Drizzle generously with olive oil (about 1/4 cup); sprinkle with salt and, more cautiously, with red pepper flakes. Mix well with your hands and spread out the vegetables. Roast until soft and lightly browned, about 20 minutes. Stir in the tomato; turn off the heat, leaving the pans in the oven.

*continued*

**3.** Meanwhile, whisk the egg in a shallow bowl. Place the bread crumbs in a similar-size bowl. Cut the cheese into 6 equal wedges or rectangles (a larger cheese could be cut into 3 equal wedges). Coat the top and bottom surfaces of the cheese first with egg, and then bread crumbs. Repeat these steps to form a fairly thick crust.

**4.** In a skillet just large enough to hold the cheese wedges, heat a generous quantity of olive oil (about ¼ cup) over medium heat. After testing the oil with a pinch of bread crumbs to make sure they sizzle, fry the cheese wedges until well browned on one side, about 20 seconds; turn and brown on the other side. (Do not cook to the point that the cheese begins to melt or you will have a mess on your hands!) Remove to a platter.

**5.** To serve: Arrange the cheese wedges in a wide, shallow bowl or on a dinner plate. Surround with the roasted vegetables.

**VARIATION**

Add 2 tablespoons ground toasted almonds or pine nuts to the bread crumbs before coating the cheese. Alternatively, flavor the bread crumbs with ¼ teaspoon dried thyme or an Italian herb blend (do not use one that contains salt and other seasonings).

# SAVORY BAKED RICOTTA with FIG, PINE NUT, and GREENS TOSS

*Ricotta al forno con insalatina di ficchi e pinoli*

MAKES 4 SERVINGS | PREP: 10 MINUTES | COOK: 20 MINUTES

*In Sicily I've most often encountered baked ricotta, sweetened and spiced, as a simple dessert. But this creamy, mild cheese can just as easily head in a savory direction. Add a quickly tossed salad with a bit of sweetness and crunch, and you have a meal.*

Unsalted butter, for the ramekins
3 large eggs
1 pound best-quality ricotta cheese
¼ cup heavy cream
½ cup grated aged pecorino cheese
½ teaspoon sea salt or kosher salt
Freshly ground black pepper
Fig, pine nut, and greens toss (recipe follows)

1. Preheat the oven to 375°F. Butter 4 one-cup ramekins or a 9-inch pie plate.

2. In a medium bowl, beat the eggs with a whisk. Add the ricotta, whisking until smooth. Add the cream, half of the pecorino, the salt, and several grindings of black pepper; whisk until smooth.

3. Divide the seasoned ricotta among the ramekins, smoothing the surface with a spatula; the mixture in each should be about 2 inches high. Sprinkle with the remaining ¼ cup pecorino. Bake in the upper third of the oven until the ricotta mixture pulls away from the edges of the ramekins, about 20 minutes. If the tops are not browned at this point, turn on the broiler, watching through the oven window until nicely browned; this will take about half a minute.

4. With a metal spatula, remove the ramekins from the oven and let them cool for 5 minutes. Place them on one side of 4 plates (if using the pie plate, cut the baked ricotta into 4 wedges). Using tongs, arrange the salad on the other side.

*continued*

# Fig, Pine Nut, and Greens Toss

MAKES 4 SERVINGS | PREP: 10 MINUTES

2 tablespoons extra-virgin olive oil
2 to 3 teaspoons white balsamic vinegar, *vincotto* wine vinegar
   blend, or white wine vinegar
Sea salt or kosher salt
Freshly ground black pepper
1 head Boston lettuce or other soft greens, torn into small pieces
   (about 6 cups)
4 to 6 fresh or dried figs, quartered
2 tablespoons pine nuts, lightly toasted

1. Combine the olive oil and vinegar in a medium bowl; whisk well. Season to taste with salt and pepper.

2. Place the greens on top and toss. Add the figs and pine nuts and toss again.

### NOTE
This recipe will serve six as an appetizer—just use smaller ramekins (1/2 or 3/4 cup).

### VARIATIONS
The ricotta-egg mixture can also be cooked like a custard, in a water bath. Place the ramekins in an ovenproof pan just large enough to hold them; pour boiling water around them halfway up the sides, and carefully transfer the pan to the oven. The finished dish will have a softer, fluffier texture than regular baked ricotta, which is slightly chewier. I like it both ways.

In place of the figs, you could substitute another fresh or dried fruit, such as ripe pear or dried cranberries.

# LAYERED ZUCCHINI-RICOTTA CASSEROLE

*Casseruola di zucchine e ricotta*

MAKES 4 SERVINGS | PREP: 20 MINUTES | COOK: 25 TO 30 MINUTES

Extra-virgin olive oil
3 medium zucchini or yellow summer squash, ends trimmed
Sea salt or kosher salt
1 cup (8 ounces) good-quality ricotta cheese
1 egg
1/8 teaspoon freshly ground black pepper, or to taste
1/2 cup fresh bread crumbs from a country loaf, crusts removed
1/4 cup grated Parmigiano Reggiano, Grana Padano,
   or aged pecorino cheese
1/4 cup snipped basil leaves
2 or 3 medium ripe tomatoes, thinly sliced

1. Preheat the broiler. Lightly oil the bottom of a 2- to 3-quart baking dish. Scrub the zucchini; peel only if the skins are thick or gritty. Angle-cut the zucchini into 1/4-inch slices.

2. Pile the zucchini on a rimmed sheet pan; drizzle with olive oil (about 2 tablespoons) and sprinkle with salt; mix well with your hands or a spatula. Dividing the zucchini between 2 sheet pans, spread them out in a single layer. Broil on an upper rack until lightly browned and just tender, about 10 minutes. As an alternative to broiling, grill the zucchini (one side only) on a stovetop grill pan. Set the oven temperature to 375°F.

3. In a medium bowl, combine the ricotta, egg, 1/2 teaspoon salt, and the pepper. Whisk until smooth and creamy. In a small bowl, toss the bread crumbs with the grated cheese and 2 teaspoons olive oil.

*continued*

**4.** To assemble the casserole: Spread the zucchini slices, browned side up, in the bottom of the casserole dish. Spread the ricotta mixture over the zucchini with a spatula. Scatter the basil on top. Overlap the tomato slices on top; sprinkle with the bread crumb mixture. At this point, the casserole can be covered and stand at room temperature for an hour or, refrigerated, for several hours.

**5.** Bake the casserole, uncovered, until heated through, 10 to 15 minutes. Place the casserole on the top oven rack and continue to cook a few minutes longer, until the bread crumbs are lightly browned but not burned.

# CABBAGE, FONTINA, and WHOLE-GRAIN BREAD CASSEROLE

*Seupa vapellinentze*

**MAKES 6 SERVINGS | PREP: 15 MINUTES** (*plus 1 hour standing time*)
**COOK: 50 MINUTES**

*One bite of this and I'm in the kitchen of Les Vieux Alpages, an agriturismo in Valle d'Aosta, where Corinne is putting the finishing touches on her seupa vapellinentze. The thick, cheesy concoction, categorized as a zuppa in Italian soup parlance, celebrates some of this small, mountainous region's most distinctive foods—the artisanal washed-rind cheese called fontina, the dense dark bread, the delicious root vegetables.*

*Apart from including these core ingredients, cooks are free to take some license. For instance, Corinne departs from the typical preparation by using only cabbage broth, not the leaves themselves.*

*The dish struck me as more casserole than soup, and my version goes all the way there. I sauté the cabbage and onions to bring out their caramelized sweetness, go easy on the cheese, and substitute mushroom broth for the usual meat broth. Despite those personal touches, I like to think of my recipe as belonging to a great mountain cooking tradition.*

2 tablespoons unsalted butter, plus more for baking dish
1 medium onion, halved and thinly sliced
½ small head cabbage, shredded (about 4 cups)
Sea salt or kosher salt
Freshly ground black pepper
4 cups cubed densely textured rye or other whole-grain bread,
   stale or oven dried (see Note)
3 cups roasted mushroom broth (recipe follows), meat broth
   (page 99), or store-bought vegetable or beef broth
2 eggs, beaten
5 ounces Fontina Valle d'Aosta, shredded (about 2 cups)

**1.** Butter the bottom and sides of a 3-quart oval or rectangular baking dish. Melt 2 tablespoons butter in a large skillet. Over medium heat, cook the onion until soft and fragrant, about 5 minutes. Add the cabbage; cook, stirring often, until it softens and begins to caramelize, browning around the edges, about 15 minutes (lower the heat if the vegetables seem on the verge of burning). Season lightly with salt and pepper.

**2.** To assemble the casserole: Place the dry bread cubes in the baking dish. Spread the cabbage mixture over them. Combine the mushroom broth and eggs in a bowl, then pour over the contents of the dish, pressing with your hand to moisten all layers. Cover and let stand for an hour at room temperature or, refrigerated, for several hours.

**3.** Preheat the oven to 375°F. Uncover the casserole and sprinkle the cheese evenly over the top. Cover with aluminum foil and bake until heated through and bubbly, about 20 minutes. Remove the foil, place the dish on the top rack, and turn on the broiler just long enough to brown the top. Cool for 5 to 10 minutes before serving.

**NOTE**

To dry the bread: Spread the bread cubes on a rimmed baking sheet. Place in the oven, turn the heat to 275°F, and cook until dry to the touch but not browned, about 10 minutes.

## Roasted Mushroom Broth

MAKES 1 QUART | PREP: 5 MINUTES | COOK: 40 MINUTES

2 cups halved or quartered white or crimini mushrooms
2 large carrots, thickly sliced
1 medium onion, thickly sliced
Extra-virgin olive oil
Sea salt or kosher salt
Freshly ground black pepper
Large pinch cinnamon

**1.** Preheat the oven to 450°F. Combine the mushrooms, carrots, and onion on a rimmed baking sheet. Drizzle with the olive oil (2 to 3 tablespoons) and mix with your hands or a spoon to coat the vegetables. Spread out in a single layer.

**2.** Roast the vegetables, stirring often, until browned but not burned, about 20 minutes.

*continued*

**3.** Transfer the vegetables to a large saucepan. Pour a little water over the baking sheet, scraping with a spatula to loosen any browned bits; add to the saucepan, along with 5 cups water.

**4.** Bring the vegetable mixture to a boil. Reduce the heat and simmer briskly until the vegetables are tender and a brown broth has formed, about 15 minutes. Season to taste with salt (I use about 1½ teaspoons) and pepper; add the cinnamon.

**5.** Cool the broth slightly and strain through a mesh strainer set over a saucepan; discard the solids.

**NOTE**
Use leftover roasted mushroom broth for soups, sauces, risotto, and so on. It will keep, refrigerated, for several days or can be frozen.

## *Breakfast all' Italiana*

In the mountain valleys of Valle d'Aosta, cheese makers and shepherds have traditionally started their day with a rib-sticking repast of fontina, blood sausages, and potatoes. A bowl of polenta, doused liberally with *brossa*—a rich-tasting, nutritious byproduct of cheese making—is another breakfast that sustains through a morning of arduous work.

A friend and I encountered quite another kind of breakfast in Modena as guests of a family with an *acetaia* (traditional balsamic vinegar operation), which we were to tour afterward. The table was laden with platters piled high with cheese, cured meats, panini, chocolates, and regional sweets such as *bensone*, cookies meant for dipping in Lambrusco. It was too much for a dozen guests, let alone two. We were a little embarrassed to be incapable of doing justice to this feast but, really, there was no expectation that we would. The display was more about making a *bella figura*, and a splendid impression was certainly made.

Neither of these examples is representative of a typical Italian breakfast, of course. From what I've observed, most Italians eat rather lightly in the morning. Standing at the counter of a bar, one might consume a brioche or *cornetto* (the Italian version of a croissant) with the first cappuccino or *caffe macchiato* of the day. I know one woman who eats a piece of Tuscan bread with mortadella every day of her life—and many whose *prima colazione* consists only of bread with jam or perhaps a few packaged cookies. You can go sweet or savory, easing into the day with whatever seems appealing.

All of this reflects an understanding of breakfast as a meal tailored to personal preferences, including the tastes of foreigners. Hotels and B&Bs are usually happy to make filtered *caffe americano* or soft-boil an egg, and those in Northern Italy might cater to guests with French Camembert or German wurst alongside the Italian cold cuts. When my husband and I were house-sitting for friends who rent out accommodations, guests from New Zealand asked worriedly where to find porridge. Oats were not in our pantry but, sure enough, a nearby supermarket had stocked them for just such an emergency.

> *"The breakfast that I'm invariably eager to eat, whether in Italy or at home, is sweet and simple."*

Rather than yearning for cornflakes or American-style coffee when in Italy, I've compiled a short list of breakfast favorites over the years. Lemon or almond *granita* stuffed in a brioche, a Sicilian street food, is one of the best things I've ever put in my mouth. I adore orange-yolked eggs basted in olive oil (page 232) and, at Villa Pilati, a B&B near Trapani, I fell for croutons made from sesame-crusted semolina bread, sprinkled lightly with dried oregano, and drizzled with oil pressed from the estate's own olives. This idea turned out to be quite portable and, back in the U.S., we regularly breakfast on croutons made with good bread and glossed with our best olive oil.

The breakfast that I'm invariably eager to eat, whether in Italy or at home, is sweet and simple: Freshly squeezed blood orange or grapefruit juice, followed by some kind of terrific bread, toasted and spread with butter, fresh ricotta, or *stracchino* cheese and preserves, in company with milky *caffe latte*. When the preserves are as special as Maria Pellizzari's lemony carrot *marmellata* (recipe follows), it's an added incentive for me (decidedly not a morning person) to leap out of bed. ๑

# LEMONY CARROT MARMELLATA

*Marmellata di carote e limone*

MAKES ABOUT 1 QUART | PREP: 20 MINUTES | COOK: 40 MINUTES

*Maria Pellizzari's lavish breakfast spread for guests of Palazzo Malaspina, her family's inn, almost always includes homemade preserves from seasonal produce. In summer you might have to choose between her fig* marmellata *and an unusual one made with fresh tomatoes. In fall and winter, it's time to mix up a batch of Maria's lemony carrot jam. I especially love to eat it over a thin layer of ricotta on crusty bread, toasted or not. Team this lustrous orange-colored* marmellata *with a hazelnut or gianduia spread or peanut butter and whole-wheat bread, and you've got one terrific breakfast sandwich.*

3 large lemons
10 medium carrots, trimmed (about 2 pounds)
3 cups sugar (see Note)

1. Use a zester to produce fine threads of lemon zest (yellow part only). (Alternatively, grate the zest; or, use a peeler to remove strips of the zest and cut into julienne strips.) Halve the lemons and squeeze the juice (about 1 cup).

2. Cut the carrots into chunks and place them in a medium saucepan with ½ cup water. Bring to a boil and simmer, partly covered, until very tender, about 30 minutes.

3. Meanwhile, combine the sugar with ¾ cup water in a medium saucepan. Heat over medium-low heat until the sugar dissolves, creating a cloudy liquid that eventually turns into a transparent syrup.

4. Drain the carrots and add with the lemon juice to the saucepan with the syrup; simmer over low heat for about 10 minutes.

5. Scrape the carrot mixture into a food processor bowl. Process until smooth. It should be thick enough to spread; if it seems too loose, return the mixture to the saucepan and cook a little longer. Cool and transfer to clean mason jars or other containers. The jam keeps well in the refrigerator for several weeks.

## NOTE

Making *marmellata* this way produces a slightly runny, not-too-sweet spread. For a thicker, jammier jam, increase the sugar to 3½ cups.

# Chapter 8
# PIZZA and PANINI

Bread: If there's a bedrock Italian food, that would be it. Take your pick—crisp-crusted, tender-crumbed rolls, densely delicious whole-wheat slices, coarse, salt-free Tuscan bread, deliciously oily focaccia—in one form or another, bread accompanies most meals in Italy. It is a key component of some soups and salads. And, in the case of pizza, savory pies, and *panini*, bread *is* the meal.

Sometimes pizza is a sit-down meal. Ideally, I'm sitting in Naples, watching the *pizzaiuolo* slide a slightly charred disk of perfection onto my plate. The aromatic steam fogs my glasses as I set upon it with knife and fork. (What I don't do is ask that the pizza be cut into slices; the waiter would comply while wondering why, like a child, I need help in cutting my food.) Most restaurants won't allow sharing of such a pizza, and first-time visitors to Italy are often surprised to discover that, even in a *ristorante*-pizzeria, pizza might be served only at dinner; given Italy's climate, firing up a pizza oven during the day has never made sense in terms of comfort or energy costs.

Pizza also exists in more informal incarnations, sold by the square or slice at a street stand or *focacceria*. A quick warm-up, and the napkin-wrapped parcel is in your hand, ready to eat. For a more elegant variant, go to Princi or one of Milan's other chic emporiums for cafeteria-style dining, where pizza is dispensed in small squares. The topping might be the familiar *margherita*, with its tomato, mozzarella, and basil, *quattro stagioni* ("four seasons" represented by four toppings), or a caramelized onion, pancetta, and *stracchino* cheese combo like the one I enjoyed in Portofino.

Open-face and double-crusted pies made with pastry dough are also part of Italian cuisine. One in this chapter, with a ricotta, asparagus, and ham filling, is ideal for a one-course meal.

*Panini*—a word that in Italy refers to sandwiches of all kinds, not just those pressed in a grill—share pizza's status as a street food, typically enjoyed sitting on a park bench or standing in a bar. Most Italians wouldn't dignify a *panino* as a meal, but to my American sensibility it certainly qualifies. Just read the stats on the most frequently eaten American meals: Sandwiches top the list, not surprisingly, given that they are quickly made, portable, and infinitely variable. So why not make them fabulous? *Gelateria* impresario Alessandro Lisciandro did just that when he treated me to a classic Sicilian sandwich calling for sharp-tasting provolone, fresh tomato, olive oil, and semolina bread. And, I would add, we ate our *pani cunsatu* with a good glass of Sicilian Merlot while sitting companionably at a linen-laid table.

The open-faced sandwiches called *bruschetta* or *fettunta*, whether crowned with cured meats or beans and sautéed greens, are encompassed in my definition of *panini*. So are generously sized *crostoni*, made from crisped bread or polenta, which serve as vehicles for inventive toppings ranging from seafood to mushrooms.

A home oven is no match for a commercial wood-burning oven, but it can produce very tasty results. I line my oven with quarry tiles, crank up the temperature as high as it will go, and enjoy what comes out.

# PIZZA and PANINI

*Four Seasons Pizza*

*Portofino Pizza with Caramelized Onions and Pancetta*

*Calzoni Filled with Escarole, Smoked Mozzarella, and Dried Sausage*

*Pizza-Panino with Eggplant and Scamorza Cheese*

*Savory Asparagus and Ham Pie*

*Friselle with Mozzarella, Tomatoes, and Basil*

*Warm Panini with Taleggio, Grilled Radicchio, and Speck*

*Tomato-Rubbed Sicilian Sandwich with Provolone*

*Fettunta with White Beans and Tuscan Kale*

*Crostoni with Sardines and Sweet-Sour Onions*

# FOUR SEASONS PIZZA

*Pizza quattro stagioni*

**MAKES TWO 9-INCH OR THREE 7-INCH PIZZAS | PREP: 20 MINUTES
COOK: 12 MINUTES**

*I get the idea of four toppings associated with particular seasons. That works for mushrooms (fall), ham (winter), and artichokes (spring), but I've always been puzzled when olives represent summer, since they are usually harvested in autumn. Tomatoes are the ultimate summer food, so when they're in season, that's what I use.*

10 ounces crimini or white mushrooms, trimmed and sliced
Extra-virgin olive oil
½ teaspoon dried thyme
Sea salt or kosher salt
Freshly ground black pepper
1 pound pizza dough, homemade (recipe follows) or store-bought
1 cup shredded semisoft cheese such as a young sheep's milk
   cheese, *caciocavallo*, or fontina
4 canned or marinated artichoke hearts, cut into slivers
2 thin slices deli ham, cut into strips
¼ cup pitted, halved Gaeta olives or other Mediterranean
   olives, or ¼ cup sliced fresh plum or cherry tomatoes

**1.** Line a lower oven rack with quarry tiles or a pizza stone if you have either. Preheat the oven to 500°F or the maximum temperature.

**2.** Place the mushrooms on a baking sheet. Drizzle with 2 to 3 tablespoons olive oil; sprinkle with thyme and season lightly with salt and pepper; mix with your hands to coat the mushrooms. Roast until browned and tender, about 5 minutes. Cool.

**3.** Meanwhile, divide the pizza dough into 2 or 3 parts, forming each into a flattened circle. Place on 2 pizza pans or baking sheets. Gently stretch and pat each piece into a round, 7 to 9 inches in diameter. Brush very lightly with olive oil.

**4.** Sprinkle the dough with half of the cheese. Spread the mushrooms over the dough. Scatter the artichoke hearts, ham, and olives (or tomatoes) in random fashion. Sprinkle the remaining cheese on top.

**5.** Place the pizza pans on the rack with the tiles (if using) for 5 minutes; once the crust has firmed up, slide the pizzas directly onto the tiles. Bake 5 to 7 minutes longer, or until the crust is lightly browned and the cheese is melted.

**NOTE**
Instead of mingling the toppings, sprinkle one on each quadrant of a single-serving pizza.

## Pizza Dough

**MAKES 1 POUND PIZZA DOUGH | PREP: 15 MINUTES** (*plus 1 1/2 hours rising time*)

**1 teaspoon active dry yeast**
**2 tablespoons extra-virgin olive oil**
**2 cups unbleached all-purpose flour, plus more as needed**
**1 teaspoon sea salt or kosher salt**

**1.** Combine the yeast with 1 cup warm water (110°F to 115°F) in a liquid measuring cup. Let stand for a few minutes, until a beige scum forms on top. Stir in 1 tablespoon olive oil.

**2.** In a large bowl, whisk the flour with the salt. Add the yeast mixture, stirring until most of the flour is incorporated.

**3.** Turn the dough onto a pastry board or other surface lightly dusted with flour. Knead with quick, light movements until soft and elastic, about 10 minutes, adding up to 1/2 cup more flour as needed. The dough will be slightly sticky. Gather it into a ball.

**4.** Clean the bowl, dry it, and coat it lightly with about 1 tablespoon olive oil. Turn the dough until lightly coated all over. Cover and let rise in a warm place for about 1 1/2 hours or until the dough doubles in size (for a slower rise, refrigerate the dough).

# PORTOFINO PIZZA with CARAMELIZED ONIONS and PANCETTA

*Pizza alla Portofino con cipolle e pancetta*

**MAKES ONE 16-INCH PIZZA OR TWO 9-INCH PIZZAS | PREP: 15 MINUTES
COOK: 40 MINUTES**

*Disembarking from a ferry at Portofino, on the Ligurian coast, we were famished and more than a little bit cranky, pushing our way through masses of fellow tourists. Before long we were sitting at a restaurant table, our mood softened as we gazed at the panoramic harbor view that had brought us all here. And, with the arrival of lunch, our spirits lifted even more.*

*My chickpea soup was delicious but I kept eyeing my husband's glorious glazed-onion pizza; eventually he relented and gave me a slice. Here's a recipe for that pie, with mozzarella standing in for the stracchino cheese used by the Portofino kitchen.*

2 ounces pancetta, diced small (about ⅓ cup, packed)
Extra-virgin olive oil
2 large onions, thinly sliced
½ to ¾ teaspoon sugar
¼ teaspoon sea salt or kosher salt
1 pound pizza dough, homemade (page 257) or store-bought
2 to 3 cups grated fresh mozzarella

1. Line a lower oven rack with quarry tiles or a pizza stone (if you have either) and preheat the oven to 500°F or the maximum temperature. In a large skillet over medium-low heat, sauté the pancetta in 2 tablespoons olive oil, until it has rendered most of its fat but is not crisp, about 8 minutes. With a slotted spoon, remove to a small bowl. Add the onions to the pan; add up to 1 tablespoon more oil and cook until the onions are soft and the edges are beginning to bronze, about 15 minutes altogether. Add the sugar and salt. Continue to cook until the onions are a medium golden (they will brown more in the oven), about 5 minutes. Cool to lukewarm.

2. Lightly oil a pizza pan or baking sheet. Gently stretch and pat the dough into a 16-inch round or two 9-inch rounds. Sprinkle the cheese over the dough. Spread the onions on top; sprinkle with the pancetta.

*continued*

**3.** Place the pizza pan on the rack with the tiles for 5 minutes; once the crust has firmed up, slide it directly onto the tiles. Bake 5 to 7 minutes longer or until the crust and topping are browned.

### VARIATION

*Pizza with Caramelized Onions and Anchovies*
Cook the onions as described above, using 3 tablespoons olive oil, 3/4 teaspoon sugar, and 1/4 teaspoon salt (you could omit the pancetta when using anchovies, with good results, but the pizza also tastes good with both). Stir in 1 clove finely chopped garlic toward the end, cooking just until fragrant. Spread the onions over the pizza. Pinch 8 anchovies in half; arrange in random fashion on the pizza. Bake as directed.

# CALZONI FILLED with ESCAROLE, SMOKED MOZZARELLA, and DRIED SAUSAGE

*Calzoni con ripieno di scarola, mozzarella affumicata e salsiccia secca*

**MAKES 4 SERVINGS | PREP: 20 MINUTES | COOK: 40 MINUTES**

*This recipe makes big, sprawling crescents filled with greens and other good things. The flavor improves once they cool off a bit; that strategy also makes it easier to pick up the* calzoni *rather than tackling them with knife and fork.*

1 large head escarole, cored
Extra-virgin olive oil
1 small onion, chopped
1 or 2 cloves garlic, finely chopped
2 ounces *cacciatorini* or other dried sausage, cut into thin strips
   (about ⅔ cup) (see Note)
1 pound pizza dough, homemade (page 257) or store-bought
1 cup shredded smoked mozzarella or *scamorza* (see Note)

1. Preheat the oven to 425°F; place racks in the center of oven. Separate the escarole leaves and wash well, changing the water until no grit remains. Stacking several leaves at a time, cut into shreds.

2. Fill a large saucepan two-thirds full of cold water and bring to a boil. Cook the escarole until tender, 5 to 10 minutes. Drain well, pressing with a spatula to help eliminate liquid.

3. Heat the olive oil (about 3 tablespoons) in a large skillet over medium heat. Sauté the onion until soft and golden; stir in the garlic, cooking just until fragrant. Stir in the drained escarole and dried sausage; remove from heat and let cool.

4. Lightly oil 2 pizza pans or rimmed baking sheets. Divide the pizza dough into 4 pieces. Shape each one into a ball and roll to make a round 9 to 10 inches in diameter. Transfer to the prepared pizza pans.

*continued*

**5.** Spoon the filling on one half of each round, leaving a ½-inch border. Sprinkle the cheese on top. Fold the other half of the dough over the filling and press along the joined edges to seal. Fold over the edges again to seal, crimping to create a narrow decorative border. With a sharp knife, slash the top of each calzone once to allow steam to escape.

**6.** Place the pans on the 2 center racks in the oven. Bake until well browned and some of the filling oozes out the vents, about 35 minutes.

## NOTES

Alternatives to the dried sausage include pepperoni, salami, and *soppressata*. The sausage can be omitted; if so, season the cooked escarole with salt and freshly ground black pepper.

You'll most likely find *scamorza*, balls with a bulblike appendage at one end, hanging over the deli counter. The smoked kind is stained a tea-brown color by wood smoke. Alternatives for this recipe include *caciocavallo* or standard supermarket mozzarella (not fresh).

To make smaller *calzoni*, divide the dough into eight or twelve pieces. The cooking time will be a bit shorter.

# PIZZA-PANINO with EGGPLANT and SCAMORZA CHEESE

*Schiacciata con melanzana e Scamorza*

MAKES 2 OR 3 SERVINGS | PREP: 20 MINUTES | COOK: 25 MINUTES

*You could argue that this Sicilian* schiacciata *is a filled pizza, but to me it straddles the line between pizza and panino. Giusto Priola explained the background of this Palermo specialty, and Alessandro Ancona, his partner at Cacio e Vino in Manhattan, showed me how to bake, split, and fill the dough. Though I don't have a wood-burning oven like theirs, my* schiacciata *always gets good reviews.*

2 small eggplants (preferably an Italian variety such as the deep
   purple oval or round lavender kinds)
Extra-virgin olive oil
Sea salt or kosher salt
4 to 6 ounces *scamorza* (unsmoked or smoked) or similar cheese
   (see Note, page 262)
1 pound pizza dough, homemade (page 257) or store-bought
1 cup marinara sauce, homemade (page 156), store-bought, or
   the sauce described on page 42
2 to 3 ounces thinly sliced *capicola* or Genoa salami (optional)
3 cups mixed greens such as shredded romaine and radicchio
Wine vinegar, balsamic vinegar, or *vincotto* wine vinegar blend

1. Line a middle oven rack with quarry tiles or a pizza stone if you have either. Preheat the oven to 400°F.

2. Peel the eggplants only if the skin is waxed or thick and tough. Cut crosswise into 1/4-inch-thick slices. Spread out on a rimmed baking sheet. Brush both sides with up to 1/4 cup olive oil and sprinkle one side with salt. Cut the *scamorza* into thin slices.

3. Roast the eggplant on the middle rack until lightly browned, 15 to 20 minutes. While it is cooling, divide the pizza dough in half and shape into balls. Lightly oil a second baking sheet. Place one of the dough balls on top; pat and gently stretch to make an 8-inch round. Repeat with the other piece of dough. Lightly brush both with olive oil. Bake on a center rack for 5 minutes.

*continued*

**4.** Slide the partially cooked dough onto a work surface. Press the tops firmly with a spatula to deflate. Using a long serrated knife, carefully cut horizontally in half (see Note).

**5.** Spread half of the marinara sauce on the cut sides of the partially cooked dough. Top with the eggplant slices, the *capicola* (if using), the *scamorza* slices, and remaining marinara sauce. Place the other pizza halves on top. Brush lightly with olive oil.

**6.** Return the stuffed pizzas to the oven; bake until the cheese melts and the top is lightly browned, 7 to 10 minutes (if it fails to brown, turn on the broiler briefly).

**7.** Toss the mixed greens with a little olive oil, a splash of vinegar, and salt to taste. Using tongs, mound the greens in the center of dinner plates. Cut each stuffed pizza into 6 wedges and arrange in spoke fashion around the salad.

### NOTE

The safest method for cutting these half-baked pizza-*panini* is to saw around the edges, one or two inches in, before cutting the center part. To repair any damage caused by cutting too deeply, trim off a thicker part of the cut side and patch the hole; use the intact half on the bottom.

# SAVORY ASPARAGUS and HAM PIE

*Torta salata agli asparagi e prosciutto cotto*

MAKES 4 TO 6 SERVINGS | PREP: 20 MINUTES | COOK: ABOUT 35 MINUTES

*Despite its resemblance to a quiche, this* torta salata *("savory pie") is definitely Italian. Not only is the filling enriched with ricotta and pecorino cheeses, but the crust is made with* pasta frolla, *an easy-to-work Italian dough containing egg. Serve it solo or with a tossed salad.*

Unbleached all-purpose flour, for dusting
Italian pastry dough for a single-crust pie (recipe follows)
½ pound asparagus, ends trimmed (see Note, page 119)
1 medium red or yellow onion
1 tablespoon unsalted butter
1 tablespoon extra-virgin olive oil
3 ounces thick-cut *prosciutto cotto* ("cooked ham" from Italy,
    available in some U.S. delis) or other good-quality ham, cut into
    ¼-inch cubes
4 large eggs
1 cup whole-milk or part-skim ricotta cheese
⅓ cup grated aged pecorino, Parmigiano Reggiano, or Grana
    Padano cheese
2 to 3 tablespoons snipped parsley or basil leaves
½ teaspoon sea salt or kosher salt
¼ teaspoon freshly ground black pepper

1. Lightly dust a marble pastry board or other smooth surface with flour. With a rolling pin, roll the dough into a disk about 11 inches in diameter, dusting the top of the dough as necessary with a little more flour to prevent sticking. Transfer the dough to a 9-inch Pyrex pie plate; press it into the pan; trim all but ½ inch of overhanging edges with kitchen shears or a knife; flute the edges or finish as you like. Chill in the refrigerator while preparing the filling.

2. Preheat the oven to 350°F. Angle-cut the asparagus into 1-inch lengths. Halve the onion, pole to pole, and cut crosswise in thin slices.

*continued*

3. Fill a small saucepan about two-thirds full of cold water and bring to a boil. Add the asparagus and cook until crisp-tender, about 2 minutes. Drain and cool under running water.

4. In a medium saucepan, melt the butter with the olive oil over medium heat. Cook the onion until soft and golden, about 10 minutes; cool. Add the asparagus and ham.

5. In a medium bowl, whisk the eggs until frothy. Add the ricotta and ½ cup water, whisking until well blended. Stir in half of the pecorino cheese and the parsley, salt, and pepper.

6. Spread the asparagus and ham mixture in the pie shell. Add the ricotta-egg mixture and use a spatula to distribute it evenly and smooth the top. Sprinkle the remaining pecorino on top.

7. Bake the pie on a rack in the lower third of the oven until the bottom crust is well browned, about 20 minutes. Move to a rack in the top third of the oven and continue to cook until the filling is set (the top will brown only lightly, if at all), 10 to 15 minutes. Cool for at least 10 minutes on a rack. Serve warm or at room temperature.

## VARIATIONS

This pie takes well to other vegetable combinations—sautéed zucchini and mushrooms, for example.

Salami or cured pancetta cut into small pieces could be substituted for the ham. It's fine to omit cured meats altogether, but the filling may need a little more seasoning (salt, pepper, herbs) if you do.

## Italian Pastry Dough

**MAKES 1 POUND** (*enough for one 2-crust or two single-crust pies*) | **PREP: 15 MINUTES**

2½ **cups unbleached all-purpose flour**
¼ **teaspoon baking powder**
¼ **teaspoon salt**
8 **tablespoons (1 stick) unsalted butter, chilled**
1 **large egg, beaten**

1. In a medium bowl, whisk together the flour, baking powder, and salt. Cut the butter into small pieces and add to the flour mixture, tossing to coat them with flour. Using a pastry blender or your fingers, work the butter into the flour until the mixture is the consistency of coarse meal.

2. Add the egg and stir until well mixed and the mixture begins to clump (if it seems too dry, add 1 to 2 teaspoons cold water). Gather the dough together with your hands and knead briefly. Divide the dough in half and press each part to form a disk. At this point, the dough can be used immediately or wrapped in plastic wrap and refrigerated for a day or two or frozen.

### NOTE

In Italy you can buy prepared dough (called *sfogliata*) packaged in a nifty triangular oblong; unfolded, the dough fits neatly into a typical Italian pie/cake dish, with higher sides than ours. Nothing could be more convenient and, what's more, it's made with butter and vegetable oil (not hydrogenated); if you have an opportunity to cook in Italy, I recommend seeking it out. I've never found prepared dough of equivalent quality in the U.S., but if you do, it could be substituted for the homemade crust used in this recipe.

# FRISELLE with MOZZARELLA, TOMATOES, and BASIL

*Friselle con mozzarella, pomodori e basilico*

MAKES 2 SERVINGS | PREP: 10 MINUTES

*The rock-hard rounds called* friselle *belong to the ingenious tradition of toasting or drying bread for long-term preservation. They're native to the South, especially Puglia and Basilicata, and have in recent years come into vogue in other Italian regions.* Friselle *make up for being a bit hard to find by their convenience—easy to store on the counter or in the freezer until you're ready to bring them to life by dunking in water.*

*This topping, with the same makings as an insalata caprese, is one of the most common and delicious for* friselle. *As for eating them, Alexandra Korey, whose husband, Tommaso, is Pugliese, advises "knife and fork, with some picking up—they need to be crispy enough not to fall apart."*

4 bagel-size whole-wheat or regular *friselle* (see Note)
Best-quality extra-virgin olive oil
8 to 12 ounces fresh mozzarella
Sea salt or kosher salt
Freshly ground black pepper
Leaves from 3 or 4 basil sprigs
2 ripe medium tomatoes

1. Fill a shallow soup bowl with water. Dip the *friselle* one by one in the water, and place 2 on each of 2 dinner plates. Drizzle with olive oil (at least 1 tablespoon for each *friselle*).

2. Cut the mozzarella into ½-inch slices and halve them. Arrange on the *friselle*. Sprinkle lightly with salt and pepper and top with basil leaves (tear larger ones in half). Cut the tomatoes into thin (¼-inch) slices; halve them and arrange on top of the mozzarella.

3. Drizzle the topped *friselle* a second time with olive oil and pass more at the table. The *friselle* can sit for up to half an hour before serving.

**NOTE**

Look for *friselle* in Italian bakeries or specialty food shops. Made the traditional way, *friselle* contain lard; many bakers substitute vegetable shortening or oil these days. If this is an issue for you, inquire or read the label carefully.

**VARIATIONS**

Can't find *friselle*? Make *bruschette* instead: Lightly toast thick slices of country-style bread, drizzle with olive oil, and proceed as directed in the recipe.

Canned tuna chunks are often incorporated into this traditional mozzarella-tomato topping. If tomatoes are out of season, roasted bell peppers make an excellent substitute; drizzle them first with a little balsamic vinegar or wine vinegar to add a tangy note.

# WARM PANINI with TALEGGIO, GRILLED RADICCHIO, and SPECK

*Panini caldi con Taleggio, radicchio grigliato e speck*

MAKES 4 SERVINGS | PREP: 10 MINUTES | COOK: 17 MINUTES

Panini, *like sandwiches everywhere, invite the maker to branch out in creative directions. This combination brings together several strong-willed ingredients, all shouting, "Taste me!" Fortunately, their insistent voices harmonize in these warm, delicious panini.*

Extra-virgin olive oil
1 medium head radicchio, cored and shredded
1 large (about 16 x5") *ciabatta* or semolina loaf, or long baguette
8 ounces Taleggio or soft Gorgonzola cheese, at room temperature
1/2 cup walnuts, broken into small pieces
4 to 6 ounces thinly sliced speck (smoked ham from northern
   Italy), prosciutto, or mortadella, or some of each

1. Preheat the oven to 350°F. Heat enough olive oil to coat the bottom of a large skillet over medium-high heat. Scatter the radicchio over the bottom of the pan and allow it to wilt and lightly char, stirring a couple of times, about 2 minutes.

2. With a serrated knife, cut the bread horizontally in half. *Ciabatta* normally has more crust than crumb; if there is a good deal of crumb on the inside of your loaf, tear most of it out and use for another purpose, such as making bread crumbs. Spread the Taleggio over both cut sides of the loaf; stud it with the walnuts.

3. Using tongs, distribute the radicchio on one half of the loaf. Top with slices of speck and place the other half of the loaf on top. Wrap the filled loaf with aluminum foil (see Note).

4. Bake the filled loaf until heated through, 10 to 15 minutes. Cut crosswise to make 4 *panini*.

*continued*

### NOTE

Once wrapped in foil, the filled loaf can be held at room temperature for up to an hour, or longer if refrigerated.

### VARIATION

You can make a toasted version of this sandwich using sliced country-style white or whole-wheat bread. Spread one side of the slices with the cheese and stud with walnuts; top half of them with the radicchio and speck as directed in the recipe. Close the sandwich with the remaining cheese-spread slices. Heat a little olive oil in a skillet and toast the sandwiches, turning once, until golden brown.

# TOMATO-RUBBED SICILIAN SANDWICH with PROVOLONE

*Pane cunsatu di montagna*

**MAKES 2 SANDWICHES | PREP: 10 MINUTES**

*Antonio Lisciandro owns Carabé gelaterias in Florence and other cities, but his roots remain firmly planted in Sicilian soil. Of his farm in the Tuscan countryside, he says, "You're in Sicily after entering my gate." I was talking about a Sicilian seaside sandwich made with sardines when Antonio interrupted to ask whether I'd tasted the mountain version. No? Five minutes later, with the help of his wife, Loredana, we were sitting at the table with the makings.*

*Antonio energetically rubbed the toasted bread—baked on the premises, naturally, with Sicilian semolina flour—with a ripe tomato. In rapid sequence, he sprinkled sea salt, crumbled oregano, drizzled olive oil, cradled the cheese in one arm, and carved toward himself with the other. After wrapping the bottom half of the sandwich with a napkin, he handed it to me, still warm and never to be forgotten.*

4 large slices semolina bread or country-style white bread
1 ripe tomato, cut horizontally in half
Sea salt or kosher salt
Dried oregano, preferably from a branch
Extra-virgin olive oil, preferably Sicilian
4 ounces imported provolone or *caciocavallo* cheese, thinly sliced

**1.** Lightly toast the bread in a toaster or toaster oven. While the slices are still warm, rub one side with the cut sides of the tomato, discarding what remains of the tomato; sprinkle lightly with salt and crumble or sprinkle the oregano on top; drizzle with olive oil.

**2.** Top 2 of the bread slices with the cheese. Cover with the other 2 slices.

# FETTUNTA with WHITE BEANS and TUSCAN KALE

*Fettunta con cannellini e cavolo nero*

**MAKES 2 TO 4 SERVINGS | PREP: 15 MINUTES | COOK: 20 MINUTES**

*One autumn Sunday, we enjoyed a lavish lunch with friends in a Tuscan trattoria, followed by a walk along country roads. There was a long interlude of sitting lazily outside our friends' apartment and dipping biscotti in vin santo. After all that, we had no right to be hungry, and yet we were. Elena built a fire indoors and over it, on a hand-held rack, toasted slices of bread. She rubbed the toasted bread with garlic, ladled on warm beans, and drizzled green olive oil over what is known elsewhere as* bruschetta *and in Tuscany as* fettunta *("oiled slice"). There were plates of local cured meats and straw-colored pecorino and, of course, Chianti wine.*

*Elena assembled the meal in less than half an hour and, I would guess, has forgotten all about this long-ago experience. What was to her an ordinary day was, for me, replete with culinary grace, and the memory returns each time I eat this dish. The kale is my addition, but I do believe Elena would approve.*

1 small bunch Tuscan kale (lacinato variety) or curly-leaf kale
4 cups white beans with garlic and sage (page 72), with some of
   the cooking liquid
Sea salt or kosher salt
Best-quality extra-virgin olive oil, ideally a peppery Tuscan oil
4 large slices white country-style bread
2 cloves garlic, peeled and halved
Freshly ground black pepper

**1.** Preheat an oven or toaster oven to 400°F. Folding each kale leaf lengthwise in half, cut off and discard the stem. Cut the leaves crosswise into shreds.

**2.** Heat the beans over low heat in a medium saucepan; season to taste with salt. Meanwhile, fill a medium saucepan with cold water; bring to a boil. Cook the kale at a brisk simmer, lowering the heat if necessary, until tender, 3 to 5 minutes; drain. Season with salt and a little olive oil.

**3.** Toast the bread in the oven or toaster oven until crisp but not browned. While still warm, rub on both sides with the garlic clove halves.

**4.** To serve: Place the toasted bread on plates. Spread seasoned kale over each slice. Spoon white beans and some of the cooking liquid on top. Season with pepper and drizzle generously with olive oil; pass a small pitcher of olive oil at the table.

## NOTE

Tuscan kale usually comes in small bunches, while curly-leafed kale bunches tend to be larger. If you have the latter, consider cooking all of it; what you don't need for the *fettunta* can become a side for another meal, sautéed briefly with olive oil and seasoned with lemon juice or wine vinegar.

# CROSTONI with SARDINES and SWEET-SOUR ONIONS

*Crostoni con sardine grigliate e cipolle in agrodolce*

MAKES 2 OR 3 SERVINGS | PREP: 15 MINUTES | COOK: 20 MINUTES

*Everyone is familiar with crostini, small rounds of bread brushed with olive oil, toasted, and topped with all manner of delicacies. This recipe calls for crostoni, big enough to be taken seriously as a meal. The sardine and sweet-sour onion topping is patterned loosely on the Venetian specialty called sarde in saor and on similar Sicilian combinations.*

2 tablespoons white or red wine vinegar

½ teaspoon sugar

½ teaspoon coriander seeds (optional)

Sea salt or kosher salt

Freshly ground black pepper

6 large slices cut diagonally from a semolina loaf or baguette

Extra-virgin olive oil

1 medium onion, thinly sliced

1 tablespoon raisins or currants, plumped in water and drained

1 tablespoon pine nuts, lightly toasted

1 cup firmly packed baby arugula or watercress leaves

1 can good-quality sardines (about 4 ounces) packed in olive oil

1. Preheat the oven to 400°F. In a small bowl, combine the vinegar, sugar, coriander seeds (if using), 1 teaspoon salt, pepper to taste, and 2 tablespoons water; mix well with a fork.

2. To make the *crostoni*: Brush the bread slices lightly on both sides with olive oil. Arrange them on a cookie rack set inside a rimmed baking sheet. Bake on a middle rack until dry to the touch but not browned, about 9 minutes. Cool.

3. While the *crostoni* are baking, heat 2 tablespoons olive oil in a medium skillet over medium heat. Sauté the onion, stirring often, until fairly soft and pale golden, about 5 minutes; add the vinegar mixture and cook a few minutes longer. The onions should be soft, with just a bit of crunch. Stir in the raisins and pine nuts. Cool in the skillet.

4. To top the *crostoni*: Divide the arugula among the *crostoni*. Top with the onion mixture. Arrange 3 or 4 sardines at a diagonal on each *crostoni*. Serve immediately or let sit up to an hour.

### VARIATION

#### Crostoni with Grilled Fresh Sardines

You'll need six sardines (about one pound), cleaned but with heads and tails intact. Rinse and pat them dry, then brush lightly with olive oil. Grill on a medium-hot fire or in a stovetop grill pan, turning once, until browned and cooked through, about five minutes. Sprinkle with salt while still warm.

## *Happy Endings*

I've always loved the buoyant atmosphere in an Italian *pasticceria* on Saturday afternoon or Sunday morning, when customers are ordering boxes filled with small delectables or a large tart topped with jewel-like fruits. They are provisioning themselves for at least one big weekend meal. Sometimes the sweet is a local specialty, such as Montevarchi's liqueur-soaked *panbriacone* or a Sicilian *cassata* decorated with candied fruits and tinted icing. Maybe it's a seasonal treat. In the Piemonte, during autumn, pastry shop windows glow with displays of *marrons glacé*, the glistening syrupy coating only partially concealing the plump chestnuts. And the winter holidays wouldn't be complete without Sienese *panforte*, dense with dried fruit, or the *panettone* now shipped around the world.

Restaurants, too, tempt customers with intricate desserts like profiteroles, cream puffs filled with *zabaglione* or whipped cream and drizzled with rich chocolate. I admire the artistry of such desserts, but what I most love to eat at the end of a meal are the simple homemade sweets served in Italian homes and small family-owned restaurants. Their flavors tend to be straightforward, not cloyingly sweet, striking just the right note.

Invite Italians to dinner and, with luck, they'll bring one of these desserts. Our Tuscan neighbor Leda arrived with a glorious *rotolo*, a sponge cake roll filled with whipped cream and wild strawberries. After dinner, suppressing my gluttonous instincts, I took some of the leftover cake to neighbors on the other side. I had barely opened my mouth to make the offer when they began nodding and reaching for the plate.

When Luciano came for dinner, he brought sugar-dusted *schiacciata fiorentina*, a plain but delicious olive-oil cake that's always on hand at his house. Lina, his mother, also makes a ring-shaped *ciambellone* that resembles a marble cake, made by swirling chocolate- and vanilla-flavored batters together.

Seasonal fruit, often served whole, is always welcome at the end of an Italian meal. Lina's *ciambellone* was accompanied by a bowlful of fresh cherries. Pears poached in red wine or vanilla-flavored sugar syrup; wild berries drizzled with a little maraschino liqueur, aged balsamic vinegar, or nothing at all; baked *amaretti*-filled peach halves: Finales such as these cannot be surpassed. ∾

# FLORENTINE OLIVE OIL CAKE
*Schiacciata fiorentina*

MAKES 9 TO 12 SERVINGS | PREP: 20 MINUTES | COOK: 30 MINUTES

*Every Tuscan cook knows how to make schiacciata fiorentina, a simple, not-too-sweet cake that takes just a few minutes to make. It stays moist for up to a week and makes a pleasant dessert, perhaps with fruit macerated with a little sugar and lemon juice— but it is equally nice with afternoon tea or for breakfast. This is Lina Romei's version.*

1/2 cup extra virgin olive oil, plus more for the pan (see Note)
1 large lemon
1 2/3 cups unbleached all-purpose flour
1 cup sugar
1 teaspoon baking powder
1/2 teaspoon baking soda
1/4 teaspoon salt
1/2 cup milk
2 large eggs, beaten
1 teaspoon vanilla extract
2 tablespoons confectioners' sugar, or as needed

*continued*

1. Preheat the oven to 350°F. Lightly oil the bottom and sides of a 9-inch square baking pan; line the bottom with parchment paper. Using a zester or grater, finely shred the lemon zest. Halve and squeeze the lemon (it should produce about ¼ cup juice).

2. In a large bowl, whisk together the flour, sugar, baking powder, baking soda, lemon zest, and salt.

3. In a medium bowl or 1-quart liquid measuring cup, combine the milk, olive oil, eggs, lemon juice, and vanilla.

4. Add the liquid ingredients to the dry ingredients, using a whisk or spatula to blend well. Use a rubber spatula to scrape the batter into the prepared pan; tilt the pan to distribute it evenly and smooth the top.

5. Place the cake on a middle rack in the oven. Bake for about 30 minutes, or until the top is well browned and a toothpick inserted into the center emerges dry.

6. Cool the cake on a rack. While it's still warm, spoon confectioners' sugar into a small strainer and shake lightly over the cake.

### NOTE
Choose a mild, extra-virgin olive oil that will not impart a bitter flavor to the cake.

### VARIATION
Omit the vanilla and mix 1 to 2 tablespoons finely chopped fresh rosemary into the batter before baking.